'Health systems in many countries, both developing and the more developed, are undergoing major reforms at a time when government involvement in health care and in providing financial support is being reduced. More than ever, all those involved in health need to understand how health policies are being formulated, adopted and implemented. This clearly written book, with its excellent examples and explanatory text, enables us to understand and analyse the complicated processes that are involved. It should prove equally valuable to health workers, managers and academics.'

Professor Patrick Vaughan,
London School of Hygiene and Tropical Medicine, University of London

'Anyone who thinks that health policy is simply a matter of finding the best way to improve health should read this book. Politics cannot be kept out of health policy. Ministers who want to stay in power inevitably have to balance the interests of different power groups within their society and outside it. The focuses of power in different types of countries are identified and analysed in this thoughtful and readable book, which is illustrated with fascinating examples drawn from real life.'

Professor Brian Abel-Smith,
European Institute, London School of Economics and Political Science

'Up to now there has been no single book concerning the study of the health policy process. Health policies result from particular combinations of political and material circumstances at different levels. Gill Walt provides the tools with which to analyse these. Her framework for international health policy analysis explores the role of the state; the way power is distributed in society; how the policy agenda is created; how policies are formulated, implemented and studied. The role of international organizations is analysed, and the case study examples provide useful practical details in this and other areas. The role which media play in interacting with the policy process is a relatively new area of study, and one for which this book provides some fascinating insight. I shall certainly use this book for teaching health planners and managers from both developed and developing countries.'

Dr Carol Barker,
Nuffield Institute for Health, Leeds

'Gill Walt approaches health policy from the perspective of actors and processes. This makes her book extremely useful to health policy makers, administrators, health workers and academics. She provides a well written analysis of how health policies are developed, enhancing our understanding of factors influencing policy formulation and implementation in developed and developing countries. There is nothing comparable for those teaching on health policy and thus Walt has done us all a great service by filling a notable gap in the existing literature.'

Professor Judith Justice, Institute for Health Policy Studies,
School of Medicine, University of California at San Francisco

Dr Gill Walt was educated at the London School of Economics. In 1979 she joined the staff of the London School of Hygiene and Tropical Medicine, where she now heads the International Policy Programme in the Health Policy Unit. She has held visiting appointments at the King's Fund Institute, London (1990), the Centre for Health Policy Studies, University of Witwatersrand, Johannesburg (1990) and the University of Cape Town (1994). Her research has taken her to many different countries and has been primarily in her principal area of concern, which is primary health care and the policy processes affecting its content, promotion and implementation. This research has been undertaken on behalf of various international agencies, including the Commonwealth Secretariat, Oxfam, UNICEF, WHO and ODA.

In addition to teaching, research and consultancy, Gill Walt is co-editor (with Anne Mills) of the quarterly journal *Health Policy and Planning* (published jointly by the London School of Hygiene and Tropical Medicine and Oxford University Press). She is also the author of numerous articles, papers and other publications – including *Mozambique: towards a people's health service* (co-edited with A. Melamed, 1984), *Community health workers in national programmes: just another pair of hands?* (1990), and *Drugs policy in developing countries* (co-edited with N. Kanji, A. Hardon, J.W. Harnmeier and M. Mamdani, 1992).

HEALTH POLICY:

AN INTRODUCTION
TO PROCESS AND POWER

Gill Walt

Witwatersrand University Press
JOHANNESBURG

Zed Books
LONDON AND NEW JERSEY

Health Policy: An Introduction to Process and Power
was first published by Zed Books Ltd, 7 Cynthia Street,
London N1 9JF, UK, and 165 First Avenue, Atlantic Highlands,
New Jersey 07716, USA, and in the Republic of South Africa
by Witwatersrand University Press, PO Wits,
Johannesburg 2050, South Africa, in 1994.

Second impression 1996

Cover designed by Andrew Corbett.
Typeset in Monotype Baskerville by Ewan Smith,
48 Shacklewell Lane, London E8 2EY.
Printed and bound in Great Britain by
Biddles Ltd, Guildford and King's Lynn.

A catalogue record for this book is available from the British Library.
US CIP data is available from the Library of Congress.

ISBN 1 85649 263 x hb
ISBN 1 85649 264 8 pb
South Africa:
ISBN 1 86814 273 6 pb

Contents

List of boxes

List of tables

List of abbreviations and acronyms

ABPI	Association of the British Pharmaceutical Industry
ACASH	Association for Consumer Action on Safety and Health (India)
ACCD	American Coalition of Citizens with Disabilities
ADRDA	Alzheimer's Disease and Related Disorders Association
AIDS	Acquired Immune Deficiency Syndrome
ALRA	Abortion Law Reform Association (UK)
ARI	acute respiratory infection
ASH	Action on Smoking and Health (UK)
BMA	British Medical Association; also Bangladesh Medical Association
BRAC	Bangladesh Rural Advancement Committee
CBI	Confederation of British Industry
CDC	Centers for Disease Control (Atlanta, USA)
CDD	control of diarrhoeal diseases programme
CND	Campaign for Nuclear Disarmament
DANIDA	Danish Agency for Development Aid
ECOSOC	Economic and Social Council
EPI	expanded programme of immunization
EU	European Union
FAO	Food and Agriculture Organization
FPA	Family Planning Association (UK)
GATT	General Agreement on Tariffs and Trade
GNP	gross national product
GOBI	growth monitoring, oral rehydration, breastfeeding and immunization
G7	Group of Seven
HIV	Human Immunodeficiency Virus
IBRD	International Bank for Reconstruction and Development (World Bank)

ICAO	International Civil Aviation Organization
IDA	International Development Association
IDB	Inter-American Development Bank
ILO	International Labour Organisation
IMCO	Intergovernmental Maritime Consultative Organization
IMF	International Monetary Fund
IPPF	International Planned Parenthood Federation
ITU	International Telecommunication Union
NGO	non-governmental organization
NHS	National Health Service (UK)
NRA	National Resistance Army (Uganda)
PHC	primary health care
SIDA	Swedish International Development Authority
TNC	transnational corporation
TUC	Trades Union Congress (UK)
UN	United Nations
UNCTAD	United Nations Conference on Trade and Development
UNESCO	UN Educational Scientific and Cultural Organization
UNFPA	UN Population Fund (formerly UN Fund for Population Activities)
UNHCR	UN High Commissioner for Refugees
UNICEF	United Nations Children's Fund
UNIDO	United Nations Industrial Development Organization
UPU	Universal Postal Union
USAID	United States Administration for International Development
WHA	World Health Assembly of WHO
WHO	World Health Organization
WIPO	World International Property Organization
WMO	World Meteorological Organization

Acknowledgements

Over the years two questions from colleagues and students have challenged me. One was 'what is health policy?' and the other 'what book will introduce me to health policy?' Neither was ever easy to answer concisely and I ended up giving lectures or making long lists of books and articles. It also became clear that most people thought of health policy in terms of the content of policy, whereas I had developed my own framework of health policy which focused on process and power. I was interested in how policy was formulated and implemented, and who influenced policy making.

This interest goes back to when I was a doctoral student at the London School of Economics, and my supervisor, Brian Abel-Smith, encouraged me to 'tell the story' of policy making in two apparently discordant areas – family planning and fluoridation of water supplies – using a policy framework which demonstrated how the comparisons could be made usefully. Later, after working in Mozambique, I joined the London School of Hygiene and Tropical Medicine where Patrick Vaughan put the idea of a book into my mind. That was some years ago and he has been unwaveringly encouraging and confident that I could write it. I am indebted to him for his wise counsel, support and optimism.

Other colleagues at the London School of Hygiene and Tropical Medicine have also been enormously helpful: Lucy Gilson was the driving force in the last stages of writing. She read draft chapters quickly, offering comments that managed to be pertinent, critical and at the same time encouraging, and asked for more! Kelley Lee and Anthony Zwi read the penultimate manuscript cover to cover and made invaluable substantive and editorial suggestions. Carol Barker from the Nuffield Institute for Health in Leeds also reviewed the manuscript and made helpful comments. I am immensely appreciative of these colleagues' gifts of time and constructive feedback.

I also received some help on the case study examples which appear in boxes throughout the text: I am particularly indebted to Catherine

Pallister, who did sterling research and writing for several examples, and to Kent Buse and Jo Macrae who allowed me to extract parts of their excellent analytical reports written for other purposes.

Given the exigencies of academic life, I might never have completed this book had my colleagues in the Health Policy Unit not filled in for me when I had three months' study leave. So a general thanks to them (including those already mentioned), to Anne Mills, and to Phil Strong, who was always cheerily encouraging about the need for policy analysis and for this book in particular. Jane Pickup was also extremely efficient and helpful in ensuring the smooth production of the book from computer to printer.

Other colleagues and friends have provided references, examples and time to talk about specific issues and I would like to thank especially David Ross, Aubrey Sheiham and Rene Loewenson. At Zed Books Robert Molteno's enthusiasm for this project and insightful comments on the manuscript were always energizing. Finally I am immensely grateful to Isky, Natasha and Lorenzo for allowing me to monopolize the computer and for being unfailingly thoughtful about my needs for quiet and a distance from domestic life. None of those mentioned can be held responsible for the views expressed or any shortcomings in the book.

1

Introduction

We sat after lunch, five of us, arguing about the meaning of health policy. For the economist from the World Bank it was about the allocation of scarce resources. For the Ugandan health planner it was about influencing the determinants of health in order to improve public health. For the British physician it was about government policy for the health service. The Brazilian smiled. 'In Portuguese the word "politica" means both policy and politics', she said. For her, health policy was synonymous with health politics.

So health policy means different things to different people. For most people, health policy is concerned with *content*. It is about the best method of financing health services (private versus public insurance systems, for instance) or about improving antenatal health care delivery. For me health policy is about *process* and *power*, hence the title of this book. It is concerned with who influences whom in the making of policy, and how that happens. Although many agree that politics cannot be separated from policy, few books on health policy or health planning talk explicitly about political systems, power and influence, and people's participation in policy making. This book is centrally concerned with those issues, and only touches on policy content as illustration or example. It offers a broad framework for thinking about policy making and although it focuses on the health sector, it can be applied to other areas too. As an introductory text, it seeks to provide a first step into the complex and analytically challenging world of policy choice and change.

Who is the book for? It is for two groups of people: the first is made up of those interested in health. They may be health professionals or they may be administrators, statisticians, planners or economists; they may or may not be working in the health sector – they could just as easily be involved in development, education, agriculture or social services and have an interest in health. The second group is composed of people concerned with politics and processes, with how policies are made, implemented, changed; with how political systems affect the outcome of policies. Of course I hope that these two groups overlap, and that the book meets their interests in both health and policy.

The book is also written for people from developing *and* developed countries. The framework of analysis is such that it can be applied to both the industrialized world and the less developed world. While acknowledging that comparative analysis is always open to criticism (for example, the use of the terms 'developing' and 'developed' or 'Third World' and 'industrialized world' hide huge variations between and within countries) I nevertheless believe that, despite widely different political, economic and social circumstances, this book demonstrates that it is possible to apply a common conceptual framework to the health policy process.

This is not to deny that institutions, available resources, the weight of state power and the capacity of the state to implement its policies all differ between developing and developed countries. For example, in many Third World countries the legitimacy of the regime is in question, and the political system quite unstable. This increases the risks and stakes for policy makers considerably: a prime minister or minister of health who incurs the wrath of important groups within the society may be ousted from power by military coup or sleight of hand; a civil servant whose meagre salary is received irregularly may only be marginally concerned about implementing current policy. This scenario is familiar to many East European countries and the southern republics of the ex-Soviet Union which used to be considered part of the 'second world'. Compared to the industrialized state, Third World state structures and institutions are weaker but also more important in relation to the society. The capacity to make and implement policy is lower, but the share of resources absorbed and controlled by the state is larger. Participation in the political process is less in some Third World countries, although this is probably changing as democratization slowly takes place. Information for policy making is much more scarce in the developing than the developed world, and because of this, many Third World countries rely on foreign advisers and transplanted solutions to problems. Again, the countries of what used to be the 'second world' are no strangers to this situation. One report on the difficulties wrought by Western advisers trying to help Russian policy makers re-orient their health policies, suggested that their main contribution had been

> to take up Russians' valuable time. The question that these visitors rarely ask themselves is: what do the Russians want from this invasion? Undoubtedly Russia has its problems ... changing the previous system of health care is made very difficult by isolation, poor infrastructure and the collapse of management. The Russians don't know what works: all they know is what

they are told by their visitors, who come encumbered by their own ideological baggage (Delamothe 1992: 1433).

Despite these differences there are nonetheless regularities in the policy process and similarities between actors who try to influence it, which transcend the differences between the developing and developed world. Centrally there is government, and the policy makers within it: politicians and bureaucrats. There are groups outside government which have a major stake in policies which affect them: they represent a wide range of interests with different levels of power and include the military, trade unions, the church, professional and business groups as well as community structures including families. In many countries they include foreign interests. How far such groups can participate in policy making is dependent on the political system and how open or closed it is.

Likewise, the policy process in different countries is itself sufficiently similar to allow comparative analysis. Many developing countries have derived their formal institutions from Western models, and it is not surprising, therefore, that the processes within those institutions resemble those of the West. Procedures and routines used in policy making are likely to be similar, even if the array of problems and their solutions are different. At the same time, we have to take into account that imported models and institutions may coexist with traditional cultures and polities. Significant incongruities may be present in habits, modes of behaviour and constellations of political and social forces (Manor 1991: 5).

The analytic framework

The approach to health policy in this book comes from the social sciences, borrowing theories from different disciplines, and using them eclectically. Thus readers may recognize the political science notions of pluralism and elitism, and the different categories of interest groups. Policy analysts (and planners) will recognize the classical models of decision making, from rationalism to incrementalism. Public choice theorists will be familiar with the state described not as a disinterested wielder of the public good, but as an actor in its own right, pursuing its own goals. Political economists will appreciate the emphasis on the interrelationship between politics and economics. This is a deliberate approach in order to give readers a flavour of the different arguments derived from different theories, and to create an over-arching framework for analysis that takes the kernel from each theory and uses it to develop a way of understanding the complex world of health policy. I hope that readers will recognize that this 'iceberg' approach does not deny the rich universe of theories, arguments and debates that exist in health policy. For those who are not satisfied with viewing only one-seventh of the story, there are full references in each chapter which appear in the multi-disciplinary and wide-ranging bibliography.

Several attempts have been made to classify how decisions are made in the political system. The most widely used general explanations are society-centred or state-centred (Grindle and Thomas 1991). Within the first category fall the *class approach* (decision making is dominated by particular social classes and outcomes always favour those classes); *pluralist approaches* (no one elite dominates decisions, different groups compete, and policy outcomes are in the public interest); and *public choice approaches* (the state is not a neutral arbiter among competing groups, but a self-interested actor itself, making alliances with other major interests, resulting in policies which are not necessarily in the public interest).

The state-centred models concentrate more on the decision process itself: the *rational actor model* derives from the position that policy makers make policy choices on rational grounds, resulting in optimum policy choices; the *bureaucratic politics* approach emphasizes policy makers' positions in organizations, and how this influences their choices of policy; and finally the *state interests* approach suggests that state policy makers are active decision makers who generate responses to problems and determine policy outcomes.

None of these approaches is entirely satisfactory in its own right, and they are the subject of much debate in the political science and policy analysis literature. Society-centred approaches grant little initiative to government policy makers, while, in contrast, state-centred approaches tend to reduce policy making to government-controlled interaction, in which external forces play little part. What is needed is a broader framework which takes account of the basic structural concerns of the society-centred approaches about where power lies, and overcomes the weakness of the state-centred approaches which concentrate too closely on government control of the policy process.

What is also striking is how far the health sector has been neglected in such approaches. Most of those writing from a political economy perspective have focused on the economic sectors. There has been little international policy analysis of reform in the health sector. Yet health is central: not only because the economic policies of the state will affect health, but because the health sector itself provides the state with one of the most visible outputs of policy, from ambulances, hospitals, health centres and pharmacies, to nurses, doctors and immunization campaigns.

The importance of international health policy analysis

In many countries the health sector is an important part of the economy: employing huge numbers of workers, absorbing relatively large amounts of national resources. It is the focus of much technological innovation and biomedical research. Most citizens come into contact with health sector institutions and personnel at several points in their lives, many of which are highly significant. Because the nature of some decision making in health involves matters of life and death, health is accorded a unique position in comparison with other social issues. Further, health occupies a special place in policy analysis because of the status of the medical profession and its role in shaping and controlling health policy.

Health is also affected by many policies which have nothing to do with health care or services: environmental pollution, insecurity and instability (whether caused by unemployment or violence), economic regulation and deregulation, contaminated water and poor sanitation all increase morbidity and mortality. Health policy traverses all sectors.

This book takes the position that health policy is best understood by looking at both processes and power, which means exploring the role of the state, nationally and internationally, the actors within it, the external forces influencing it, and the mechanisms within the political system for participation in policy making. This draws on theories from both society-centred and state-centred approaches, placing them within a global context.

The first layer of analysis is the international level. States increasingly make policy in an interdependent world, and are not always sovereign decision makers, especially in the economic sphere. Multinational companies, the World Bank and donor agencies have had considerable effects on health policies all over the world. State politicians and bureaucrats are key policy makers, but they are influenced by international actors, even where the state often takes the lead in defining and directing society towards particular development goals. In particular, foreign donors have a clear influence on health policy in many countries. In the 1970s, as part of the policy impetus to promote primary health care, Western donors offered financial aid to build up rural health networks in Africa, often against ministry of health preferences for improved central hospital facilities. The resulting expansion of primary health facilities to previously neglected rural areas undoubtedly represented foreign influence on health policy. In the 1980s many Third World ministries of health were forced to consider an increased role for the private sector in health care as a condition for being able to renegotiate overdue interest repayments or new loans from the

International Monetary Fund (IMF) or the World Bank. It is not only the Third World policy process which is affected by being part of a global village. The countries of the former 'second world' have been flooded with advice and aid for particular policies. Domestic policy in the industrialized countries is sometimes influenced by the activities of pressure groups working at the international level, or regional organizations such as the European Community. An example of the latter is in the regulation of pharmaceutical products.

The next layer of analysis is the national one. Understanding the nature of the political system, and the extent to which participation is tolerated or not, provides an explanation of how power influences policy. Clearly an authoritarian state allows participation only through clearly defined channels. The communist states, until the end of the 1980s, allowed significant participation but only through mass national movements such as women's or youth organizations, or local bodies such as Tanzania's ten cells, or China's brigades or communes. Liberal democracies, on the other hand, encourage participation both through a system of voting for representatives who make policy, and through the formation of pressure groups which can try to influence policy makers' choices with regard to specific issues. But how much people actually participate, even in liberal democracies, is a much debated issue. Participation in Indonesia's democratic system has been likened to compulsory consensus (Godwin 1992: 18). By focusing on the political system it is possible to build up a picture of the complexities of how societies allow people within them to express demands and wishes and how these are translated into policy by their governments. In the 1970s and 1980s health policies in Cuba and the apartheid regime of South Africa were profoundly affected by the political systems that designed and implemented them. These two examples are touched on further in the next chapter.

The final layer of analysis is the closest to where we stand, as members of groups, of institutions, of political parties, of professions. Most of the book is focused at this level, and looks at the actual processes of policy and the actors involved at each stage. We ask questions about how problems are recognized, and turned into issues that get on to the policy agenda. How are policies formulated, implemented and evaluated? We ask how far the policy process is a rational search for the best possible solution to a particular problem, or whether, in fact, policy is made up of small, incremental changes that are hardly ever innovatory or revolutionary. And since processes do not have a life of their own, but are dependent on actors to give them expression, analysis of the policy process is interwoven with an exploration of which actors are involved, and how far each may be exerting influence on policy.

This book is about the policy process, not about health policy options (or content), and not about planning. Many writers do not distinguish between policy and planning, but for me, planning follows policy: planners help to put policies into practice, although the planning process itself may help to develop and refine health policies. Those concerned with the components and techniques of planning will have to turn elsewhere: Green (1993) gives an excellent starting point for those from the Third World, and Lee and Mills (1982) still provides a classic introduction to the subject. There is room for much more institutional, organizational analysis of policy, of policy processes, and the implementation of policy. I hope this book will serve as a stimulus to a greater exploration of the submerged six-sevenths of the health policy analysis iceberg that so few have, up to now, pursued.

The structure of the book

Chapter 2 explores the political system as a whole, starting with a systems approach, which stresses the demands made on the political system from political parties, pressure groups, other institutions, research, individuals, and the media. Systems analysis attempts to assess the interaction of all the different parts of the political system that affect health policy. This general framework offers a comprehensive way of approaching the political system and people's direct and indirect participation in it. This is followed by a look at different types of political system. Everyone talks of democratic or conservative governments, and in so doing refer to the norms of that country, and sorts of policies those governments pursue. Blondel's identification of five types of political system is used, which clusters countries into different groupings. They are not fixed, and over time countries may change from one to another. Finally we look at a number of exogenous factors (such as the role of foreign donors) that exist outside the political system, but which may affect policy.

In the third chapter we reach the next layer of analysis, and explore the way power is distributed in society, and how far it influences the policy process. Debate revolves around the extent to which policy making is dominated by a few elites at the national (or even international) level, or whether there is competition among different groups to influence policy. In order to understand how influence is exercised, we define what we mean by policy and the policy process, through problem identification to policy evaluation, noting that different actors may be involved at different stages. We also explore the extent to which policy making is a rational process or one of 'muddling through'. The basis of the rational approach is a belief that policy makers can make rational choices by a judicious use of information and option appraisal, thereby reaching optimum policies, and exercising control over their futures. At the opposite end of the spectrum the incrementalist approach provides a description of a policy process in which 'muddling through' is the norm, and in which policy makers take short cuts, small steps, and only introduce incremental change when necessary.

From the fourth chapter on, we explore a real world in which we start looking more closely at the interface of policy making and policy makers. Given that every society faces many varied problems at any one time, how do we explain why some issues get taken up and placed on the policy agenda by policy makers, whereas others are left at the wayside? We examine what is meant by the policy agenda and the process of agenda-setting, and focus on two of the main actors in the process: the government and the mass media.

In the fifth chapter we look at the formulation of policy, and because we see government as being central to public policy making, we concentrate on the institutions that make up the government, exploring the relative control over policy between politicians and civil servants, between ministries of health and other government sectors. The sixth chapter is concerned with a vast array of different pressure or interest groups outside government, which may want to put their point of view, or change the government's view, on particular policies. We explore the relative power of each of these groups and examine how far they are accepted as legitimate or not by government policy makers, and what sort of tactics they use to get attention for their views. We include in this chapter non-governmental organizations (NGOs), which are not usually thought of as interest or pressure groups, because many have evolved from being merely involved in service delivery to being active in lobbying for particular policies.

Because this analytical framework sees all countries as part of an interdependent (although not equally interdependent) world, in the seventh chapter we focus on interaction at the international level, to assess how far this affects policy making at the national level. We look at international organizations (such as the World Health Organization or UNICEF), international interest groups, and the relationship between countries at the global level.

The eighth chapter returns to processes, and to the most important part of the policy process: implementation. Can we assume that once policies have been formulated they will be implemented? We look at central–local relations, examining whether decentralization gives subnational health authorities room to manoeuvre in execution of policy. Chapter 9 is focused around policy makers' need for information, and questions how far research and evaluations feed into policy, and whether they lead to policy change or transformation. The final chapter is a reminder that the analytic framework used in this book must be used as a starting point: that power and process are concepts of great complexity, and current paradigmatic changes in political economy and health are challenging, and will continue to challenge, much received thinking.

Caveats

If this book were a painting, it would be described as being of the primitive school. The subject is recognizable, the figures bold, the colours bright: it aims to leave a strong impression. Subtle shadings, perspective, details, are missing, and it is up to the viewer to imagine them. I have avoided semantic squabbles. I am as unhappy as many of my colleagues with the words we use to describe a complex world and the differences between and within the societies in it: developing and developed; industrializing and industrialized; north and south; rich, middle-income and poor; first, second and Third Worlds. I agree we need to reformulate our paradigms of thinking, but in this book I rely on the familiarity of the old terms, which to some extent continue to describe relationships between parts of the world. I therefore use the words interchangeably and not pejoratively, aware of their power:

> Words describe the realities of human life. But words also have the power to create and shape realities. The words of the strong carry more weight than the words of the weak. Indeed, very often the weak describe themselves in the words coined by the strong. Over the last two centuries or more the strong have been the technologically advanced nations of the West. As they imposed their military, political, and economic power over most of the world, they also imposed the power of their words. It was they who named the others, in a sort of negative baptism. Who were the others? When the West was still Christian in its outlook, the others were 'the heathen'. Then they became 'the uncivilized', or more optimistically 'the less civilized' as Western imperial power came to be conceived of as a 'civilizing' mission. Before the Second World War the most common appellation was 'backward'. After the Second World War, with the coming of the United Nations, those others began themselves to participate in the naming game. 'Under-developed countries' became 'developing countries'. Since the Bandung conference, in the mid 1950s, the term 'Third World' has generated a mystique all its own. Although the ideological implications of all these appellations were shifting, sometimes rapidly, the basic empirical referents have not really changed over the last few decades: The basic division is between rich and poor countries, rich or poor not necessarily in possession of natural resources, but in ability to utilize those resources for themselves (Berger 1974: 23).

If words are used eclectically, then theories are too. I have chosen those models which seem to me to be most useful in building up a framework for international health policy analysis. While theoretical and methodological debate has its place, I am not attempting to test the validity of the different theories or their empirical bases. Unless details are germane to the conceptual framework of process and power, theories have been pared down to their central core. I am struck by the richness and variation in models, typologies, and approaches to problems both within and between disciplines. Since the end of the 1980s there has been a spirited unravelling, remoulding, and reorganization of concepts and theories to help explain what seems to have been a paradigmatic change in health policy all over the world. Again, I have chosen simplicity and familiarity where classic concepts still serve well. I have also used examples prolifically, and case studies where possible – in order to clarify and illustrate abstract notions. Although these are biased and limited by experience and reliance on English language publications there is no reason to suppose that the issues and processes they describe would be much different given other sources.

In writing this book I have had to come to terms with some conflicting ideas in my own theoretical approach to process and power. On the one hand, it seems to me that very small groups of elites control much policy making at all levels of society: global, national and subnational. This seems clearly the case with economic policy, which sets the framework for sectoral policies. On the other hand, I see, and describe, many different groups trying to influence policy at all those levels, and sometimes succeeding. I have therefore used a 'bounded pluralist' approach (Hall et al, 1975) in presenting the framework (see Chapter 3). I have argued that while issues of high politics (policies of macro or systemic importance) may well be formulated and imposed by narrow elites or a ruling class, issues of low politics (routine, day-to-day sectoral or micro policies) can be influenced by many different groups.

Many years ago a Catholic priest said to me that he could not understand how anyone who did not believe in God could get up in the morning. 'What would make them get out of bed?' he asked. I feel a bit the same about politics and the ability to influence change. If we, as health workers, or teachers, or students, or civil servants do not feel that we, and the groups or organizations we belong to, have some power to alter policy that affects our lives, or the lives of those around us, why get up in the morning? This book offers a framework for thinking about the various influences on health policy, and can be used as a first step in acting to influence change.

2

How does politics affect participation in health policy?

This chapter sets out a broad general framework for thinking about how far the political system affects health policy and people's participation in public policy making. Two simple 'snapshots' of countries in 1980 go to the heart of the subject. In Cuba the state perceived health as a right of all citizens, and society was structured to allow for maximum participation in health, through mass mobilization campaigns and other mechanisms such as neighbourhood committees. In South Africa the state left health to market forces and disenfranchised the black majority population. The resulting health policies (and health status) of both countries reflected the political system. In Cuba, everyone had nearly equal access to health services, and infant mortality rates fell from about 60 to 14 per 1,000 between 1954 and 1980. The best indicators of equity were statistics which showed that differences within and between rural and urban areas were small (Valdes Brito and Henriquez 1983). In South Africa, in contrast, health services were used as an instrument of apartheid to uphold the social, economic and political institutions structured along legally defined racial categories. The political system allowed some activity by anti-apartheid progressive health groups, which attracted attention to the adverse effects of apartheid on health, and may have had some influence on the state. Nevertheless, access to health services was unequal, as were health status differentials between ethnic groups: in 1985 infant mortality rates were 61 per 1,000 for blacks and 9.3 per 1,000 for whites (Benatar 1991).

Why a concern with the state?

These two snapshots illustrate why understanding the state is crucial to the formation of health policies. The political system provides the framework for people's participation in policy: it illustrates the mechanisms through which people are encouraged (or discouraged) to participate. In this chapter we are centrally concerned with the state or government because it extends deeply into people's lives, and does more than any other body to decide what policies should be implemented.

The state's role in many areas of economic management expanded in both developed and developing countries, between the Second World War and the late 1970s. Guided by Keynsian ideas about employment, social welfare and industrial policy, most developed countries saw the state assume central responsibility for most public utilities and social services, including health. In the UK, for example, the National Health Service was created. In Canada universal access to health care was formalized. The private sector, where it existed, became heavily regulated through legal and economic controls.

A similar strengthening of the state occurred in developing countries, particularly in the newly independent countries of Asia and Africa, under orthodox theories of development. Public sector employees in Tanzania grew from 27 per cent of those in formal employment in 1962 to over 66 per cent in 1974 (Perkins and Roemer 1991: 16). Throughout Latin America the extension of minimum wages and social security enabled alliances to form between industrialists, urban workers and the middle classes during the 1950s and 1960s (Ghai 1992: 3).

By the 1980s, however, considerable disaffection with this extended role of the state had emerged. Global economic recession was entrenched, state administrations were increasingly criticized as being undemocratic, unresponsive and unaccountable, and many developing countries were in debt. The contraction of the state began in the USA and spread to other industrialized countries, then to developing countries. Publicly owned industries were sold, public expenditure reduced, and private industry deregulated. Internationally, conditions set down by the global financial institutions such as the World Bank and International Monetary Fund (IMF) pressured developing countries to accept structural adjustment programmes for their economies, led by privatization policies and other ways to diminish the role of the state. Thus by the end of the 1980s, governments throughout the world were reducing their responsibilities in the public sector, moving away from providing services directly while retaining regulatory and financial control.

However, even as the state is relinquishing its role in many areas of public life, governments will continue to affect the lives of their citizens in many ways, ranging from the relatively trivial to the chillingly arbitrary. Extrapolating from Leichter's (1973) list of laws and regulations that governments have imposed on their citizens we can point to governments over the past decade that have:

— demanded children be given names only from a prescribed, approved
list (Argentina);
— demanded all children be immunized before entering school (USA);
regulated the number of children a couple may have (China); pro-
hibited private medical and legal practice (North Korea);
— had one law for black citizens and another for white (South Africa)
and countenanced the 'disappearance' of hundreds of thousands of
their citizens (several Latin American countries).

All governments attempt to control economic policy, whether they
preside over industrializing, post-industrial or developing economies. So,
while contemporary wisdom has the state divesting itself of many of its
functions in order to increase the role of market forces, the reality is
that in many countries government remains a major and direct actor
in the society. It is likely to continue as a major employer of labour,
responsible not only for the bureaucratic apparatus of government, but
also for many services including transportation, energy, education and
health, as well as for some industrial production.

Government determination to encourage the expansion of the private sector into new areas is itself a public policy of great significance.
Even if current state services are taken over by the private sector,
governments are likely to want to exercise their authority to regulate,
monitor or inspect private provision of those services. Public policy will
remain of critical importance. Thus governments will continue to play
a central role in policy making.

The state's role in health

In both developed and developing countries governments have been
centrally involved in health regulation and provision, ranging from public
health measures that ensure safe water and unadulterated food, to border
controls that attempt to regulate the spread of communicable diseases.
They are concerned with injury and accident prevention (seatbelts, crash
helmets, speed limits) as well as with safety at work. They regulate
industries such as pharmaceuticals, and license suppliers, production,
labelling, testing, patent production. They pass laws about pollution and
noise. They fund research, and are concerned with the ethical implications of research.

In most countries governments are intimately involved in the provision of preventive, promotive and curative health services, and the
scope and range of tasks and responsibilities of health authorities has
broadened over the past years. Doctors, nurses and community health

workers have been joined by health planners, economists and managers. The recognition that health services alone will not improve people's health has led to greater governmental efforts to find mechanisms for the discussion of the multi-sectoral nature of health policy, although coordination between sectors has been more difficult to implement than was predicted. Nevertheless, some governments have been willing to insist on health warnings on cigarette packets, to control lead levels in petrol or advertising of alcohol and cigarettes, to improve food labelling, and to increase health education and information on risky (unhealthy) behaviour.

Major health questions demand attention from governments. The Chinese and Thai governments have been involved with American companies and the US military regarding HIV vaccine trials in their countries. Malaria continues to preoccupy ministers of health. Desowitz (1991) describes how he revisited villages in Papua New Guinea in 1984 and 1990, having been absent since 1962. In 1962 virtually all villagers had been affected by malaria, and twenty years later nothing had changed. Malaria still affected nearly everyone in the villages. But in 1962, there were potent chemotherapeutic and insecticidal anti-malarial weapons. In 1990, all over the malarious world, drug-resistant parasites, insecticide-resistant mosquitoes and disillusioned health authorities had rendered those weapons impotent. Malaria threatens tourism and production, which worries governments.

As the fever to reform the health sector infects the developing and developed world alike, governments are concerned about, and challenged on, specific policy issues: the effectiveness of health care (especially as the private sector grows); the costs of providing health services and how to contain them; and how to improve and sustain equity between public and private sectors.

Governments are also not alone in health decision making. Regional organizations such as the European Community (EC) play a limited but important part in health policy by harmonizing regulations on pharmaceuticals, for example, or encouraging health-promotive legislation such as a ban on cigarette advertising or legislation on the tar content of cigarettes. Primarily a regulatory body with responsibility for trade policy, the EC can promote legal and fiscal regulations or policies in a number of areas that affect health, such as safety at work (Joffe 1993).

Most governments are closely involved in the training of health workers, from doctors at universities to para-professionals in schools of health sciences. Many have devised policies to encourage professional graduates to practise in rural areas. Even where governments may be retreating from mandatory controls on medical graduates, they may still be concerned with geographical inequities, and be looking to fiscal or financial compensation for working in unattractive areas.

Defining the political system

So far we have talked about the political system, the state, and the government without differentiating between them. What do we mean by the political system? It is an abstract notion of many forces which impinge upon the state and government. It includes the private sector (interest groups such as health insurance or social security companies; professional organizations; private hospitals; the pharmaceutical industry), political parties and individual voters. It also includes the *state* – another abstract idea – but one that most people recognize as a society within a geographically bounded territory. The state is concerned with domestic policies, affecting its national society, and with international policies, affecting its place in the world. Some states have a stronger identity than others. For example, the rural citizens of some Third World states do not perceive themselves as part of a nation-state, and the state's apparatus may not reach the whole territory. The 1990s were witness to the fragmentation or the destruction of the role and function of the state in Somalia and in the former Yugoslavia, for example.

By and large, when we talk of the state we mean the institutions that make it up:

— legislative assemblies, including parliaments;
— central or national ministries or departments of state, including regional or local authorities;
— the armed forces;
— the courts of law;

and the functions they perform:

— providing services, such as health and education, roads and rubbish collection;
— raising revenue;
— making and keeping law and order.

The state is thus made up of all the authoritative decision-making bodies of the society; it is legally supreme and it can use coercion to achieve its ends. *Government* is a narrower concept than the state, and includes the public institutions in which collective decisions are made into laws that affect the whole society. These are usually parliament, the executive, the bureaucracy, and ministries or departments of state.

The *political system* was represented in an analytical model by a political scientist (Easton 1965; see Figure 2.1) and although it has flaws it provides a useful overarching framework. Easton denotes the political system as one which contains all the institutions and processes involved in what he calls the authoritative allocation of values for society. Values are those things which have significance and importance to people. They may be material (consumption goods such as refrigerators or telephones), or services (good-quality education or health) or symbolic or spiritual (the right to speak your mind publicly, the right to a fair trial, the possibility of not bearing an unwanted child). Allocation of values is the process whereby governments choose which values to grant, and which to deny: the process of making or altering policies. Authoritative value allocations are those choices which are accepted as legitimate by the people affected by the policies – usually made by government.

INPUTS   OUTPUTS

Demands   ⌐ Institutions ⌐   Goods
Support   ⇒ | of | ⇒   and
Resources   ⌊ government ⌋   Services

Figure 2.1 Easton's model of the political system

The reason we need governments to allocate values is that the number of values which might be allocated is larger than the number of values which can be allocated – scarcity and competition exist. Scarcity may be of a physical kind – the economy simply has insufficient resources to provide all the goods and services people want – or of a spiritual or moral kind – competing ideas of what people consider good and valuable. Governments have to make both physical and moral choices (for example, whether to provide nursery education or to allow abortion on demand).

In the middle of the systems model is what is called the black box of policy making, which includes all the institutions of government. Outside government there are inputs to the system, which result in outputs in the form of different policies.

Demands are made by individuals or groups seeking particular policies that favour the things they want and value. They may be expressed as broad wishes to see lower crime rates, or a good system of secondary education, or a national health service, or specific desires for family planning services. These preferences become demands when they are articulated through interest groups or political parties and are made known to government.

Resources help the government respond to demands being made. They may be natural: oil, gold, fertile land; or from taxation, or loans or external aid; or they may be from production, which will in turn depend on the availability of trained and skilled workers. Without sufficient trained midwives and maternity beds, women will not be able to deliver in hospital even if they want to.

Support is more elusive, but refers to the support of the majority for the political system. In many countries this support is symbolized by national voting for political parties or candidates in elections, or by the willingness to pay taxes. This is often quite complex, however, and many governments stay in power without being ostensibly supported by the people. Much will depend on the perceived legality of the government: if it is seen to be legally in power, then its legitimacy is more accepted. If not, then the government may choose to use coercion to secure its will.

Demands, resources and support are fed into the black box of policy making – the institutions which formulate and implement policy, and which include national government as well as local authorities – and what come out are policies that affect goods and services as well as symbolic aspects of life. These public policies are put into effect, feed back to society, and may lead to different demands.

The major systems analysts assume that a balance is needed between the inputs and outputs of a political system if it is to survive. In other words, governments do not respond to all demands for a host of reasons – including lack of resources – but if they consistently do not satisfy demands or ignore them, or are unable to meet them, then the system will have to adjust – the government or the constitution will have to change.

And this is one of the main flaws of the systems model. It takes little account of conflict and the imperfect balance of power and influence, of *who* benefits from the state's outputs. It assumes that the state is neutral in its handling of demands, balancing the different values according to availability of resources rather than according to the relative power of those making the demands. It also overlooks the persistence of certain governments – and their ability to use force to repress or create demands or to coerce compliance. Even if they do not use force, it is often easy for governments to hear only the demands of those closest to them – the urban rather than rural population, or the majority ethnic groups, for example.

So, while Easton's systems model is useful as a conceptual tool, we need to pay more attention to who exercises power and influence. And in order to do that, we have to understand what mechanisms exist for the expression of demands. There may be many channels or few. Support may be relatively stable or very unstable. Some states may be tolerant of criticism or dissent, allowing dissatisfaction or disaffection to be voiced and even demonstrated publicly, allowing groups to be formed which will mobilize support for their cause. There are other states, however, which are more authoritarian, or dogmatic, which tolerate little, or no, dissension, and which offer few channels through which demands can be made legitimately.

Participating in public policy making

Our main question is how does the structure of the political system affect participation, affect people's potential to influence public policy? So far we have talked very generally about the state, and the extent to which the state affects its citizens through its laws and regulations, the services it provides, the functions it undertakes. But clearly governments differ. Much depends on the history of the country, its sense of national sovereignty, the political system in place, the degree of stability and so on. Political culture and structure differ considerably between countries and impose different constraints on policy. How does the political system affect policy? Is it so structured that ordinary citizens can influence the allocation of values through the policy process? In this section we ask two questions:

— How far does the structure of the state allow or encourage people to participate in public policy making?
— What are people's beliefs about, and attitudes to politics and the government? How far do these attitudes affect their participation in public policy making?

Forms of participation

It is useful to distinguish between *direct* and *indirect* participation. *Direct* participation refers to those means by which people try to influence the course of government policy by interacting with government policy makers or officials, face to face. Members of pressure or interest groups attempt to lobby politicians about their views on, say, measures to control cigarette smoking, abortion policies, or on the state of health care. Or community members form health committees to promote better preventive messages in their neighbourhood, or to lobby the local hospital to allow women to take husbands into the delivery room. In Chapters 6 and 7 we look at direct participation through interest groups.

Indirect participation consists of those political activities which are aimed at influencing the selection of government representatives and the policies they are likely to pursue. Traditionally such activities cover voting in elections, campaigning for particular candidates or parties, or joining political parties. In this chapter we look at indirect participation in policy.

How far do citizens influence policy making through indirect participation – through voting for the political representatives who support their views, for example? This is complex, and subject to long debates among political scientists. For example, in Mexico voting in elections is compulsory. This means that when people apply for passports or to enrol children in school they have to demonstrate that they have complied with their civic duty and voted at the last election. Compulsory voting is not only a developing country phenomenon: voting is also (at least theoretically) compulsory in Australia and Belgium. Thus opportunities for indirect participation depend to a great extent on the norms of the political system. It is helpful, therefore, to try to draw a distinction between different political systems.

Drawing on Blondel (1990) we can identify three basic questions to be asked in trying to characterize the differences between political systems:

— Who is involved in the political system? Who makes the decisions? That is, how *democratic* is the system?
— How are decisions taken and disseminated? Is there much discussion of alternatives? That is, is the system *liberal* or *authoritarian*?
— What is the substantive aim of policy? To distribute goods and services equally or maintain inequalities? That is, is the system *egalitarian* or *inegalitarian*?

Using these concepts, Blondel (1990: 28) places political systems in five clusters:

1. liberal-democratic;
2. egalitarian-authoritarian;
3. traditional-inegalitarian;
4. populist;
5. authoritarian-inegalitarian.

A word of warning before we continue. Many scholars have tried to construct typologies for classifying and comparing different kinds of political systems and most of these typologies have weaknesses. Clearly any characterization is imprecise: political systems are dynamic, and no system looks exactly like another. But there is considerable agreement on salient features. For example, all contemporary Western European countries are described as liberal democracies, characterized by relatively high levels of participation and openness. Most post-colonial political regimes in Africa have been unstable and ephemeral yet have exerted a powerful influence over society. Many communist regimes were authoritarian. Healey and Robinson (1992: 38) suggest a useful typology of African political systems that describes four regimes: military, authoritarian, populist and pluralist, categorizing these into further, overlapping sub-categories. Thus military states may be characterized by tyranny, dictatorship, or Leninism, and authoritarian states by Leninism, autocracy, monarchy, oligarchy, guided democracy, or social democracy. For our global overview, Blondel's five rather general categories offer a way of thinking about different political systems, as long as we keep in mind that they are not static categories.

Liberal democratic systems

Those countries whose governments operate within a stable framework of institutions – which together provide numerous channels for participation: political parties, elections, interest groups, and 'free' media – are generally referred to as liberal democracies. The 'models' include the countries of Western Europe and North America as well as Japan and India, amongst others. The countries falling into this category have varied considerably over time: Greece, Spain and Portugal became liberal democracies in the 1970s and 1980s, while Chile was a liberal democracy until 1973, when it became a military dictatorship, and reverted to being a liberal democracy again in 1990. Many of the ex-communist states of Eastern Europe and Africa are attempting to move in the direction of liberal democracies in the early 1990s.

Liberal democracies are characterized by the diverse number of groups which participate in public policy. It should not be assumed that this relatively open system necessarily leads to mass participation: in many countries substantial numbers of people do not vote even if they have the opportunity to do so. For example, in the American presidential election in 1988 only one person in two of voting age turned out to cast their ballot (Danziger 1991: 192). However, even if individuals do not exercise a vote for a political party, they may participate as a member of a group in order to express their preferences and influence government policy in this way. Liberal democracies are thus characterized by competing interest groups which attempt to negotiate and bargain with government to fulfil their own goals. The extent to which the diversity of pluralism equates with influence on policy, is, however, greatly debated. Policies in liberal democracies are normally regarded as neither highly inegalitarian nor truly egalitarian. There is usually some attempt to redistribute income and social services, although this has been less true of many liberal democracies, such as the UK, over the last decade, where differences between social classes have grown rather than diminished.

Structurally there are clear constitutional arrangements, and clear differences between parliaments or congresses, the courts, the executive, the bureaucracy and the church. There are many institutions which are respected, legitimate, and independent of the state.

Health policies in liberal democratic states are characterized by diversity, with public and private sectors competing to a greater or lesser extent. At one end of the continuum countries such as the United States rely almost entirely on the market to provide health care, treating it as a commodity. The state only steps in to cover the very old and the very poor. At the other end of the continuum – among the countries of Western Europe, for example – the public sector has played a significant role in health care financing and provision (although in the 1990s this is diminishing) and health care has been seen as an essential part of the welfare state. Health policy has been dominated by health care or medical services, but public health has received some recognition.

Egalitarian-authoritarian systems

Not many of these regimes exist today. They were characterized by the communist states: the Soviet Union, China, Vietnam, Cuba, Angola, Mozambique, although all these countries look very different in the 1990s. In the 1970s they were described as having closed leadership, authoritarian bureaucracies and highly regimented popular participation. However, even in the Soviet Union government could not ignore major interest groups and the movement away from authoritarianism began in the 1980s. In 1982 observers concluded cautiously that

> Mature socialist industrial states remain politically closed but the ruling elite must increasingly take into account a host of social, economic and institutional interests (Hague and Harrop 1982: 41).

The unprecedented mass demands for more say in government policy led to revolutionary change in these countries in the late 1980s and early 1990s; however, greater participation has resulted in greater instability, which will itself affect policy.

These states were *intendedly* egalitarian, even if there are doubts as to the extent and scope of equality. Full employment policies were accompanied by highly developed social security systems guaranteeing mass provision of education, health, childcare and pensions. Structurally such societies were more bureaucratic than liberal democracies, with much greater links between political and state structures, with the main (often only) political party playing a dominant and controlling role. Thus while it was sometimes argued that several institutional mechanisms existed for citizens to express their views and preferences, many described such participation as regimented, a form of social control rather than of democratic opportunity.

In these countries, health care was funded and provided almost entirely by the public sector (in some countries the private provision of health care was illegal) and as a basic human right. Though it was theoretically available to all on an equal basis, there were differences between rural and urban provision and in quality of care between facilities and groups. Through endeavours to redistribute resources these countries made some attempt to support general health through full employment, universal education and food subsidies as well as through the development of health services. Such redistributive effects (among other things) resulted in significant declines in infant mortality in countries such as Cuba and China. Neglect of environmental pollution and of preventive policies on alcohol and smoking, however, took their toll in some of the Eastern European socialist states.

Traditional-inegalitarian systems

Few political systems fall into this category in the modern world, although a few remain, largely in relatively remote or closed parts of the world. These systems are traditional: they preserve inequalities and oligarchical structures, and concentrate wealth in the hands of a few. Examples might include Saudi Arabia under the Saud family. Until 1990 Nepal was described as dynastic, with the king as chief policy maker. There was no contest for leadership, and few opportunities for mass participation. Although since 1979 there had been direct election to Nepal's legislative body, the national Panchayat, the king still appointed the Council of Ministers from this body. According to Panday (1989) it was common knowledge in Nepal that all major and many minor decisions were taken at the Royal Palace. A more democratic system was introduced in early 1990 after mass street demonstrations demanding more say in government. By and large, in times of stability, these regimes are supported (if passively) by the people, and are therefore not necessarily authoritarian. However, they may become so when crises emerge and threaten traditional legitimacy.

Health policy in such countries depends heavily on the private sector, and health services are largely urban and relatively under-developed: elites and their families are flown out to friendly neighbours or ex-colonial powers in acute or rare emergencies. Often such countries boast a great diversity of non-governmental organizations offering health services – ranging from religious organizations to international charities.

Populist regimes

Familiar to many African countries, in particular, populist political systems are based upon a single or dominant party which is predominantly nationalist. Leadership tends to be heavily personalized, and the opportunities for participation are often regulated through mass movements (of women, youth) which are allied to the single political party. Coercion prevails over consensus. Elites, either through kinship or membership of the party, exercise some influence on government, as long as they operate within its nationalist framework. Where the regime is able to exercise sufficient control over the populace, it may become totalitarian, with the state penetrating into all aspects of social life.

Many newly independent states of Africa and South America began life as populist regimes, typically born out of resistance to colonial or traditional powers. Strong leadership is often necessary to mobilize the population, especially where the society is strongly heterogeneous, with many different ethnic or religious groups. Expectations for egalitarianism are often high, but seldom realized, and such regimes may be fairly authoritarian while the leader retains popularity.

An example of autocracy is Malawi, ruled by Hastings Banda, who started as prime minister in 1962, became president in 1966 and was made life president in 1970. At the time of writing Malawi was undergoing political change, but Banda still had the power to dismiss members of parliament, and appoint, transfer and dismiss senior officials and ministers. As a result, policy initiative was very tightly controlled, and officials hesitated, until very recently, to articulate any misgivings for fear of being perceived as disloyal (Gulhati 1990). Korten (1989) quotes an Indonesian colleague describing many Third World countries as experiencing the law of the ruler instead of the rule of law. This was true of many European fascist states earlier this century.

Many of these regimes came to power after gaining independence from a colonial power, and in contrast to the colonial health systems which were restricted largely to colonialists and their families, they offered health services as a right to their populations. In parts of Africa (south and east), this was offered without direct charges to patients. In west and north Africa people expected to pay small amounts for health care. Initially the newly independent countries built major hospitals – what Morley and Lovel (1986: 164) have called 'disease palaces' – but in the 1970s embraced primary health care in an attempt to move health care closer to rural communities. Some of these countries, for example Tanzania, were the inspiration for the primary health care approach introduced internationally in the late 1970s. However, although many achieved significant extension of rural health facilities and trained many new health personnel in the 1970s and early 1980s, they were unable to sustain their expanded systems or to guarantee quality of care in economic recession. In the 1990s health policies were dominated by an increasing call to the private sector and to systems of cost recovery.

Authoritarian-inegalitarian systems

These regimes are often established as a reaction to a liberal demo-cratic regime, as occurred with the rise of fascism in Europe in the 1930s, or in Latin America periodically since 1945. In Africa, and to some extent in Asia, they have occurred as reactions to populist regimes – often regimes which have become corrupt. In these cases the military then takes over government.

Many developing countries have experienced military regimes over the past decades – with varying dimensions of authoritarianism or repression. Political violence wielded by paramilitary forces and 'death squads' against political dissidents (often very broadly defined) clearly limits participation. The longer a military regime stays in power, the more likely it is to involve civilians in government but they are likely to be members of an economic (business and landed) elite. Koehn (1983) argues that in Nigeria civil servants have always shaped and determined government policies, and under military regimes have gained even more power because of the military leaders' comparative lack of experience in government. Often top civil servants formed powerful coalitions with the armed forces:

> many career civil servants took advantage of the opportunity provided by the replacement of politicians with military men, who shared common ad-ministrative values and depended upon their support and expertise to ex-pand their already powerful role in fashioning public policies (1983: 6).

In the mid-1980s over 50 per cent of sub-Saharan governments were military or quasi-military (Sandbrook, quoted in Gulhati 1990: 1148).

Many of these states were characterized by autocratic personal rule, developed powerful machinery to enforce control, and are known to-day as 'soft', 'weak' or 'decayed' states because they lack legitimacy among the population and, far from initiating development, are its main constraint. Zaire is an example of the decayed state, with President Mobutu holding on to power ruthlessly, having personally enriched himself at the country's expense.

These regimes are highly authoritarian; 'normal' political life is reduced to a minimum, 'and there is even the widespread belief among the authorities that politics can be abolished altogether and be replaced by management and administration' (Blondel 1990: 32). They are inegalitarian because they protect the interests of a narrow class of elites, although there are a few examples – such as the Velasco regime in Peru – where a military government attempted to introduce redistributive land policies between 1968 and 1975 (McClintock 1980).

In the 1980s military governments were replaced with civilian gov-ernments in Peru, Bolivia, Argentina, Uruguay, Brazil, Guatemala and El Salvador, but the military elite, with large-scale business executives and landowners, continued to define the rules of the political game (often with financial and other support from the United States of America).

> Although claiming to favor democratic regimes in the Third World, most US government officials since World War II have actually supported military rule by professional soldiers, particularly when left-wing leaders espouse egalitar-ian economic policies that threaten capitalist interests (Andrain 1988: 23).

Health policies in such countries were diverse, with a tendency to rely on the private sector for citizens, but to protect the armed forces and their families. Escudero (1981) has argued that Argentina's health levels deteriorated with military takeovers because of the treatment of medi-cal care as a 'commodity', with the increase of imports of high tech-nology, and the takeover of health systems run by the labour unions. Almost all countries (whatever their political persuasion) provide sepa-rate health services for the armed forces, and these are often well supplied and financed.

In summary, classifications of political systems such as those used above are necessarily crude: they appear static, which they are not, and they take no account of history. For example, in those Third World countries that gained independence only after 1945, the confidence in national sovereignty may not have been very strong. In these countries, which were carved up rashly by colonial powers that showed little respect for existing legal or ethnic boundaries, independence resulted in multi-ethnic, multi-lingual states. In the 1990s, as the one-party states were encouraged to move towards more democratic structures (often a condition of continuing donor aid), they were faced with political difficulties stemming from their own traditions and history. In analysing Mozambique's attempts to move from a one-party to a multi-party system, Jorge Rebelo of the Frelimo Party noted that:

> national consciousness is still weak, and permitting several parties, several political forces, might encourage the creation of parties along tribal, regional or religious lines ... plus the danger that foreign forces could try to buy or corrupt Mozambicans so that they would set up parties obeying instructions coming from outside the country (Rebelo 1990).

Such issues are not peculiar to Mozambique, as is clear from the break-up of the former Yugoslavia and the Soviet Union.

From the above we can see that the political system encourages or discourages participation, and results in significantly different health policies. But even in the liberal democracies, in which it is accepted that indirect participation is an inherent part (since not all citizens can play a direct role in government and must therefore choose others to represent their views), there is a great deal of debate about the extent and degree to which citizens really can affect policy, and how far they believe that they can influence government. Concepts and theories about democracy are currently under review (Birch 1993).

The culture of politics

In all countries of the world people have beliefs about politics and the part they can play in influencing governments. There is enormous diversity in beliefs, even within the same country. Rural populations, to whom government is remote, may have very different notions from those held by people in cities. Wood illustrates this vividly in *Third Class Ticket*. A group of villagers from Bengal are taken on a tour of the Indian Assembly in Delhi, where a deputy asks:

> Did you come to see your great government? Here India, the greatest democracy in the world, is ruled. Here we make the plans for your crops, we make the arrangements with foreign countries to give us aid, and we preserve the ancient traditions of political wisdom which have been known in India for longer than anywhere else in the world. This is where everything you do is governed. This is the people's assembly (Wood 1980: 131).

A little later one of the villagers asks:

> — 'Please tell us what is democracy and why is India the biggest democracy?'
> — 'It is government by the people, and we have the most people who vote of any country in the world.'
> — 'But you said voting was a choice?'

— 'Yes, of course.'
— 'But we are always told by the money-lender where to put the mark on the paper. Where is the choice?'
— 'You should not be told by anyone.'
— 'Then how would we know where to put the mark?'
— 'You should put it by the man you think is the best, who will do what is right for you here in the assembly.'
— 'But why should any man in Delhi be concerned with our village? We have seen no one who knows our village.' (Wood 1980: 133)

For many rural dwellers what happens at the village level has far more meaning, and may be based on very clear hierarchical relationships that do not mirror the national political system – may, indeed, run parallel to it. For example, a chief or headman may be valued far above anyone in central government. In Botswana, the traditional decision-making body, the *kgotla*, is recognized as the legitimate forum for community decision-making.

> Perhaps the best proof of the central role of the *kgotla* is the fact that all organizations which claim to have a community-wide constituency hold their elections at the *kgotla* and bring their proposals to the *kgotla* for approval. Likewise, when officials from outside have a message for the village, whether Members of Parliament or researchers, they bring it to a *kgotla* meeting (Brown 1982: 90).

However, even though the *kgotla* is seen as the most directly legitimate decision-making body at community level, its influence is waning. Most rural people know that government politicians or officials have authority to induce change (to move homesteaders to communal villages, for example), or bring in external resources to assist the village. Politicians and officials may thus be feared, or politely ignored (they make promises they do not keep) or the opposite – they may instil enormous loyalty because they offer patronage. Not only do local politicians attract the resources for a new well, bridge, road or school, but they may be crucial for supporting villagers' applications for places in higher education or training, or for employment.

In the industrialized world political beliefs have undergone enormous changes over the past decades. There appears to be much greater disaffection with politics in both Britain and the United States than there was twenty years ago, discontent focusing on particular policies (for example, the Vietnam War in the USA in the 1970s, the Poll Tax or Community Charge in Britain in 1990) as well as with systems of voting. For example, in 1993 Italy voted to change from proportional representation to a mainly 'first-past-the-post' majority system. New Zealand, on the other hand, voted to abandon their first-past-the-post system in favour of a mixed system. In both countries it seemed that voters were criticizing what they perceived to be the vested interests of the political establishment.

As individuals, people may vote for representatives in local, regional or national authorities. One survey of seven liberal democracies in the mid-1960s showed that voting in national elections was the *only* form of participation in which the majority of each population engaged (Verba et al. quoted in Hague and Harrop 1982: 68). In Britain on average four out of ten people vote at local elections, although the percentage voting at national elections is usually much higher – nearer to 70 per cent. Similar ratios are reported elsewhere, although developing countries tend to have lower figures: the proportion of people who voted regularly in national elections in Nigeria was 56 per cent, with lower figures for local elections (Verba and Nie 1975, quoted in Danziger 1991). In India over 60 per cent of people have voted in general elections over the past decades (Curtis 1990). In some Third World countries votes have cash value: for example in the Philippines under President Marcos, 10–20 per cent of the electorate literally sold their vote, handing over signed ballot papers to local patrons in exchange for money or favours (Hague et al. 1992: 190).

Yet, in spite of relatively low turnouts for voting, the cynicism expressed in the title of a book by a British member of parliament, *If voting changed anything, they'd abolish it* (Livingstone 1987), is relatively unusual. While critics such as Livingstone argue that elections are in essence a device for expanding the power of the elite over the population, research suggests that competitive elections do make a difference to public policy. Parties do differ in their domestic policies, and prefer to implement their promises when they are elected. Hague et al. (1992: 183) point to the different policies emanating from right- and left-dominated liberal democracies in the post-war period in Europe. They suggest that Sweden, where the left has been more influential (compared with Italy, where the right has dominated), has had lower unemployment but higher inflation, more students in higher education, lower military expenditure and a larger public sector.

The most dramatic changes in political culture were seen in the demands for democracy in eastern European countries in 1989. Political crises in those countries in the 1950s (East Germany, Hungary, Poland), in the 1960s (Czechoslovakia, Poland) and continuing with Solidarity into the 1980s in Poland, indicated a severe disaffection with the authoritarian regimes in power, which came to a head in the years after 1989.

There are some countries where voting may be seen largely as symbolic – in one-party states, for example, there may be very little difference between competing candidates, and a vote may be a way of showing support for the ruling regime. Indeed, in more authoritarian regimes, *not* voting may be considered an act of dissension. In some countries citizens may not be allowed to vote. As late as 1993 South Africa still had a majority disenfranchised black population. Women in Switzerland, Portugal and Spain only got the vote in the 1970s.

If people do not use their votes as individuals, they may utilize other options. They sometimes take part in mass demonstrations, boycotts or strikes. In the last decades the media have brought home the drama of mass protests: Americans against the Vietnam war; Chinese in Beijing's Tiananmen Square; Czechs, Poles, Hungarians, Romanians and East Germans in the cities of eastern Europe. In many countries of Africa there have been mass protests as the price of food has risen under structural adjustment policies.

Disillusion with voting at elections has also been countered by alternative means to influence government. Over the past two decades there has been a great increase in the formation of interest groups to pressure governments to change their policies in particular areas. Jordan and Richardson (1987) point to the growth of new pressure groups as well as the increase in membership of established groups all over Europe – the environmental movement being one of the obvious examples. Many Third World countries have seen a huge multiplying of non-governmental organizations, many of which are service-related, but which may act as pressure groups too.

Indeed, Czechoslovakian sociologists have argued that the revolution in 1989 came about because there were a number of small groups, institutions and individuals (nature conservationists, environmentalists, students, actors, writers, painters, and scholars) who formed 'islands of positive deviation' during the 1980s, and had been proposing an alternative definition of the state (Wright 1990). Even under authoritarian communist regimes, people joined interest groups in spite of the fact that their ability to influence government was limited. We look more closely at the way interest groups work in Chapter 6.

From the above it is clear that the type of government or political culture within which people live makes an enormous difference to the extent to which they do, or can, participate indirectly in public decision making.

Exogenous factors that affect policy

So far we have talked about the extent to which the political system affects participation in policy. But other, exogenous, factors may also affect policy formulation and implementation. The range of factors that influence or determine what governments do, or what they choose not to do, are virtually infinite. Aside from the effects of the political system, public policy may also be influenced by international tension, a country's climate, economic wealth, degree of ethnic conflict, historical traditions, and the level of literacy among other things. Leichter (1979) orders the factors influencing policy into four different areas: *situational factors*, which are more or less transient, impermanent or idiosyncratic conditions that have an impact on policy; *structural factors*, which are the relatively unchanging elements of the society and polity; *cultural factors*, which are the value commitments of groups within communities or the society as a whole; and *environmental factors*, which are events, structures and values that exist outside the boundaries of a political system but which influence decisions within it.

Thus, *situational factors* such as violent events or sudden change may affect policy. Wars, for example, may allow governments to introduce policies which would not be considered legitimate under other circumstances: the UK government was able to annex the private, voluntary hospitals during the Second World War in order to provide a coordinated and national health service. War in Nicaragua mobilized people to great effect in the social sector: giving voluntary services to improve community health. Thus it was possible to mobilize thousands of volunteers to help improve the delivery of preventive services such as vaccinations (Frieden and Garfield 1987), so much so that infant mortality rates decreased from 113 to 73 per 1,000 between 1979 and 1985. On the other hand, war in Mozambique steadily undermined a decade of positive health policies to extend the primary health sector. Deliberate targeting of health workers and rural health facilities resulted in irregular supplies of drugs and equipment to peripheral health facilities, withdrawal of some health workers into urban areas, and considerable insecurity in rural areas (Cliff and Noormohammed 1988). The unremitting antagonism of the United States government to Cuba under Castro, while not erupting in violent war, mobilized the population throughout the 1960s and 1970s to support actively its own government's policies because of perceived enemy hostility.

Other changes, such as a coup or a radical change in political leadership, may also legitimate policy change which would not otherwise be sanctioned. It has been argued, for example, that military takeovers in Argentina led to reorientation in health policy, resulting in poorer health status for the population (Escudero 1981). When Zambia's new democratic movement government came into power in 1992, replacing the single political party headed by Kenneth Kaunda which had been in power since independence in the 1960s, it was able to remove sub-sidies on some foodstuffs with no major public demonstrations against the rise. This contrasted markedly with violent demonstrations against a similar attempt by the past government a year before.

Thus war and major political change can expand the role of the state, or distort, divert or limit state activity. They may legitimate changes which would otherwise not be accepted. In the 1930s the depression led to the introduction of social insurance in Europe. In the 1980s slow economic growth led to many liberal democracies turning to the pri-vate sector as a way of shifting resources away from the public sector towards 'managed markets' in the health field.

However, this does not mean that change is only possible under crisis situations. McPherson and Radelet (1991) describe how the Gambia introduced an Economic Recovery Programme in the mid-1980s which, in spite of many uncomfortable effects on certain sections of the com-munity, nonetheless drew no opposition. This was partly explained by the political environment of disorganized opposition forces and weak labour unions, and partly by a heightened perception on the part of government and military policy elites that the economic stability of the nation was endangered. Threats came from foreign donors, on the one hand, who had supported the IMF's attempt to get the Gambia de-clared ineligible to borrow unless it introduced economic reforms, and on the other hand from its larger and richer neighbour, Senegal, which had always looked towards incorporating the tiny Gambian nation within its borders. Opposition was also tempered because liberalizing rice importation at a time when world rice prices fell sharply meant that the price of rice in the Gambia was actually lower after the economic recovery programme was introduced.

Structural factors clearly affect policy, and we have already discussed how far the type of political regime may affect participation and there-fore policies. The economic base of a country will affect its policies: for example, whether it is primarily agrarian or one-product dependent. Cuba is ambivalent about health education in relation to tobacco and sugar, because they are its two main export crops. Technological change can have all sorts of unanticipated effects on policy: the diffusion of technology in the health sector can completely distort countries' health budgets. For example, the growth of sophisticated machinery for imaging – from ultrasound to nuclear magnetic resonance – has affected health budgets as well as demands and expectations for treatment.

A fascinating example from Brazil is related to caesarian sections. In Brazil, many doctors are trained but salaries are relatively low, so doctors may have three or four jobs – in both the public and private sector. In the mid-1980s it was observed that the number of caesarean sections had risen to 30 per cent of all births. Research suggested that many of these operations were unnecessary (50 per cent occurred among high-income and low-risk women). Decisions to undertake caesarean sections were taken on financial grounds (doctors' fees for operations were higher than for natural births) rather than medical need. In order to change this, the state introduced a policy of equal fees for operations and natural births. However, the rate of caesarean sections continued to rise. The reason was structural. Because the labour market was so organized, and doctors felt they had to have several jobs to gain sufficient income, they needed to control the timing of giving birth, and this was easier to do with operations than with natural methods, which were less predictable (Barros, Vaughan and Victora 1986). Clearly structural change, in terms of the labour market for doctors, was necessary before change in the numbers of caesarean sections would alter. The fact that caesarians are rising elsewhere, as in the UK, suggests that the issue is even more complicated. Here it seems the increase has more to do with the reluctance of some doctors and midwives to take risks, because of greater reliance on technology (and resulting loss of clinical experience) and fear of litigation.

Other structural factors may affect policy considerably: the type of economy has had clear repercussions for the sorts of health services countries have developed. In the United States, the reluctance to provide public services except for the indigent or very poor was grounded in the structure of a free market system. At the other end of the spectrum, the centrally planned economies until the 1990s assumed responsibility for health care for all. Obviously a country's national wealth or gross national product (GNP) affects its ability to allocate resources to health. Although both Thailand and Sri Lanka's public expenditure on health was less than 2 per cent of GNP, Thailand's total GNP was eight times larger than Sri Lanka's – US\$ 64.4 billion as against US\$ 7.3 billion (UNDP 1992).

Also social and demographic factors can affect policy. The degree of urbanization affects the feasibility of providing services, while the birth rate and age structure of the population have long-term consequences for health policy. Significant migration can affect the transmission of diseases such as malaria and the Human Immunodeficiency Virus (HIV), and many other aspects of health.

Culture also has its influence on policy. Political culture affects people's participation and belief in government and change. If people do not trust the government, or feel some pride in the political system, an 'alienated political culture' may result, such as in Italy in the 1980s and

1990s as corruption and dirty dealing by the state were uncovered. The effects on behaviour may be extremely complex, but they are unlikely to lead to open participation. Language, religion and traditional social values all play a part too. In those parts of the world where women are kept in purdah, it may be difficult for health services to reach them. In many countries the national language is not spoken throughout the country and women, in particular, may be limited to one or two local languages. This creates difficulties in training and recruitment which may affect the utilization of health services and communications between professionals and communities.

And finally there are what Leichter refers to as environmental factors which affect policy, but which I prefer to call *external* or *international* structural factors. There is increasing interdependence among states, which for the health sector is observable in many forms. It has long been understood that transnational corporations – in the pharmaceutical industry, for example – can have profound effects on national policy making. Trade agreements (or rather disagreements), such as the General Agreement on Tariffs and Trade (GATT), can also impact considerably at the national level. Bilateral and multilateral aid flows are an influential component of policy making in many developing countries. For example, many such countries receive aid because they occupy an important strategic position for the donor: over 30 per cent of US aid goes to Israel and Egypt. Similarly, multilateral financial institutions such as the IMF, in conjunction with bilateral institutions, can lay down ground rules or conditions for recipient countries. These are often demands to adopt certain economic reforms (reduction in the public sector) or political reforms (introduction of multi-party systems). Indeed, many developing countries will argue that national policy is being driven by external donors who often do not understand the specific conditions of the recipient country, and, more importantly, are not held accountable when policies go wrong. We still have little understanding of the extent to which policies are diffused through such multilateral institutions, through meetings, missions to countries or exchanges of information.

Conclusions

Many of these issues we will pick up again as we look at the various actors in the policy process. The main purpose of this chapter is to draw attention to two major considerations that have to be taken into account when looking at policy making. First, that an analysis of the political system will help to ascertain how far participation in policy will be encouraged or allowed. While liberal democracies, at least in theory, encourage both direct and indirect participation, authoritarian regimes may formulate policy with very little public consultation or participation. People's beliefs about the political system will also affect their levels of participation. And second, all policy will be affected by exogenous factors. Situational factors such as wars, or a change of prime minister, may provide opportunities for change not usually perceived possible. But structural factors, such as a country's geography or its ethnic heterogeneity, will also affect policy. Such factors provide the context within which policy making occurs, and have to be taken into account when considering policy change.

3

Power and the policy process

Theories about policy making are concerned with processes. They are modes of analysis which focus on decision-making processes, but some take a macro-view and others a micro-view. Macro theories are concerned essentially with power in political systems, and can be differentiated by theme: consensus or conflict. In the last chapter we looked at Easton's systems approach, which stressed the responses of the whole political system to demands made on it from the environment, and how policies are fed back to the political system to ensure consensus is maintained. In this model, political power is perceived as the ability of government to decide collectively and to put agreed policies into practice. The second theme – the conflict approach to the political system – focuses on who makes policy: a small number of elites or many different groups. From this perspective political power consists of the ability to impose policies that may be opposed. It is a 'question of power over others, rather than power to achieve shared objectives' (Hague et al. 1992: 9).

The micro theories of policy making focus less on political systems and more on the mechanisms and administrative routine of policy making. These theories range along a continuum from decision-making models of rationality at one extreme, to incrementalist models at the other.

In this chapter we bring together the macro theories of consensus and conflict, and the micro theories of policy making, because even the micro-theories about how decisions are made have to deal with who influences policy. They raise the question: is it possible to devise rational policies if many different groups are insisting on their demands being met?

Power: who influences policy?

A commonly held view of democracy is that there are many ways in which people can participate in the policy process and so influence governments to promote the policies they want. This view is not universal, however, and some argue the opposite: that power is in the hands of a few, and most policy is decided by a small group of elites within government or even outside government. This chapter explores these theories to see what seems most relevant for health policy.

The pluralist view

The classical pluralist view is that power is diffused throughout society: that no one group holds total power over others. Pluralists base their arguments on the following observations within liberal democracies (Smith 1977):

1. Political equality and individualism are protected by the fundamental political rights to vote and to free speech. Access to government is guaranteed through electoral choice, through lobbying and other forms of pressure group activity and through politically free mass media.
2. The weakness of the individual citizen is compensated for by the right and ability of all to organize groups and associations for political action. This level of citizen participation allows a certain level of expression of opposition which serves to control or direct political dissent.
3. The state in a pluralist society is not monolithic: it is regarded as a neutral set of institutions, adjudicating between conflicting social and economic interests. The state does not defend the interests of any one particular class or group, nor show any marked bias towards particular interests.
4. Even though the state has its elites, the pluralist state is characterized by a plurality of elites. No one particular elite dominates all the time.

The expectation from a pluralist policy process is that policy outputs are wise and in the collective public interest because they have achieved majority support, and because the government is the unbiased arbiter between many competing interests. However, many question the view that the state (or government) is a neutral negotiator between different interests. For example public choice theorists argue that, far from seeing the political system as one in which government holds the balance between different groups who jostle and bargain for their own interests, the government in fact has substantial power which is strongly linked to the interests of other powerful institutions such as the military, sources of capital, boards of banks, large or transnational corporations and even international organizations outside the state. These institutions form powerful coalitions of interests, and only promote policies that serve their own interests.

For example, in the 1970s many observed the existence of coalitions of interests from industry (representing capital) and labour (representing workers), which together formed powerful corporate interest groups. Such groups became so large (especially employer–employee groups) that they were ruled by a few leaders, who conferred with government, but were very distant from their largely passive members (whom they represented). It was argued that governments welcomed corporatism because it was easier to deal with one powerful group than with many – and the state could also then expect the leaders to control any conflicting interests between members. This was not always the experience however: the Trades Union Congress (TUC) in Britain, a corporate body which negotiates with government on behalf of many different unions throughout the country, was systematically undermined by government in the 1980s, and the main corporatist relations remaining were between government and the business community. In Thailand the government established Joint Public Private Coordinating Committees (JPPCCs) for different sectors and a central one for the economy as a whole, in order to facilitate close coordination between public and private sectors. JPPCCs have been used by business to forward complaints or requests to central government (Bennett and Tangcharoensathien 1994).

The elitist view

Marxism provides the theoretical base for many elitist theories, which suggest that policy choice and change is dominated by particular social classes, and that the primary function of the state is to ensure the continuing dominance of these classes.

Such theories are supported by some empirical evidence which suggests that the links between certain classes in society and top policy-making positions are very close. One study in Britain in the 1970s showed that 40 per cent of the top three ranks of the British army were connected by birth or marriage to members of the economic and state elite – cabinet ministers, senior diplomats, major financiers. A classic study in the USA suggested that three overlapping groups dominated top positions at the federal level: political, corporate, and military leaders, and that many of them had attended the same schools and universities, and some even had ties through kinship (Wright Mills 1956). Today Wright Mills' theory could be regarded as a form of corporatism, which maintains that elected representatives have been losing power to institutional interests (big business, the military and, in some cases, the trade unions) and a small inner core of government policy makers (Hague, Harrop and Breslin 1992).

In many Third World countries, bureaucrats, businessmen, professionals, military and government make up tight policy circles that form, to all intents and purposes, a ruling or dominant class. In some countries, they may be so few in number that they can be recognized as elites by their family names.

Elitists thus conclude that pluralist views of power and influence in the policy process are wrong, and base their arguments on the following claims:

1. The political elite is only open to members of the dominant economic classes – it is they who really influence policy. Clearly in some countries this elite is very small – it includes the military, and may have a stranglehold on power. This is a familiar pattern in some Latin American and African countries.

2. Interest groups are clearly not equally powerful. They all command different levels of resources, and such inequalities affect how far their influence extends. Groups representing business (the alcohol or pharmaceuticals industry, for example, or large producers such as tobacco farmers) which affect national trade and economic growth have more leverage with government policy makers than groups representing service industries (hairdressers or nurses). In the health field, high-status medical professionals may have an important direct or indirect effect on, for example, health manpower policy. Doctors often hold the last card in negotiating with governments – they can leave the country and practise their profession elsewhere. Where they are in short supply, as in many Third World countries, this represents a real, if indirect, threat to government. Hospital porters or midwives do not have the same level of influence. The potential power of a trade union (which can call its members out on strike, with potential damage to the national economy) is far greater and more directly felt than a peace group concerned about the growth in nuclear armaments.

3. Pluralism focuses on the government policy process, but ignores the power that economic domination confers outside the areas of state activity (especially among transnational companies and international organizations). Transnational corporations operate across national

boundaries, and can exert considerable pressure on governments, their ultimate weapon being to remove their investment. In later chapters we see how the tobacco and alcohol transnational corporations have influenced health policy in many east European and Third World countries. Many international organizations are dominated by the powerful industrialized countries, which have not only influenced conditions of world trade to the detriment of the Third World, but have also been able to force some Third World countries to introduce drastic changes in domestic economic policy. Many ministries of health in Africa attest to the influence of international organizations in setting their policy agendas. For example, throughout the 1980s UNICEF's enthusiastic promotion of the GOBI interventions (growth monitoring, oral rehydration, breastfeeding and immunization) precluded the pursuit of other policies in some countries.

However, in analysing the way policy develops, many believe that the elitist view of the political system overstates the capacity of elites to wield power. Non-elites *do* challenge elites – and government policies are so wide-ranging and cover so many areas that it is easy to observe there are multiple groups competing for attention on specific issues. Even in developing countries, where interest groups are not always sufficiently well organized to put effective pressure on government officials, certain groups will have access to government through, for instance, professional bodies or the church. Hall et al. (1975) suggest a compromise theory of power. Their notion of *bounded pluralism* suggests that issues of high politics – largely economic questions – are decided within an elitist framework, but that most domestic, routine policies on health, education, transport and housing are likely to be developed along pluralist lines, with some participation of different groups at different stages of the policy process. It may be that with non-controversial issues there is room for manoeuvre in the policy process, and government may be open to influence from different sources as long as government policy makers perceive them as legitimate. Of course, it can be argued that even domestic policies are affected by economic policies, and that therefore ultimately all policy is in the hands of a ruling elite. However, this is such a strong negation of the ability of people to change policy that I would still support the notion of a bounded policy space in most liberal democracies and some other political systems in which there is room to manoeuvre, to challenge and change government policy.

The same question is addressed by Lindblom (1979) who concludes that policy issues are divided into two categories: those on ordinary questions of policy, and those that constitute the grand issues pertaining

to the fundamental structure of politico-economic life. On the first set
of issues he sees many groups actively participating. On the grand issues
he suggests that participation is weak or even absent:

> The treatment in politics of the grand issues is governed by a high degree of
> homogeneity of opinion – heavily indoctrinated, I would add (Lindblom 1979:
> 523).

Many of these issues are pursued further in Chapter 6.

Process: what is policy and how is policy made?

Up to now we have deliberately used the words decision making and
policy making synonymously. Some analysts differentiate policy from
decisions largely on the grounds that policy is larger than decision –
that policy usually involves a series of more specific decisions, sometimes in a rational sequence (Hogwood and Gunn 1984). Harrop (1992:
1) suggests that a decision is a 'more or less explicit selection from a
range of options', while policy involves 'a bundle of decisons and how
they are put into practice'.

However, in everyday life the distinction between policy and decision is often blurred: they cannot simply be differentiated as macro and
micro levels of reality. Policy makers never start with blank sheets of
infinite possibilities – previous decisions affect present policies. Governments' *ad hoc* decisions (on maternity leave, nursery schools, school hours)
may together add up to forceful implicit policy (discouraging women
to join the labour force). For these reasons, in the general framework
used in this book, decision making and policy making are often used
interchangeably.

There is also confusion over what policy means and the context in
which it is used. One commentator of the British economic scene at
a time of particular uncertainty noted caustically:

> A curious word is being used to describe the Government's latest round of
> economic improvisation. It is being called a 'policy' ... What policy? A policy
> ought to be something more than a galvanic twitch. It ought to have legs for
> distances longer than those implied in 'a dash for growth'. It ought to have
> some end in view larger than seeing an addled Government through the
> next month (Ignatieff 1992: 25).

He went on to say that:

> policy is not about surviving till Friday. Nor is policy to be confused with
> strategy, which is about getting through to Christmas. Policy is the selection
> of non-contradictory means to achieve non-contradictory ends over the

medium to long term. Policy is the thread of conviction that keeps a government from being the prisoner of events ... (Ignatieff 1992: 25).

Other uses of policy observed by Hogwood and Gunn (1984) are as a *label for a field of activity* (for example, talking about the government's economic policy, or social policy), or as an *expression of general purpose* or a desired state of affairs (for example, 'the government's policy is to build a new society, free of exploitation') or as a *specific proposal* (for example, 'the university's policy is to give students the right to sit on all governing bodies within the university from next year', or sometimes policy is used meaning *programme*. For example, the government may talk about its school health programme, which includes legislation precluding children from starting school before they are fully immunized against the major vaccine-preventable childhood diseases, and providing for medical inspections, subsidized school meals and compulsory health education in the school curriculum. The programme is thus an embodiment of policy for schoolchildren.

In this book policy is used to denote *a series of more or less related activities and their intended and unintended consequences for those concerned*, rather than a discrete decision. Policy is usually directed towards the accomplishment of some purpose or goal and is defined as:

> a purposive course of action followed by an actor or set of actors in dealing with a problem or matter of concern (Anderson 1975: 3).

Public policies are those policies developed by governmental bodies and officials, and thus focus on purposive action by or for governments. Policy involves the decision to act on some particular problem, but includes subsequent decisions relating to its implementation and enforcement. Policy should involve more than intention or statement of intent – it should represent what governments actually do. However, given that government's choice *not* to do something may represent a policy (successive United States governments chose not to introduce a universal health system, but to rely on market forces to meet people's health needs), policy must include what governments say they will do, what they actually do, and what they decide not to do. In looking at public policy, we are concerned with the formal institutions of government: they provide the structure within which the public policy process takes place.

Health policy embraces courses of action that affect the set of institutions, organizations, services, and funding arrangements of the health care system. It goes beyond health services, however, and includes actions or intended actions by public, private and voluntary organizations that have an impact on health. This means that health policy is concerned with environmental and socio-economic effects on health as well as with health care provision. However, many books on health policy focus narrowly on the health care system only. Nancy Milio (1987) prefers to talk about *healthy public policy* in order to differentiate the broader definition from the narrow.

Types of policies

Policies vary, and the type of policy may affect political behaviour. One simple way of differentiating policies is to divide them into 'high politics' and 'low politics'. These terms are borrowed from the field of international relations, where high politics is defined as:

> the maintenance of core values – including national self-preservation – and the long-term objectives of the state (Evans and Newnham 1992: 127).

Low politics are issues

> not seen as involving fundamental or key questions relating to a state's national interests, or those of important and significant groups within the state (Evans and Newnham 1992: 184).

Thus major economic decisions (devaluation of the currency) or perceived national security crises (border disputes) are high politics, and may be influenced by a few powerful groups who essentially make up what could be called a ruling class. In these situations, government is likely to confer only with groups considered important for the nation's economic and political security (representatives from the financial and military sectors), and the policy process is likely to be relatively closed. In health, reform of the health sector may be treated as high politics, depending on how far it is perceived by policy makers as being crisis determined. Introducing essential drugs policies or restricted lists of drugs may also be high politics, with policies being decided by a few elites (see Box 8.1 on Bangladesh). In this book I refer to policies addressing high politics issues as *systemic* or *macro* policies. These policies are usually the domain of the government, formulated by government and passed as law through the legislature.

However, on a whole series of ordinary issues – or low politics – the policy process may be much more open. Groups with special interests may have considerable access to government, and may be given opportunities to influence policy. This clearly varies hugely, and is generally more common in developed countries than in developing countries. Nevertheless, even in the more closed policy environments of many Third World countries, non-government organizations, the church and professional groups may influence some types of low-politics policies. In health many policies would come into the category of low politics. Policies addressing low politics issues are referred to as *sectoral* or *micro* policies. Sectoral policies may not be considered by the government as a whole, but rather by the department responsible for that sector or at sub-national levels, and may be communicated through circulars or letters rather than through legislation. These different policy types and levels are set out in the Table 3.1, with examples.

Table 3.1 Policy types and policy levels

	High politics	Low politics ('politics as usual')
Policy type	Macro policy Systemic policy	Micro policy Sectoral policy
Policy level	National government State government Regional authority	Ministry of health Local health authority Institution (e.g. clinic, hospital)
Policy example	Regulation of private sector Reform of civil service salaries and conditions	Introduction of breast screening Change in vaccine policy

While this conceptual visualization is useful, it must be remembered that policies may change with circumstances: what appears to be a low-politics issue (the closing of a hospital) may become a high-politics issue because of the actions of various interests, including the media. Similarly, systemic policies may not be perceived as high politics at one point in time, but will be at another. Also sectoral or micro policies may cause incremental shifts in policy which, over the longer term, add up to a systemic policy change.

Another way of thinking about policy types is to define them by their effects. One typology divides policies into distributive, regulatory, self-regulatory and redistributive policies (Lowi 1964, adapted in Palmer and Short 1989), although these are not exclusive. *Distributive* policies consist of the provision of services or benefits to particular groups in the population, which do not result in any obvious disadvantage or reduction in benefits to other groups. As such they are not particularly controversial, and the policy process may be quite open, and meet little resistance from the interest groups involved. The introduction of village health worker schemes would be an example of a distributive policy. *Regulatory* policies involve the imposition of limitations or restrictions on the behaviour of individuals or groups (forbidding private practice among nurses and licensing physicians, for example). Because they are aimed at a relatively narrow section of the population, even if they are controversial they are unlikely to attract the participation of many other interest groups. *Self-regulatory* policies are generally sought by an organization as a means of controlling its own interests, and may be introduced to avoid interest group activity. The International Federation of Pharmaceutical Manufacturers Associations introduced a Code of Marketing Practices for its own members in the 1980s in order to stave off an onslaught from many different groups, and some pharmaceutical companies established new procedures for the advertising and labelling of drugs after strong criticism from consumer groups. And finally *redistributive* policies are those which consist of deliberate government attempts to change the distribution of income or wealth (by means of progressive taxation, for example). They are often extremely controversial, and may engender strong interest group activity both in opposition and in support.

In health policy, where policies are more usually likely to fall into the category of low-politics, distributive or regulatory policies, it seems reasonable to see the policy process as pluralist rather than elitist. Many different interests may be expressed in relation to health policies, ranging from strong groups such as the medical profession or the pharmaceutical manufacturers, to relatively weak groups representing consumers of particular services (diabetics, or those who need renal dialysis), and government will take notice of some of these groups at some points in the policy process (although not always). This does not mean that health policies are always non-controversial or low politics. Current changes in the financing of health systems, for example, have been the subject of great controversy in many countries, and interest groups such as the medical profession have been notably weak in dealing with determined governments. As we will see in Chapter 6, pluralist inputs to health sector reform in Britain in the 1980s were also limited.

The four stages of policy making

Because policy making is so complex, there have been various attempts to outline a framework which simplifies a process often described as messy, fortuitous, random and therefore not open to systematic analysis. The most common framework used describes the process of policy making by stages or phases, going from problem identification to policy evaluation.

PROBLEM IDENTIFICATION AND ISSUE RECOGNITION   How do issues get on to the policy agenda? Why do some issues not even get discussed?

POLICY FORMULATION   Who formulates policy? How is it formulated? Where do initiatives come from?

POLICY IMPLEMENTATION   Arguably the most important aspect of policy – yet often gets short shrift. What resources are there available? Who should be involved? How can implementation be enforced?

POLICY EVALUATION   What happens once a policy is put into effect? Is it monitored? Does it achieve its objectives? Does it have unintended consequences?

These different stages of policy making are described variously. Kingdon (1984: 3), for example, talks of a set of processes that include at least:

1. the setting of the agenda;
2. the specification of alternatives from which a choice is to be made;
3. an authoritative choice among those specified alternatives; and
4. the implementation of the decision.

Hogwood and Gunn (1984) provide a more detailed set of processes:

1. Deciding to decide (issue search and agenda-setting);
2. Deciding how to decide (issue filtration);
3. Issue definition;
4. Forecasting;
5. Setting objectives and priorities;
6. Options analysis;
7. Policy implementation, monitoring and control;
8. Evaluation and review;
9. Policy maintenance, succession or termination.

While there is little disagreement among policy analysts about the different stages of the policy process, there is a great deal of dissension as to how far policy follows a rational or logical process from problem identification to policy evaluation. Many would argue that the above models give a false impression, because they imply that policy making follows a linear process through sequential phases, starting with identifying a problem and ending with a set of activities to solve that problem. Also, because so much attention is given to decision making, it

appears that there is often an invisible line between stages 2 and 3 of
the first model: that once the decision is made, implementation is
assumed to occur.

Obviously this begs many questions. Policies may remain intentions
that are never put into practice, or may be implemented in ways that
distort the original intentions of the policy makers. Indeed, anticipation
of the means of implementation may well affect policy. For example,
in the mid-1970s the government of India wanted to extend primary
health care throughout rural communities, and believed that the way
to do this was to train village inhabitants for short periods, after which
they would be able to provide rudimentary health care to their own
neighbours. However, the Federal Government knew that most of the
states of India were sceptical about the value of such workers and
therefore not interested in training them, and it was the states that were
responsible for health care services. The Federal Government therefore
offered additional financial resources as an incentive to encourage states
to start training and employing village health workers.

Is policy-making a rational process?

So far we have suggested that policy making is not controlled entirely
by government. If it is accurate to think of the health policy process
as essentially pluralist, is it possible to assume that such a process will
be rational, taking into account all the different views, and coming out
with an optimal and rational policy? Much attention has been focused
on the micro-level aspects of the policy process. Here policy analysts
have looked closely at the actors – the policy makers – within an
organizational setting, and asked how far policy makers are rational
actors who accumulate information, choose between policy options, and
then take the 'best' course of action. Three basic models have been
suggested to consider the question of how rational policy making is: the
rational or synoptic, the incrementalist, and mixed scanning.

Rational or synoptic models

Many believe that policies or decisions are made in a rational way. That
is, policy makers go logically through certain stages to reach the best
possible policy:

1. The policy maker is faced with a particular problem, which can be
   separated from other problems, or compared with other problems
   (for example, there are insufficient financial resources to provide good
   quality primary health care services).

2. The goals, values or objectives that guide policy makers are clarified and ranked according to their importance (for example, equity goals – providing good services for everyone – may be seen as secondary to efficiency goals – providing services at the least cost).

3. The various alternatives for dealing with the problem are considered (for example, raise taxes, introduce fees at primary health care facilities, increase charges for drugs or in-patients, among other things).

4. The consequences (costs and benefits) following from the selection of each alternative are investigated (for example, the balance between raising revenue by introducing user charges for health services and the resulting decrease in utilization of services).

5. Each alternative, and its consequences, are compared with other alternatives.

6. The policy maker chooses the alternative (and its consequences) that maximises the attainment of his or her goals, values or objectives.

The result of this process is a rational decision – that is, one that most effectively achieves a given end.

However, many question the usefulness of rational models which prescribe how policy ought to be made. They argue that policy makers are constrained from behaving rationally in many ways. First, policy makers do not always face concrete, defined problems – they have to identify or recognize the problem first. Or even if a problem is identified – for instance, insufficient funds for health care – it may be difficult to identify the specific problem: is it caused by reluctance or inability to pay for services, or by excessive demand? Defining the problem may be difficult for the policy maker. The whole issue of environmental deterioriation and global warming is so huge, and the effects so unknown, and so international, that policy makers may be at a loss to know where to start analysis except at very local levels (for example, lowering tax on lead-free petrol in order to encourage drivers to use it). In many of the newly industrializing nations, where levels of pollution are reaching uncomfortable if not dangerous levels, the complications (and conflicts) of knowing how to formulate policy are huge. And if defining the problem is not simple, nor is clarifying goals and objectives and turning these into operational policies that can be implemented.

Second, it is unrealistic to think that policy makers have the time, imagination and information available to allow them to make comprehensive predictions about the costs and benefits of the various alternatives. The complexity of the task is too great and unintended consequences cannot, by definition, be anticipated.

Third, policy makers themselves are not value-free. They are not objective. They have their favourite types of solutions, specific ways of thinking about problems. Neo-liberals will promote privatization policies, and may be reluctant to introduce censorship of books or films. Also organizations are not homogeneous – the individuals within and their values may differ from each other or from the values of the organization (for example, civil servants in the UK may belong to any political party but must serve the government in power, which may mean formulating policy which is in conflict with their own ideas).

Fourth, past policy determines present policy. It may not be possible to draw up a perfect list of alternatives – some of these will be foreclosed because of past commitments or investments.

In answer to these sorts of criticisms, the rational theorists have argued that the rational–synoptic model of policy making is an ideal model and that as such it is unfair to criticize it as being unrealistic or impracticable. Simon (1957) argues, for example, that the rational model gives a deliberately idealized view of how decision making occurs in organizations – and provides an ideal to strive towards. He suggested that in actuality most policy making should be described as following a process of 'bounded rationality'. This involves the policy maker in choosing an alternative intended not to maximize his values but to be satisfactory or good enough. The term *satisficing* describes this process. In other words, Simon and others say that policy makers are intendedly rational, but work within many administrative and bureaucratic constraints (such as inadequate information), which means that they are not always perfectly rational in their policy choices.

In summary, the rational–synoptic model of policy making is an ideal model – with strong prescriptive overtones – providing a theory of the way policy makers ought to behave in making decisions. The second approach to policy making takes a quite different, descriptive approach, and is a response in part to the rational model.

The incrementalist model

Incrementalism avoids some of the problems of the rational-synoptic theories and is more descriptive of the way policy is actually made. It can be summarized as follows:

1. The selection of goals or objectives and the means of implementation are closely allied – and not distinct from one another. In fact, policy makers often avoid thinking through or spelling out their objectives. This may reflect an awareness that to do so would precipitate conflict rather than agreement.

2. Policy makers look at a small number of alternatives for dealing with a problem and tend to choose options that differ only marginally from existing policies.

3. For each alternative only the most important consequences are considered.

4. There is no optimal policy option: the test of a good decision is that there is agreement among policy makers about the option chosen, without assuming it is necessarily the 'best' decision.

5. Incremental policy making is essentially remedial, and focuses on small changes to existing policies rather than considering future major policies (e.g. national environmental policy). Policy makers accept that few, if any, problems are ever solved once and for all time. Policy making is serial – you have to keep coming back to problems as mistakes are corrected and new lines of attack developed.

The best known of the incrementalists is Lindblom (1959) who describes the policy process as one of *disjointed incrementalism* or *muddling through*. This process derives from Lindblom's pluralism: he notes that the policy process is affected by *partisan mutual adjustment* – the process of negotiation, bargaining and adjustment between different interest groups (or partisans) to influence policy. What he is concerned with is the empirical policy process – what *is* happening, rather than (as with the rational theories) what *ought* to happen.

Thus Lindblom argues that usually, although not always, what is feasible politically is only incrementally or marginally different from existing policies. Drastically different policies fall beyond the pale. He argues that this is not necessarily bad because:

— it concentrates the policy maker's analysis on familiar, better known experience;
— it sharply reduces the number of different alternative policies to be explored; and
— it reduces the number and complexity of factors policy makers have to analyse.

In his 1979 essay 'Still muddling, not yet through', Lindblom said that it had become textbook orthodoxy that in policy making only small or incremental steps are ordinarily possible. But he went on to say:

> Most people, including many policy analysts and policy makers, want to separate the 'ought' from the 'is'. They think we should try to do better. So do I. What remains as an issue then? ... Many ... believe that for complex problem solving it usually means practising incrementalism more skilfully and turning away from it only rarely (Lindblom 1979: 517).

In other words, Lindblom defends incrementalism as designed, deliberate and conscious incompleteness of analysis, which accepts that policy makers have to make decisions in a political world which introduces many constraints to the process.

The strongest critic of incrementalism is Yezekial Dror (1989), who accuses incrementalists of being conservative – content to make such small changes that they reinforce inertia and the status quo. This may be all right, Dror argues, in conditions of high social stability, where policies are being implemented relatively well. But where such conditions do not prevail or where significant social changes are sought, incrementalism would not be appropriate.

Lindblom's reply is that very little policy making is revolutionary – most falls into the incremental category. He quotes from Abraham Lincoln and Thomas Jefferson, who believed that the people should have the right to overthrow a government and that occasional revolution was healthy for the body politic. But he goes on to say:

> It is not to dissent from them that I have been claiming that 'muddling through' or incrementalism ... is and ought to be the usual method of policy making. Rather it is that neither revolution, nor drastic policy change, nor even carefully planned big steps are ordinarily possible (Lindblom in McGrew and Wilson 1982: 125).

Dror's argument about incrementalism being essentially conservative is supported by many, although incrementalists maintain that significant changes can be brought about through a series of small changes. Lindblom says:

> Incremental steps can be made quickly because they are only incremental. They do not rock the boat, do not stir up the great antagonisms and paralyzing schisms as do proposals for more drastic change (Lindblom in McGrew and Wilson 1982: 131).

Dror favours a model which can act as an ideal model for policy makers, and includes the idea of *extra-rationality* (use of judgement, creative invention, brainstorming, the brilliant idea that comes unexpectedly in the bath). Thus, although he sympathizes with the validity of incrementalism as a descriptive theory, he still wants a more normative model to act as a way of strengthening and improving the policy process.

Mixed scanning and normative optimal models

Etzioni, too, looks for a middle position between the rational and incrementalist theories, and introduces the notion of mixed scanning which he suggests is both a good description of the policy process and a way of guiding the policy process. Essentially, mixed scanning divides decisions into a macro (fundamental) and micro (small) classification. Mixed scanning involves the policy maker in undertaking a broad review of the field of policy, without engaging in the detailed exploration of options as suggested by the rational model. The idea comes from a military example: that is, soldiers are trained to scan the area in front of them to see if the enemy is there, not taking everything in in detail, just looking for major signs. Etzioni uses an example of setting up a worldwide weather observation system using weather satellites. He describes the rational approach as seeking an exhaustive survey of weather conditions using cameras capable of detailed observations, and by scheduling reviews of the entire sky as often as possible. This would yield an enormous amount of detail which would be costly and take a long time to analyse. The incrementalist, on the other hand, would focus only on those parts of the skies of which knowledge existed from past experience, ignoring all formations which might deserve attention if they arose in unexpected areas. Mixed scanning would employ two cameras: a broad-angle lens that would cover all parts of the sky but not in great detail, and a second one which would zero in on those areas revealed by the first camera to require a more in-depth examination (Etzioni 1967).

An artificial debate?

How real are the differences between these different models of policy making? Is it largely an artificial debate (Smith and May in McGrew and Wilson 1982)? On the one hand, most observers accept that rational models are accurate pictures of widely held images about ideal policy-making procedures. Criticism centres on the fact that rational models are empirically inaccurate or unrealistic: THAT IS NOT THE WAY THINGS ARE.

On the other hand, there is a broad degree of sympathy for the view that the incrementalist approach has much validity as an empirical model of how policies are made. Criticism centres on its conservative defence and acceptance of the *status quo*: THAT IS NOT THE WAY THINGS SHOULD BE.

But the point is that one model is really describing an ideal model of policy making (how it ought to be made) and the other is describing what actually happens in the policy process (how policy is made). Both have validity, but should be understood separately: one as a normative or prescriptive model, the other as an explanatory or descriptive model.

The mixed scanning approach may encompass both prescription and description, although this is open to argument. The problem with the rational and mixed scanning models is that they restrict policy making to the organizational context, and allow little room for external pressures on policy makers. Lindblom, on the other hand, is explicit in his view of the policy process being influenced by a plurality of participants, and therefore being partisan and partial.

Conclusions

Two main conclusions follow from this view of power and process in policy making. The first is that the chance to influence health policy does exist in many societies, although clearly this depends on the nature of the political system. Participation may be weak or even non-existent in the grand issues or high politics – which may be dominated by small groups of elites. But on the ordinary issues of policy – the low politics – the potential for participation often exists.

The second conclusion is that formal analysis of the policy-making process is useful in as much as it makes us aware of the gap between rational procedures and what mostly happens in practice. However, public policy making has to be understood essentially as a political process, rather than an analytical problem-solving one. The rational theorists, including Dror and Etzioni, tend to focus on the dynamics of the process of solving problems, while Lindblom has struggled with the idea of different interests influencing the policy-making process.

4

Setting the policy agenda: who influences what?

In this chapter we ask how policy issues are identified. Why do some issues gain government attention? How do issues get onto the policy agenda, and become enshrined in law, or regulations, or policy statements? And why are some issues ignored? Our primary focus is on public-sector policy making and our concern is with why government chooses to act on some issues and to ignore others. Because the media are often perceived as agenda-setters, we pay particular attention to their role.

What is the policy agenda?

We may use the word agenda in a number of different ways: for example we might say 'The agenda for the committee today is examinations'. At other times we may refer to a 'hidden agenda' or 'an agenda for the 1990s'. Here we use the term agenda as:

> the list of subjects or problems to which government officials and people outside of government closely associated with those officials, are paying some serious attention at any given time (Kingdon 1984: 3).

Within the general domain of health, for example, the minister of health will be considering, at any one time, a range of problems or issues: the inefficiencies of hospital services, the rise in the number of people smoking, the distribution of pharmaceutical products, how to regulate a fast-growing private health sector. Out of the set of all conceivable issues or problems, some get attended to seriously in preference to others. The agenda-setting process narrows down the set of possible subjects to those that actually become the focus of attention.

Obviously the list of problems differs and varies from one section of government to another. The president or prime minister will be considering the major items – international crises, managing the economy.

The ministry of health will have a more specialized agenda, which will include a few 'high-politics' policies, such as reform of the health sector (in the UK, for example, into providers and purchasers) and many more ordinary, 'low-politics' issues, focusing on problems in biomedical research, preventive health services, or hospital costs.

Why do issues get onto the policy agenda?

This is a question that plagues policy analysts. Why do policy makers take action when they do? Clearly they sometimes react to crises (although we need to establish criteria to define what constitutes a crisis), but much policy making is, as Grindle and Thomas (1991) put it, 'politics-as-usual changes': routine, day-to-day problems that need solutions. Where does the impetus for change or reform come from when there is no crisis? Several scholars have tried to provide models that explain how, and why, some issues are taken seriously by government officials when there is no apparent crisis. The Hall model identifies three conditions that help to explain why governments might act on any particular issue or give precedence to a specific issue (Hall et al. 1975). The Kingdon model uses a 'three streams' approach, suggesting that complex policy processes occur in three separate streams and only when these come together does an issue make the policy agenda (Kingdon 1984). Both models are useful in their own ways, and serve to illustrate how different people approach explanations of the policy environment.

Agenda setting in politics-as-usual circumstances

The Hall model: legitimacy, feasibility and support

This model (Hall et al. 1975) uses the concepts of legitimacy, feasibility and support to suggest that only when an issue is high in relation to all three concepts does it become an agenda item. They provide a simple and quick model for analysing what issues might be taken up by governments. For a more complex but similar theoretical model, see Cobb and Elder 1983.

Legitimacy refers to those issues with which governments feel they should be concerned, and in which they have a right to intervene. These represent issues where governments feel most people will accept state intervention. Issues range from high to low legitimacy. For example, most citizens will expect governments to keep law and order in the streets, or to defend the country from attack. These would be widely accepted as highly legitimate state activities. However, there are many other areas where legitimacy may not be so easily conferred. For example, there is a long ideological debate about the boundaries between individual freedom and the right of the state to curb that so-called freedom.

This differs greatly from country to country. It appears that China's one-child population policy has been accepted as a legitimate government concern (on the whole), and in the urban areas of China most people over the last three decades have adhered to it. Clearly the authoritarian political system of China was crucial for compliance, and it is difficult to see many other countries accepting the right of the government to decree how many children a couple may have.

Feasibility refers to the potential for implementing the policy. It is defined by prevailing technical and theoretical knowledge, financial and other resources, availability of skilled personnel, capability of administrative structures, and existence of necessary infrastructure. Does the state have the capacity to ensure implementation? There may be technological, financial, or personnel limitations that suggest a particular policy may be impossible to put into effect, however legitimate it is seen to be. For example, many countries may feel that where families are separated, fathers should be made to be financially responsible for the upkeep of their children. However, the administrative complications of tracing separated partners and ensuring regular payments are considerable, and such policies may simply be seen as impossible to implement. Poor countries may wish to introduce systems of personal or business taxation in order to increase the state's revenue, but this may not be considered logistically possible because so many people work in the informal sector.

Finally, *support* refers to the rather elusive, but important, aspect of public support for, or public 'trust' in, government. This may be strong support of important interest groups, or it may be relatively weak (even passive) support for policy. If support is lacking, or discontent is high, it may be very difficult for government to implement policy. Neither the Irish nor the Argentinian government proved able, in the 1980s, to introduce divorce law reform in those countries, in the face of implacable church opposition. As we will see in Chapter 8, when President Ershad of Bangladesh tried to introduce a radical health policy in 1990 he was strongly opposed by the medical profession. The reform included, among other things, a ban on private practice by junior doctors and university lecturers. The Bangladesh Medical Association immediately declared a strike, and this action, among other factors, led to the downfall of the Ershad government.

Governments can challenge important interest groups such as the church, but only if they have sufficient support elsewhere. For example, as we shall see in the next chapter, the Thatcher government in Britain in the 1980s successfully introduced a restricted drugs list – against the wishes of the majority of the medical profession and the pharmaceutical industry – because the government was in a particularly strong position.

So, using these three conditions, governments will calculate whether the issue they are considering falls high or low on the continuum. If it has high legitimacy (government has the right to intervene), high feasibility (there are sufficient resources, personnel, infrastructure) and high support (the most important interest groups are positive – or at least not negative), then the issue may well come onto the policy agenda, and fare well, once enunciated as policy.

Sometimes governments will put an issue onto the policy agenda because they wish to make a statement about it, to show they have a position – but they do not expect it to be translated from policy into practice because it has low support, or low feasibility. Then it may remain policy on paper only and not in practice.

The Kingdon model: agenda setting through three streams

Kingdon's three-stream approach (1984) is a much more complex model of how issues reach the government policy agenda. He conceives of policy being made through three separate streams of processes – the problem stream, the politics stream and the policies stream. Policies are only taken seriously by government when a major 'window of opportunity' opens up in each of the three streams at the same time. Kingdon is fond of watery analogies, likening policy making to a primeval soup, in which 'many ideas float around, bumping into one another, encountering new ideas, and forming combinations and recombinations' (Kingdon 1984: 209).

In the problem stream, for example, he asks why some problems occupy the attention of government officials more than other problems. The answer for him lies in the way in which officials learn about conditions, through indicators, focusing events or feedback. Indicators may include routine information on health statistics – for example, showing an increase in heart disease or the rising costs of a particular programme. Focusing events may be a crisis – a cholera outbreak, or even a personal experience (a cousin gets a rare disease, and attention is drawn to the costs of medicines to treat it). Feedback comes from programmes already in place (complaints from staff or patients, or an evaluation). Of course many conditions are not necessarily perceived as problems. Just as the community used to living with malnutrition does not recognize infant pot bellies as a problem, so policy makers will only define an existing condition as a problem when they feel (or others persuade them to feel) that something needs to be changed.

In the politics stream there are what Kingdon refers to as visible and hidden participants. The first group are organized interests – Lindblom's partisans – who put a particular point of view, highlight a specific problem and use the mass media to get attention. Visible participants may be inside and outside government. For example, new presidents or prime ministers may be powerful agenda setters because the newness of their position allows them room for manoeuvre. Equally an interest group with strong statistics backing their story may be an important agenda setter. The hidden participants are the specialists – the community of academics, researchers, consultants – who work less on getting issues onto the agenda, and more on proposing alternative options for solving problems that do get onto the agenda. Hidden participants may, however, also play active parts in getting attention for problems – especially in partnership with the media. A researcher with interesting findings, especially if they challenge current policy, may 'leak' information to the press, or call press attention to an article in a scientific journal.

Finally, the policy stream selects from problems and politics the proposals which will become public policy. Selecting from among the problems and the alternative policy solutions, policy makers will use a number of different criteria: technical feasibility, congruence with existing values, anticipation of future constraints (including financial restraints), public acceptability and politicians' receptivity.

The main point Kingdon makes is that the separate streams of problems, politics and policies each have lives of their own. But there comes a time when the three streams are joined, and then policy change occurs. Thus Kingdon argues that policies are certainly not made in stages, steps or phases. The independent streams flow through the system all at once, each with a life of their own and equal with one another. If they all meet, and become coupled, then a window opens, and the issue is likely to be taken up seriously by policy makers. What causes the three streams to come together at any one point may be due to one or many reasons: individuals, media attention, a particular crisis or the dissemination of research results. Thus participants in the policy process do not proceed from identification of a problem, and then seek solutions for them. Agendas are not first set and then alternatives generated. Alternatives may be advocated for long periods before the opportunity arises for them to be accepted.

Both models give a relatively complex set of conditions that might affect what issues come onto the policy agenda. But sometimes in politics-as-usual, reforms may be introduced with apparently minimal effort. Grindle and Thomas (1991) give the example of health reform in Mali, introduced by external advisers, but with no particular event or sense of urgency for change perceived by health policy makers. In the absence of any real involvement of the Mali Ministry of Health, the plan for change took two years to develop, and was designed almost entirely by the United States Administration for International Development (USAID) personnel and consultants. According to the authors, the dominant concerns of policy makers were with the problems and benefits which would accrue to the Ministry of Health and its personnel if change were introduced.

> Thus, bureaucratic infighting (which involved considerable tension with USAID), reluctance of technical personnel to commit themselves to the change, and the desire to acquire project resources such as vehicles, supplies and regular paychecks figured prominently in decision making (Grindle and Thomas 1991: 112).

Mali is an extremely poor country, and in the economic climate in which reforms to the health sector were being discussed, it is probably fair to assume that Ministry of Health policy makers were concerned primarily to attract the foreign funding offered by USAID because it offered support for salaries or per diems, supplies, vehicles and so on, and only secondarily to reform the health sector. Thus, there were no challenges to the Ministry's legitimacy to change health policy, support was dependent on getting agreement among the bureaucrats and professionals who would be implementing any change, and the feasibility of introducing policy reform was dependent on American dollars flowing into the Ministry. As long as resources (in the form of vehicles, supplies and salaries) were guaranteed by reform, then support for change existed.

Policy change under crisis

A crisis exists when the important policy makers perceive that one exists, that it is a real and threatening crisis, and that failure to act could lead to even more disastrous consequences. Events that do not have all these characteristics are likely to be tolerated, until the worst has blown over. However, where the gravity of a situation is confirmed by pressure from outside government, such as rioting in the streets or threats from international agencies to withdraw foreign aid or a dramatic fall in the price of an export crop, and the government has access to information from its own technical experts or advisers, then the chances are they will perceive the problem as a crisis, and act to reform existing policy.

Many examples of policy change due to crisis are of economic policy. One example is that of the Ghanaian government's decision to devalue its currency in December 1971, where the stakes for policy makers were high.

> For them the future development of the country was at stake, as well as their own reputations as managers of the economy and as leaders of a popularly supported political party. Thus, for them, the stakes involved fundamental conditions of economic stability and growth and the legitimacy and durability of their hold on political power (Grindle and Thomas 1991: 77).

They were right to be worried. Less than a month after the devaluation the government was overthrown by the military, who cited the decision to devalue as one of its reasons for taking over.

Crises are not always acute, however. During the 1980s many countries came to a gradual realization that a chronic financial crisis existed, and that this could no longer be ignored. Where changes in policy had been incremental shifts (such as the introduction of primary health care), policy makers began to talk of radical change – of *policy reform*. In the health sector, the World Bank's *Financing for health care: an agenda for reform* set the framework for the extent of change considered necessary. Once the magnitude of the economic crisis was admitted, policy makers were forced to accept the advice and technical analysis of the global financial institutions, whose role was significantly enhanced during this period. The sense of crisis was not limited to developing countries. Policy reform became the byword in the industrialized world too, with a clear focus on planning for change or implementing strategic change. In the UK the nature of the National Health Service was transformed through a series of policy reforms (such as introducing the concept of purchasers and providers, fund-holding general practices, trust hospitals) that made past major organizational change of the NHS such as that in 1974 (uniting all local level health services under area health authorities) seem relatively minor.

Non-decision making

While both crisis and politics-as-usual models are useful for asking how issues come onto the policy agenda and are acted upon, or why they do not (because they lack legitimacy, feasibility or support or because the three policy streams do not come together to provide a 'window of opportunity'), it is not sufficient to stop there. Observable action provides an incomplete guide to the way policies are decided. In other words we need to think about *non-policy making*, or *non-decision making* – which is how the scholarly literature refers to it – as well as policy making.

It is easiest to start with what we do *not* mean. If policy issues do not come onto the agenda, it may be because policy makers are unaware of the issue or have decided not to act for a series of reasons which are provided by the above two models. Policy makers may also decide not to decide on a particular issue, but to delay it.

Non-decision making on the other hand is more subtle. It is when

> the dominant values, the accepted rules of the game, the existing power relations among groups, and the instruments of force, singly or in combination, effectively prevent certain grievances from developing into full-fledged issues which call for decisions (Ham and Hill 1986: 64).

That is, issues remain *latent*, and fail to enter policy-making processes because they are against the interests of those in power. So a non-decision results in the suppression or thwarting of any challenge that seems in conflict with the interests of the decision maker. Non-decision making can take many forms, starting with the use of force to prevent demands entering the political system: the apartheid regime in South Africa used imprisonment, exile, censorship and torture to suppress demands for political rights for its black population. More likely, however, non-decisions revolve around neglect or ignoring particular issues or groups. For example, in many societies the needs of ethnic minorities are ignored – especially if they are particular to that minority, such as high infant mortality rates among Gypsies.

Non-decision making may be very subtle, as one of the classical examples in the political science literature shows. Crenson (1971) studied two cities in the United States with respect to action taken to control air pollution. The two cities were adjacent steel towns, called Gary and East Chicago. East Chicago passed a law controlling air pollution in 1949, but it took another fourteen years for Gary to act. In East Chicago there were many steel companies, but steel production in Gary was dominated by a single corporation, US Steel. Crenson suggests that the fragmentation of the steel industry in East Chicago meant that it was relatively easy for policy makers to pass a law on air pollution (which people felt strongly about). But in Gary, US Steel was in an extremely powerful economic position, and anticipating the corporation's negative response to any attempt to control the pollution they were creating meant that policy makers did not even consider this as an issue for the policy agenda.

This example of indirect influence at the level of a city can obviously be true too for other levels of policy making. A ministry of health in a developing country may not even mention the long-term negative effect on the nation's health and the cost to the health services when

new contracts for tobacco and alcohol manufacture are being negotiated because of the anticipated response from other (stronger) sectors
of government (the ministry of industry, the ministry of finance) which
are more interested in building up industrial capacity and increasing
government revenue.

Who sets the agenda?

So far we have looked at general explanations for how issues get onto
the policy agenda, or how they may be prevented from getting there
– sometimes by quite indirect means. Let's now turn to the actors in
the policy process. Many actors may be agenda setters, but one of the
most important is the government, which has control over legislation
and the policy process. Others include organized interests, whether they
are international, such as the World Bank or USAID, or national, such
as the business community. The structural adjustment policies of the
1980s were a good example of international agencies forming a coalition of interests with donors and pressuring some governments to introduce economic reforms and changes in government administration
and political systems. Another example is the way population protagonists in the US put family planning onto the global health policy agenda
in the late 1960s, as described in Box 4.1.

Box 4.1 'Development is the best contraceptive': setting the
family planning agenda

Until the early 1960s concern about population growth was limited to a relatively small, largely American, policy community. By
1965 the US government had assumed leadership of this network
of population protagonists, and was determined to place the issue
of population growth firmly on the international policy agenda.
Twenty years later, in a dramatic reversal of policy, the US government stepped away from the helm. What are the politics behind this
policy shift?

In the mid-1960s the US government played an active advocacy
role, encouraging developing countries to adopt policies to reduce
population growth (India was particularly receptive given its large
and growing population), eliciting the participation of other Western donors, and mobilizing UN support for family planning (which
until then had taken a cautious approach to population issues).
Population activities were largely defined as family planning prog-

---

rammes, influenced by the advent of the oral contraceptive, which had been tested in several developing countries and was being used by over 4 million women in the US by 1965. From the mid-1960s the US government was the largest donor of funds, technical support and expertise to family planning programmes around the world.

Internationally the President of the World Bank added his weight in 1968 by noting that the 'mushrooming cloud of the population explosion' would 'explode in suffering, explode in violence, explode in inhumanity' unless action was taken (McNamara 1981: 35). The World Bank established a Population Projects Department a year later, and began making loans for population activities in the early 1970s. This was accompanied by the creation of the United Nations Fund for Population Activities (now known as the UN Population Fund – UNFPA) in 1969 to channel additional resources to population activities.

However, putting the issue on the agenda was one step. Keeping it there, and translating policy into practice, was another. At the World Population Conference in Bucharest in 1974, American assumptions that the population issue was no longer controversial, and that the rationale for family planning had largely been accepted, were shattered. At the conference not only was the political nature of the population question reaffirmed, but Third World countries redefined the problem in the context of broader political and socio-economic changes. Karan Singh, then Minister of Health in India, said 'Development is the best contraceptive' (The Lancet 1992: 1155). It was argued that population problems were symptoms of underdevelopment which in turn was a consequence of the international system. In other words what was needed was not population policies but a New International Economic Order.

The agenda-setting role of the media was part of the story. In 1974, the debates about population at the Bucharest conference were widely covered by the mass media, giving them a high degree of visibility. In the mid-1970s, birth control was still a controversial subject, even in industrialized countries. For example, in 1977 a UK television film on public attitudes to contraception and different methods of birth control was banned at the last minute because the British Broadcasting Corporation feared it would offend viewers (Karpf 1988: 165). Thus media coverage of population issues was limited because of its close equation with birth control, which was still seen as a private rather than public concern.

At the 1984 International Population Conference in Mexico, politics and ideology again drove the policy process. Developing countries continued to favour broad development programmes that stressed reproductive choice. However, the US government under the Reagan administration now had a very different view of population growth as a 'neutral phenomenon'. This new position suggested that a reduction of government intervention in public policy would promote economic growth and thus a decline in fertility (Camp and Lasher 1989). The rise of right-wing pro-life interest groups in the US, and increased interest in individual human rights, were important in leading the Reagan government to reverse its commitment to population issues. As Camp writes (1993): 'A powerful anti-abortion lobby wrung a series of major concessions on population aid policy from the Reagan administration and then bullied the Bush administration into vetoing all congressional attempts to overturn them.' Again the media played an active role in bringing public attention to what were called 'forced abortions'. In January 1985, a series of articles appeared in the Washington Post, a prestigious American newspaper, claiming that China's population policy was 'rooted in coercion, wanton abortion, and the intrusion by the state into the most intimate of human affairs (Crane and Finkel 1989: 37).

As a result, support for the International Planned Parenthood Federation (IPPF) and UNFPA was withdrawn, and aid for population control significantly decreased. Although President Clinton overturned many of these decisions after 1992 (the US once more contributes to UNFPA), American funding for population activities is much lower in the 1990s than it was in previous decades. The US's role in consciousness raising about population, however, had clearly become more accepted by the 1990s. A meeting held in India in 1992 to review forty years of family planning activity was closed by Karan Singh, who suggested reversing his Bucharest aphorism to read 'Contraception is the best development' (The Lancet 1992: 1155).

While international agencies or foreign governments may raise issues to be addressed, as described in Box 4.1, they are not the only groups vying for position on the government's policy agenda. National interest groups may also manage to get significant attention for issues they consider important. Environmental groups, for example, have been

relatively successful over the past few years in focusing increasing attention on environmental issues. The media may also play an important part in forcing issues onto the policy agenda which might otherwise
be ignored. However, government clearly has a major control over what
issues reach the policy agenda, and may accept or reject particular issues.

Government as agenda setter

Government clearly decides what policies need changing, revising, or
introducing. But how far do governments pursue an active programme
of issue search – looking for items to go onto the policy agenda?
Hogwood and Gunn (1984) make the case that governments *should* pursue
an active programme of issue search, because they need to anticipate
problems and their ramifications before a crisis occurs. Also information and needs change (in almost all countries the growth of an ageing
population will have major implications for health policy in the future
– from the growth of the incidence of chronic diseases to caring for the
very old and frail); new problems arise (increased migration from the
former Soviet Union to other countries in Europe and from Africa to
Europe); new solutions become available (new technology replaces long
stays in hospital with day surgery); attitudes change (restricting smoking
in public places is now feasible in many countries where previously this
would have been opposed by many community interests).

Therefore, Hogwood and Gunn suggest that governments should go
through a series of steps to define issues and decide whether they should
go onto the policy agenda, by setting out to 'search for issues' and
defining the conditions under which they are likely to be effective. They
use a *prescriptive* approach – arguing that this is what governments *should*
do.

In issue search, government would consider some of the following
factors:

1. Who says this particular issue is a problem? Why? Where is the
   initiative coming from?
2. Is it a 'real' problem, treatable by government? (Is it legitimate for
   government to act on this? For example, the boundaries of when to
   intervene in domestic violence is a hugely contested area of action
   for the state (the police, the judiciary, social workers) and governments may be very reluctant to devise new legislation which some
   see as an invasion of privacy.)
3. Is there likely to be agreement on the problem? (How much support
   exists, and from where does it come?)

4. Is the time for policy making premature? Is it too soon for action? Does there need to be considerable public debate, in order to ensure support? For example, in Britain, making the wearing of seat belts mandatory was attempted for years before it finally became law in the mid-1980s. One of the reasons for procrastination was to educate the public sufficiently so that the majority of people would obey the law once it was introduced. The police argued that they would not be able to enforce the law – i.e. it would not be feasible – if it were not supported by the majority. In the event, seat belt wearing rose from 32 per cent before the law was passed to 95 per cent just after the law was introduced (Leichter 1986).

5. Is the policy context or policy framework correct? Is the issue seen from the perspective of efficiency, ignoring other aspects, such as equity? Can an alternative perspective be sought? How are others (beneficiaries for example) likely to view the issue?

6. Is the issue being framed at the appropriate level of aggregation? If it is too global – too aggregated – it may remain at the level of a slogan or a call to arms – it is too big to grasp, difficult to act on. For example, the issue of global warming needs to be broken down into smaller issues if it is to get onto the policy agenda and be acted upon.

7. Is the causal structure of the problem understood? Governments may or may not understand the problems that contribute to, or predispose to a particular problem (for example why does vandalism occur, why do children sniff glue?). Even if there is some understanding, there may be reluctance or inability to tackle the underlying causes. For example, it is clear that, in order to control urban pollution, most very large cities of the world need comprehensive transport and industrial policies that restrict individual car use and industrial pollution. Instead, most governments disaggregate the issue and put catalytic converters or unleaded petrol on the agenda because to tackle the major causal determinants would be seen as threatening to many important interest groups (such as the motor and oil industries). The same would be true in many parts of the world where industrial and vehicle pollutants create major ill health.

8. Can the implications of the issue be specified and quantified? How far can the scale or intensity of the problem be specified? What is its incidence? How quickly is the problem changing? What is the degree of uncertainty? With policies related to HIV disease or AIDS, all governments faced difficulties with answers to these issues in the 1980s, making it easy to undermine policy or detract from the importance of the issue.

Of course, we have already learned that policy making seldom proceeds as a rational linear process: governments may search for issues to put onto the policy agenda, anticipating crises and changes in needs in the population. But it is likely that this is a simplification of a very complex process. A new government, for example, may take the opportunity afforded by the goodwill generated at the beginning of a new regime, put an issue onto the agenda *and* drive it through to rapid implementation. This occurred with the Bangladesh national drugs policy introduced in 1982 and described in Chapter 8, Box 8.1.

A potentially important catalyst for making governments take notice of issues which have been ignored is provided by the media. Of course the media also may legitimate or criticize issues that government identifies as belonging on the agenda. The rest of this chapter is devoted to exploring to what extent the media may exert an influence on what appears on the policy agenda. In many liberal democracies they are perceived as a potent force in drawing attention to issues, and forcing politicians to act.

The media as agenda setter

How far do newspapers, television, magazines and radio guide our attention to certain issues and influence what we think about? How much leverage do they have over policy makers in their choice of issues of political concern and action? The media receive major attention in this chapter because they are often underestimated as actors in the policy process.

The mass media are of two types: print and electronic. Print media are magazines and newspapers; electronic media are television, radio and films. Referring to them as *mass media* implies that their communicative realm is extremely broad, often encompassing the whole society (although this is clearly less true in the Third World). They serve several vital functions: they are agents of socialization (instructing people in the values and norms of society, generally transmitting the society's culture); they are sources of information; they function as propaganda mechanisms (they seek to persuade the public to support particular policies, or buy consumer goods); and finally they serve as agents of legitimacy, generating mass belief in, and acceptance of, dominant political and economic institutions (Marger 1993).

The role of the media is affected by the political system. In many countries, the media are entirely state-owned, and exercise significant self-censorship, fearing government reprisals for covering what are considered to be inappropriate issues. Their impartiality may be in doubt. For example, there are many countries where populist heads of state have presided over newspapers of cringing obsequiousness, and where, if criticism has been voiced, journalists have been dealt with harshly. In Chinua Achebe's novel *Anthills of the Savannah* he describes one scene in which the Minister for Information telephones the editor of the national daily newspaper, asking him to send a photographer to cover a goodwill delegation from Abazon. In fact, the delegation from Abazon is a dissatisfied group of peasants who have brought a petition to the President. The editor exclaims:

— 'That's a new one. A goodwill delegation from Abazon! A most likely story! What shall we hear next?'
— 'And for God's sake let me see the copy before it goes in.'
— 'And why, if one may have the temerity to put such a question to the Honourable Commissioner?'
— 'You've just said it. Because I am the Honourable Commissioner for Information. That's why.'
— 'Well, that's not good enough, Mr Commissioner for Information. Not good enough for *me*. You seem to be forgetting something, namely that it is *my* name and address which is printed at the bottom of page sixteen of the *Gazette* and not that of any fucking, excuse my language, any fucking Commissioner. It's me who'll be locked up by Major Samsonite if the need arises, not you. It's my funeral ...'
— 'Quite irrelevant, Ikem. You ought to know that. ... I'm getting quite sick and tired of repeating it. I am doing so now for the last time, the very last time. Chapter Fourteen section six of the Newspaper Amendment Decree gives the Honourable Commissioner general and specific powers over what is printed in the *Gazette* ...' (Achebe 1988: 26).

In the liberal democracies, the independence of the media is just as hotly defended, but the government uses more subtle means of getting the media to toe the line. Both television directors and newspaper editors act as gatekeepers, deciding what events to cover or what issues are important. In communist regimes the media were used by the government to inform the population about achievements and priorities. Alternative views were extremely limited and many observers were cynical about the quality of information provided. The Moscow newspaper *Pravda* meant 'truth', but for decades most Russians believed it told anything but the truth. In most political systems where the press is owned by the state doubt has been expressed about the ability of the press to criticize and survive. Indeed, some suggest that the old-style censorship is long abandoned, but that a more insidious trend of 'internalized censorship' has taken over.

In poorer countries, the media tend to be less developed, and focus largely on urban populations who are literate and have access to radio and television. Competition between the media is limited, and even as African countries move towards multi-party democracies in the 1990s, and take steps to establish independent media, they are hampered by a weak capital base, high levels of illiteracy, few opportunities for advertising, and a lack of professionals.

Even in the liberal democracies, there are debates about how independent the media are and what sort of influence they have on public thinking. Two reasons are given for a 'less-than-anticipated' role of the media in agenda setting. First, many argue that the media are not nearly as free as they seem, and second, that they do not have a strong influence on policy makers who get their information from many different sources.

THE AUTONOMY OF THE MEDIA   The democratic postulate is that the media are independent, and committed to discovering and reporting the truth. However, there are many who reject this view. Herman and Chomsky (1988) say that, on the contrary, the media are controlled very deliberately to give information that basically supports the state and important interest groups. This requires systematic propaganda, and they have evolved the 'propaganda model' to show how it works. Although based on the American mass media, it has general (and increasing) relevance for other countries too. The propaganda model demonstrates several ways (for example, through size, ownership and profit orientation; advertising; and sources of information) in which news is filtered so that what is mostly disseminated is in the interests of the state and of powerful groups. Thus news coverage is systematically based on its serviceability to domestic power interests. This model clearly has particular value in relation to the 'grand' or 'high-politics' issues, but it is nevertheless useful to bear in mind when we are thinking of controversial health issues, and the way the media portray particular views. Not everyone agrees with the propaganda model. Many reject the notion that information is deliberately filtered, while accepting that it is produced within an ideological framework which often supports conventional wisdom and powerful groups' views.

THE RESPONSIVENESS OF THE MEDIA TO LESS POWERFUL GROUPS   In spite of the view expressed above that the media are largely controlled by the state and major interests in it, many groups see the media as a way of reaching both the general public and policy makers. Pressure groups, for example, are convinced that they need to attract media attention for their causes and, indeed, they gain political status in this way. As we see in Chapter 6, they often draw in professionals to attract media attention. Through media exposure, some groups may become the focus of opposition to government policy (or the lack of it), while others will become legitimate sources of information. For example, a UK group conducted a survey into intensive care services for babies, and published its findings. One press headline following publication was 'NHS shortages cause deaths of 1,000 newborn babies a year' (*Guardian* 1993). Certainly there are examples where the media have forced governments to change policy, or put an issue on the agenda. In the UK in 1978, for example, the environmental group Greenpeace intervened in a proposed seal cull in Orkney. The media coverage of the event – resplendent with pictures of defenceless, dewy-eyed, baby seals – forced the Secretary of State for Scotland to call off the cull (Negrine 1989: 164).

But while environmental stories often get attention from the media, more political stories do not. Those groups lobbying on behalf of the disabled, AIDS victims, drug addicts, or battered women have more difficulty in attracting and keeping media attention. The media do not treat everyone equally and fairly. This is nowhere more clear than looking at reporting on disasters. Often serious disasters are not covered only because reporting teams are not present, or they are not considered 'newsworthy', perhaps because there have been several recent disaster stories. Reports in the UK on the Somali famine were completely overshadowed in 1992 by civil war in the former Yugoslavia. Furthermore, press interest may be quixotic, transitory, and press copy necessarily simplifying and sometimes distorting the multifaceted nature of events and proposals.

As agenda setters, then, the media may play a role, especially in conjunction with other groups such as researchers or interest groups. However, how long they have to sustain interest in a subject in order to assure its place on the policy agenda is subject to some doubt. Anthony Downs (1972) describes the *issue-attention cycle* of the media and predicts that problems begin to fade from media attention (and the public) when their solutions imply major change or a redistribution of wealth in the society. Downs suggests that initial alarm and reaction to a specific problem is met, at least in the American context, with a belief that a solution can be found by government. When it becomes clear, at a later stage, that the problem is too difficult to solve without a major restructuring of the society, the issue becomes 'business as usual', and both the media and the public look for more interesting, new issues. For a few weeks in the summer of 1993 the UK media highlighted the need to bring sick or wounded Bosnian children to Europe for medical treatment: the numbers of such children needing help did not diminish and the story faded from the front pages.

Some issues, however, do not go away, and the media may have long periods of troughs and peaks. Nelson (1990) describes the ups and downs of media interest in child abuse; the issue was first taken up by newspapers in 1874, which led to the establishment of the Society for the Prevention of Cruelty to Children. A long period off centre stage was ended when a paediatrician published a paper in 1962 on 'the battered child syndrome', giving cruelty to children a medical significance. Nelson makes the point that professionals may have considerable power to attract the media, who consistently monitor scientific journals in search of new stories. Indeed, she argues that child abuse achieved a place on the policy agenda because a few pioneering researchers crossed the bridge to mass-circulation news outlets. The public's interest in this social problem prompted state legislatures into action. But how often do the media influence policy makers?

THE IMPACT OF THE MEDIA ON POLICY MAKERS   Obviously there are occasions when the media do influence policy makers: to act in a particular way, or to take notice of a particular issue. Occasionally they campaign like pressure groups. For example, a British newspaper, the *Sunday Times*, took a particular stand on thalidomide, the drug which caused birth deformities when given to pregnant women, by running a deliberate campaign to win higher compensation for the affected families than they believed the lawyers would do. The newspaper began in 1972 with an article, an accompanying editorial and an opening headline 'Our Thalidomide Children: A Cause for National Shame'. They also hired a researcher for four months to study the literature on tranquillizers, other drugs and experimental work on their reproductive effects in order to be able to counter the scientific consensus that the congenital malformations had not been foreseeable (Karpf 1988).

Nevertheless, the extent of influence on policy makers by the media is open to question. First, policy makers have many different sources of information. A report about a particular issue may be covered in different ways in different newspapers or television programmes, and may be perceived by the policy maker as 'biased' depending on which newspaper or television programme reports on it. On the other hand, the media may act as communicators within a policy community: a concern expressed as a story or an editorial in a quality newspaper may be used by a policy maker to draw attention to a particular issue.

Second, it is difficult to separate strands of influence. The mass media are not external agencies acting upon the political process – they are part of that process itself. They are thus implicated in agenda setting and in giving meaning to events – but not alone. What they may do is magnify movements that have started elsewhere – that is, they help to shape an issue but they do not create it. This fits with the Herman and Chomsky model – that the media basically mirror the views and values of the state and the major interests in it.

Third, policy makers are less likely to be moved to action by a single press account. It is concerted action by the press that may make a difference, and a competitive press (providing both left- and right-wing opinions) is unlikely to take one view of issues that are political. However, the question then arises about how far the media are really competitive, and how far they can influence public opinion. These are burning questions for which there are no simple answers.

In the Third World, the influence of the media on policy makers is less easy to discern. Journalists, editors, radio broadcasters and television producers may make up part of the urban elite, and have close ties with policy makers in government. Where the media are owned directly by government, policy makers would not expect to see much critical expression, or discussion of alternative policies in the media, and may not encourage any such discourse. Policy circles are small in many Third World countries, and those journalists who are perceived as being critical of a political regime are often the first to be arrested when repression strikes. Although this is changing, the independence of the press and television remains vulnerable both to political whim and to a weak capital base.

However, this is not to say that the media do not influence policy makers. Sen (1983) compared the role of the media in reporting famines in China and India. In the years 1959–61, when there were very poor harvests, China suffered a massive famine in which millions died. The mass media were silent on the famine, and it was only later worked out that the death toll was between 14 and 16 million extra deaths in those years. India, on the other hand, has not had a famine since independence. The crux of Sen's argument is that India cannot have a famine, even in years of great food problems, because of the nature of Indian democracy, and the role of the press.

> The government cannot afford to fail to take prompt action when large-scale starvation threatens. Newspapers play an important part in this, in making the facts known and forcing the challenge to be faced. So does the pressure of opposition parties (Sen 1983: 55).

In China, where the press was not free, the instruments for challenging government were a great deal more hidden and less explicit, and government did not act to avoid the catastrophe. Ironically, however, Sen goes on to point out that while the press plays an important role at times of acute starvation, forcing government to save the really disastrous losers in the food battle from dying of hunger and related illness, non-acute, regular starvation, even though extremely widespread in India, unlike China, does not attract attention in newspapers.

> The system works powerfully to prevent catastrophic losers in the food battle. But it comfortably accepts, and takes in its stride, the quiet presence of an immense number of ordinary losers – the chronically ill-fed who are rather more prone to disease and death than their better-fed compatriots (Sen 1983: 56).

The Chinese have been much more committed to making public provision for food distribution to guarantee some food to all, and in normal circumstances, this commitment has the effect of avoiding the widespread malnourishment and non-acute hunger observed in India. It also helps to explain the improvement in China's health status indicators: for example, infant mortality rates fell from approximately 90 to 30 per 1,000 over the years 1950–91.

Conclusions

As with all aspects of policy making, there can be many actors involved in the policy process, and agenda setting is clearly not necessarily dominated by government. Policy change or reform may occur through crises or through politics-as-usual, but in both cases, certain factors will be important. A crisis will have to be perceived as such by the most important policy elites, and they have to believe that failure to act will actually make the situation worse. In politics-as-usual, many different reforms or changes may compete for policy makers' attention, and which one actually gets considered seriously will depend on a number of different circumstances including who gains and who loses in the change. Timing is important, and issues may be around a long time before all the 'streams' come together and are propelled onto the policy agenda.

The media can be important for drawing attention to issues, and forcing governments to act, but this is more likely to be so in the 'low-politics' issues. On major or 'high-politics' issues topics that concern national enemies, or perceived threats to security, the great majority of the media are likely to support the basic thrust of government policy, if the government is seen to be legitimate.

5

The government policy arena: the heart of policy making

Once a problem has been recognized, government may decide to act on it. This is the initial stage of policy formulation. However, as we have seen, public policy making is a political process, not simply an analytical problem-solving process: it is a process of negotiation, bargaining, and the accommodation of many different interests which reflects the ideology of the government in power. Formulation of policy will usually take into account those interests, and will also be affected by prior or related policies, the financial and other resources available, and expected resistance or support. Formulation of policy is thus closely affected by those who take part in it.

In this chapter we look at those structures or institutions of government which are involved in policy formulation: political parties (although not strictly part of government, they may set the agenda for government prior to election); the legislature, the executive, and the bureaucracy or administration. We also look briefly at the ministry of health, the regional, federal or local structures of government, and the role of other political institutions such as the judiciary and the military. Our main concern is the role of each in policy making. Where are decisions being made? Who is influencing policy formulation and implementation? What are the relative strengths and weaknesses of each? Let's look briefly at each of these areas.

Political parties: promising *and* delivering?

In the liberal democracies, where two or more parties compete for power, they usually produce policy documents or statements before each election to demonstrate their intended policies if they are voted in as government. Their policies will usually be discussed at party congresses, where activists from local constituencies will get the chance to suggest amendments or changes. They are not, however, bound by such policy statements and may not pursue a particular course of action once in office. On the other hand, political parties gain support by disclosing what they intend to do, and lose it if they do not carry through their intentions. Since they depend on support as well as revenue raised from their constituencies, through membership and donations, they often couch policies in sufficiently general terms, catering for a broad front of opinions.

In multi-party systems political parties are most often involved in the initial stages of policy identification – stating what changes they plan to introduce, or what new items they will add to the policy agenda. Only when they are in power will they actually formulate policy. It is only at the stage of taking office (whether as a follow-up term or as a new government) that they will be exposed to details or to the various interests affected by changes being proposed.

Thus, a political party may promise reform, but not be able to deliver when in power. 'Australian government retreats from health promises' was the headline given to a story in 1993 suggesting that the Australian government was reneging on one of its main pre-election promises to buy beds in private hospitals (*British Medical Journal* 1993: 163). Curtis (1990) describes the Janata (People's) Party which was founded in 1977 in India, through the amalgamation of a number of smaller parties, which was able to promulgate a credible programme in 1977 that satisfied its constituent groups and their members. Most important was the common opposition to the emergency rule introduced by the Prime Minister, Mrs Gandhi, with its limitations on the judiciary, suspension of civil rights, press censorship and forced sterilization. The Janata Party said it would introduce policies that encouraged self-reliance, the alleviation of poverty and redistribution of wealth. However, once it was in power, the fragile unity of the new governnment collapsed, and it was unable to meet the promises it had made as a political party:

> Some leaders wanted to press forward toward rapid economic development; others considered modernity the ultimate expression of spiritual corruption, and sought instead to favor home industries and agriculture. One group wished to assimilate the science and technology of the West; another group rejected Western materialism and resolved instead to revive and fortify Hindu culture (Curtis 1990: 493).

However, not all multi-party systems provide opportunities for policy debate before elections. In Botswana, parties have not used elections for raising or debating policy issues or for presenting alternative policy agendas (Holm 1988).

In single-party systems the political party formulates all policies and it becomes the task of the government to find the best ways of implementing them. Parliament thus acts as a forum for debate but it is the Party which is the supreme policy-making body. On the whole, and especially in Africa, elections in single-party systems do not provide voters with choices or policy alternatives, and criticisms of the ruling party are often mute or stifled. In Mozambique, before the introduction of a multi-party system (due in 1994), the Party could directly intervene in policy making if it felt that a ministry was deviating from its political course. On two occasions (in 1976 and 1979) the health services were criticized and, in speeches delivered by the president, attention was drawn to what were seen as deficiencies in the quality of care being provided. The first speech, made soon after independence, resulted primarily from grass-roots complaints about the central hospital in Maputo, the capital city. The number of people seeking care had trebled, resources had not grown proportionately and trained health workers were in short supply. However, the problem was seen in terms of poor management and attitudes. The Ministry of Health's response to this criticism from the Party was to reorganize the hospital along more democratic lines, making health workers more accountable for their actions.

The second speech in 1979 again expressed the Party's displeasure with the way health services were organized and delivered, and was part of a more general campaign against other sectors too, which were also accused of lack of leadership, negligence and corruption. The government's response to Party criticism was to dismiss the Minister of Health, and introduce different work methods in the ministry – more decentralization, more delegation of decision making and responsibility (Walt and Cliff 1986).

In one-party states, the separation between party and government is not always simple: many people hold important positions in both, and the party provides broad policy guidelines for government. But also, as in the Mozambican example above, the Party intervenes in government policy where it feels it is contravening, or not reaching, required standards. In liberal democracies, once the political party gains political power, the government is in charge. While governments may not flaunt party policy, they may seek to persuade the party that from the standpoint of government, past policy positions may need adaptation. And they can introduce new policies, through the legislature and executive. Let's look more closely at these roles.

The role of the legislature: bark without bite?

In the overwhelming majority of countries, constitutions state that the legislature is the expression of popular sovereignty and the top decision-making body of the country. Three-fifths of countries have unicameral legislatures, called variously the Chamber of Deputies in Chile, the National People's Congress in China, the National Assembly in Egypt and Tanzania. Bicameral legislatures (such as those of the UK, USA, India, Mexico, Venezuela, France, Japan) have two legislative chambers: the House of Commons and House of Lords in the UK, the House of Representatives and Senate in the USA, the Lok Sabha and the Rajya Sabha in India (Danziger 1991). Most legislatures are supposed to have three functions: to represent the people, to enact legislation, and to oversee the executive (the top leadership). The legislature is the location of constitutionally established responsibilities for elected representatives (or members of parliament, deputies, senators, etc.), the object of media and public attention. It is the body through which the government's policies are enacted and enshrined in law. And finally, it is the body which scrutinizes executive performance, or questions specific plans or actions of the executive.

Are these ideal expectations of the legislature met? Obviously, countries have a variety of constitutional arrangements, and different powers of legislature *vis-à-vis* executive power. However, legislatures are viewed increasingly as bodies that rubber-stamp decisions reached elsewhere. In a review of the literature on elections and legislatures in Africa, Healey and Robinson (1992) suggest that elected representatives are seldom more than marginal in the policy process, and in some countries are inhibited by a history of detention without trial for criticizing proposed government policy. They quote Le Vine (1979) as suggesting that in francophone Africa the legislature has become just another instrument (and a dispensable one) of the ruling elite. In Europe, one observer has accused most European legislatures of being ceremonial, full of 'masculine pomp, ritualised debates, public school behaviour and preoccupation with trifling details' (Keane 1988).

Five main reasons are given for this, some of which apply elsewhere. First, there is such a strict control of proceedings by the party machine and the executive that this represents a stranglehold on the ability of ordinary elected representatives to exercise much control over, or even to examine, major policy decisions. Second, the executive uses a system of patronage and party discipline to reinforce executive domination. Third, radio and television have taken debate away from legislative chambers, into a world of television studios, confidential briefings and editorial conferences. Fourth, bureaucratic power has expanded so much that much decision making operates outside the legislature. And finally, the globalization of the world means that supra-national bodies such as the EC or the IMF limit or foreclose parliamentary policy choices.

In the industrialized world this is largely in relation to investment and defence policy, but in many Third World countries external influence may affect health sector policy.

However, while there is a great deal of pessimism about the role of legislatures and the extent to which they can perform their three vital functions, they nevertheless survive. They survive because they have great symbolic value, and uphold the idea of democratic representativeness. And they are not all the same. Some legislatures are relatively docile, but others, such as the US Congress (and legislatures in some Latin American countries), are stronger, even if they are not truly determinant in policy making. They may be effective in scrutinizing, delaying, and from time to time blocking executive proposals. Some elected representatives are extremely active, and may try to influence the policies presented to the legislature, although for quite diverse reasons. Jeffery gives the example of Indian politicians proposing motions to cut the health budget because of the behaviour of doctors in specific clinics or hospitals – using the parliamentary opportunity 'to settle scores' (Jeffery 1988: 172), and harass or embarrass government. The strength of the legislature is derived not only from its legal status but also from its ability to attract publicity, and its blend of substantive information from a variety of sources which converge on it: journalists, pressure groups, academics and the bureaucracy.

If the legislature does not have a great deal of say in policy formulation, who does? Let's look at the politicians who make up the government, and the civil servants who advise them. Is this where the centre of power lies?

The executive: is it in control?

In most countries with multi-party systems, most of the power for policy making lies with the executive – the elected officials who become prime minister or president, and the ministers (or deputies, or senators) who are responsible for certain sectors of government.

There is some debate, however, between those who believe that the executive (or top leadership) dominates policy making and those who believe that it is really the civil servants, or bureaucrats, who control the policy process. This is an ongoing debate which provides no definite answers. It depends strongly on which country you are looking at, and over what time period.

In the USA the legislature (or Congress) is relatively separate from the president's office. The executive consists of the president, the staff in the executive office (a group of supporting bodies which include the

White House office with a staff of about 400), and the political appoint-
ees the president makes to top policy positions in government departments and agencies. The USA is a typical presidential form of
government, in which the president is both head of state and chief
executive, who has considerable power, but has to persuade the legislature to agree to proposed policy, and who can be rejected by the people
through elections. In Mexico too the keystone to the political system
is the presidency. The president is the dominant figure in policy making, the prime mover, the motivator and the tone setter for all government activity. His or her power is wielded directly, through the
appointment of cabinet members, and indirectly, through the appointment of individuals to particular positions:

> Each time a new president comes to office in Mexico, there is an extensive
> turnover in government jobs. The fact that the ruling party doesn't change
> does not make much difference in this, nor does the fact that the incoming
> president was picked by the outgoing one. Indeed, the fact that new presi-
> dents are picked by the predecessors seems to impose a particular psycho-
> logical obligation on them to demonstrate that they are independent and
> not simply puppets. Moreover, they want to demonstrate that they will avoid
> the errors of the predecessors, so a great deal of ostentatious change in per-
> sonnel and policy orientation is mixed in with the inevitable continuity from
> incumbent to incumbent (Curtis 1990: 553).

Premier Deng Xiaoping is like an emperor and head of the communist
party. In the French presidential system the president and the prime
minister share leadership, often leading to trials of strength between the
two.

In a parliamentary system like the UK Westminster model, the
executive is closely linked to the legislature – members of the cabinet
are members of the legislature. In the UK and India the executive is
composed of the prime minister and the cabinet of ministers, often
including the minister of health. In these countries the prime minister
does not usually make political appointments to government departments, which are run by career civil servants who do not change even
at the top levels, when governments change. What may happen is that
the prime minister may bring in her or his special advisers – but they
sit in a separate policy unit attached to the prime minister's office, and
not in government departments.

In all these systems there are a number of checks and balances to
control the power of the executive and the ruling party. One of the
most important is the separate judicial system which may overturn laws
made by the legislature where it can be shown that they have contra-
vened the constitution.

The role of the chief executive

One of the much debated questions in political science relates to the relative strength of prime minister *vis-à-vis* other members of the executive. How far do they decide questions of policy collectively, how far can the prime minister impose his or her own view on executive colleagues? In those countries of the Third World where political leadership is personal and unaccountable – where constitutional rule is the exception rather than the norm – most major policy decisions will be left in the hands of the chief executive.

Sometimes the executive may be very small: an inner group of politicians who cluster around the chief executive. Those who make up the cabinet or council of ministers (whatever the inner decision-making body is called) are the real policy makers. How authoritarian this inner kernel of decision makers is, is of major interest. In the UK during the 1980s, for example, much was made of the fact that cabinet members changed significantly during Mrs Thatcher's years in office, and that there was little room for manoeuvre for those not committed to what has been called the 'conviction politics' of those years. In other words, many political observers felt that the prime minister was a key policy maker, and dissidents, even from her own political party, were not tolerated. Both Mrs Gandhi in India in 1977, and Mrs Thatcher in Britain in the late 1980s, were seen as virtual dictators within democracies. In general, the powers of prime ministers *vis-à-vis* their ministerial colleagues have tended to increase.

Not only will the executive in this position be the main formulator of policy, but she or he may also be the primary agenda setter. Talking of the 'impoverished policy process' of the Thatcher years, Rosenhead uses the introduction of health service reform as an example of slipshod agenda setting:

> In late 1987 the Government was under intense public pressure over the National Health Service. It was in this atmosphere that Mrs Thatcher launched a 'boomerang'. In a television interview with Jonathan Dimbleby in July 1988 she announced that there would be a fundamental review of the NHS. The initiative was one of which the entire NHS and the Department of Health, even to their top echelons, had no advance notice (Rosenhead 1992: 17).

In this situation, civil servants were faced with a *fait accompli*, and were left having to review and develop a new health policy which was clearly in line with specific ideology. In Britain it is not common for civil servants to express their views on policies, and when in mid-1991 the chief executive of the National Health Service, Duncan McNeill, made headlines in the top newspapers by denying that the Conservative government's reform of the health sector meant privatization of the health service, the government was accused of illegitimate tactics of 'hiding behind' or 'using' a civil servant to present its case. In the British system it is an important principle that civil servants remain as impartial as possible, serving whichever government is in power.

The civil service: running the show?

However, the other side of the argument is that politicians and prime ministers come and go, while civil servants stay. Without the machinery of government – the administration, or the bureaucracy – the political system could hardly function. The bureaucracy is the institution that administers the functions of the state. It is made up of the civil servants or bureaucrats working in departments or ministries, agencies or bureaux, who collect information and records, plan how policies can be disseminated, enacted, monitored, interpret and apply public policies that provide public goods and services, regulate and enforce policies, collect taxes and other revenue. Although supposed servants to their political masters, bureaucrats may have huge power because of their expertise, knowledge and competence. The bureaucracy has been credited with maintaining political systems when the executive or legislatures are ineffective.

Clearly the power of the bureaucracy *vis-à-vis* the politicians differs from country to country. The Conservative government which won the general election of 1979 in the UK remained in power for an unbroken period over the decade of the 1980s and into the 1990s. In this period they built up huge knowledge of, and experience in, government, easily matching that of their civil servants. In the USA and most Latin American countries top civil servants change with changes in government. Civil servants in these systems are not seen as 'neutral' but 'supportive' of one party or ideology. In these systems of political patronage, civil servants and politicians may form very tight policy circles, with all policy initiatives coming from within. Indeed, during the Reagan administration in the USA, this tight circle of policy makers was even able to act unconstitutionally, and break their own government policy in relation to Iran, in order to supply arms to the Contra forces they were supporting against the Nicaraguan governnment.

In those systems where civil servants have careers as such, and stay in position when politicians change, politicians may be highly dependent on civil servants. Although it is conventional wisdom that civil servants carry out the wishes of ministers, and merely advise on policy, some have argued that bureaucrats actually play very important roles in policy initiation and formulation. Ministers arriving at a government department are never faced with a blank sheet of paper. Policies have been laid down by former ministers, and are being implemented. Even if ministers come into departments with clear views on what sorts of policies they would like to see, or what changes are needed, they may be thwarted by civil servants who make them aware of the pitfalls of such action. Many ministers, in fact, endorse what the bureaucrats say. In looking at the causes and consequences of variance in ministers' performances as leaders in the UK, Headey (1974) devised a typology of ministerial roles, and concluded that while a few were equipped to serve as policy initiators most acted as:

—minimalists;
—policy selectors;
—policy executors; and
—policy ambassadors.

Minimalists limited their role to basic departmental work; *policy selectors* saw themselves as intelligent laymen happy to choose from a series of alternative policies; *policy executors* were largely concerned with management roles and efficiency; and *policy ambassadors* acted in a public relations role promoting the work and policies of their department. After a spell as a minister in a UK Labour government in the 1970s, Meacher (1980) argued that British civil servants had enormous power. He characterized their ability to control policy by manipulating information to keep ministers at a disadvantage. They did this by using one or several tactics.

RULES OF THE GAME PLOY   With this tactic, civil servants enforce routine meticulously. Officials control speeches made by ministers, and determine what ministers can and cannot say. The example given above, of Mrs Thatcher announcing in a television interview that a major reform of the health sector would be undertaken, was unusual.

FAIT ACCOMPLI PLOY   When ministers are new to a department, a range of policies will have been decided. Ministers are dependent on officials who may reject change by saying it is too late: the forms have been printed and distributed, the training has taken place.

EXPERT ADVICE PLOY   Ministers depend on civil servants for advice, and where this is professional or technical advice, may feel out of their depth and unable to challenge the departmental view. This may be particularly pointed in departments of health, where the minister is not a physician, but is advised by physicians.

TIMING OF PAPERS PLOY   By making available detailed papers on important policies only a few hours before the meeting to decide the issue, civil servants keep the minister at a disadvantage.

While these are all characterizations, and half in jest, there is nevertheless sufficient truth in them to suggest that the higher echelons of the civil service are by no means neutral when it comes to policy making, and may have considerable influence in relation to the politicians who are their 'masters'. These are all the more apparent with newly elected governments, especially if they have never held office before, or not for a long time.

In some countries – the communist states for example – the notion of an impartial bureaucracy was rejected from the beginning: all bureaucrats were expected to work within party guidelines, and at the top echelons civil servants were expected to be members of the party. In other countries, too, the classic model of the civil service, with loyalty owed to the state, is at variance with what actually happens. Because of a long history of factional alliances, it has been said that the bureaucrats in the African country of Chad are loyal first to personal, political allies, and only second to the government. Where political allies are the government, then policy making proceeds. Where they are not, bureaucrats may act against the interests of the ministry in which they are employed (Foltz and Foltz 1991).

Many colonial systems left nascent bureaucracies which continued and grew in expertise, becoming the mainstay of the state through political upheavals. In Nigeria, which adapted the British model of administration, top civil servants are supposed to elaborate policies and plans and to assist in determining the best means of implementation. In practice it is argued that more senior civil servants play a central role in policy formulation. This is explained by a number of different factors which include political instability (change in ministers), the delegation of broad discretionary authority and, in comparison with politicians, the superior knowledge and expertise of the administrative classes who have made up the civil service (Koehn 1983). Such was the perceived power of the civil service that in the year that followed a coup in 1975, more than 10,000 civil servants were dismissed from the federal and state ministries and parastatals in an unprecedented sweeping purge of all ranks in the public services. In spite of this, observers conclude that during the three decades following independence civil servants have constituted the main political actors and exercise relatively uninterrupted influence over the fashioning of public policy in Nigeria, even where a military government is in place.

In Nepal, up to 1990, when democratic reforms were introduced, all major and minor decisions were taken at the Royal Palace, and although civil servants were answerable to the Council of Ministers, in practice the civil service was

> more likely to emphasize its relations with the Royal Palace secretariat which presides over not only the destiny of a given policy or development programme but also the fate of individual bureaucrats (and ministers) (Panday 1989: 319).

From this we can conclude that the civil service is hardly neutral, and that top bureaucrats may play an important part in policy making. This power derives from their proximity to ministers and their own expertise and competence. As we shall see, bureaucrats also have extremely important links to other departments in government and to external interest groups which increases their areas of influence.

However, a final caveat is in order. When it comes to major policies (economic policy for example), and smaller countries, where the political system is relatively limited, bureaucrats may be less able to influence the policy process at least when it comes to the 'high' politics issues. In those countries where ministers have had to deal with the World Bank and IMF, it is often ministers who are the major negotiators. Here the pull of power is not so much between bureaucrat and minister, but between minister, his ministerial peers and foreigners. Klitgaard points out the tensions in such roles. Talking of Equatorial Guinea, a small country in central Africa, he notes that the Finance Minister, who was himself a trained economist, was often in a difficult position:

> ... the Minister of Finance was caught in the middle. To creditors and aid givers he represented the government and was therefore the breakwater for waves of criticism and conditionality. On the other hand, inside the government he had to report and to some extent represent what the creditors and aid givers insisted upon. He bore bad news to both sides and could easily be seen by both as the embodiment of the enemy (Klitgaard 1991: 281).

But even in sectors such as health, where the policies being negotiated are not systemic, but sectoral, or micro policies, government ministers and officials may be highly dependent on external donors' preferences. Cliff (1993) concludes that in Mozambique the Ministry of Health has been forced to change several health policies to adapt to donor demands, and that some districts' health services are in fact controlled by foreign non-government organizations rather than by the state.

In the case presented in Box 5.1, it is clear that policy in the health sector was to a great extent decided by the foreign donors who came in to assist the Ugandan government in the mid-1980s.

Box 5.1 'Donors could do whatever they wanted': international influence on government policy

From 1971, when Idi Amin seized power in a military coup, until 1986, when the National Resistance Army (NRA) government was formed under the presidency of Yoweri Museveni, Uganda suffered years of factionalized political violence, war and economic chaos. Between 1965 and 1989 gross domestic product per capita halved (Save the Children Fund 1993). Western donors largely withdrew from or substantially reduced assistance to Uganda during the period, and it was only after the establishment of the NRA government that they began to return. Rehabilitation of the country began in the 'post-conflict' period after 1986, although insurgency continued in significant areas until the early 1990s. 'Post-conflict' appears in quotation marks because of the long period after 1986 when peace and stability were still fragile.

The response of national and international agencies to the task of 'post-conflict' rehabilitation occurred in the absence of a clear national health strategy. International agencies rapidly designed, funded and implemented programmes reflecting their own objectives and government lacked effective mechanisms for their coordination. Policy thus became fragmented. As one observer said: 'donors could do whatever they wanted in the immediate "post conflict" period. The government said "yes" to EPI [expanded programme of immunization] "yes" to the rehabilitation of hospitals, "yes" to CDD [control of diarrhoeal diseases programme]. There was no attempt to redirect programmes because there was no central health policy.'

Policy in this period might be described as being in a state of free fall. Interestingly, major donors such as the World Bank did not seek to impose conditions on aid flows to stabilize health policy at this time. One World Bank official said that in the immediate 'post-conflict' period the Bank sought to be helpful and not to impose difficult conditions on loans. Government was in need of a great deal of money, quickly, and there were vast needs for reconstruction of the physical infrastructure to provide basic services such as health and education.

Given the absence of clear government policy and its dependence on aid, donors were in a strong position to determine priorities and allocate funds. In contrast, government was in a weak position to counter donor bids for programmes, both because the demand for any type of input was overwhelming and because of the limited bureaucratic capacity to regulate and coordinate aid.

Donors therefore sought niches for their own activities. For example, UNICEF initiated a universal child immunizaton programme, the Danish Agency for Development Aid (DANIDA) supported essential drugs for health facilities, and NGOs carved out their own projects in particular areas. Many foreign representatives of international agencies, donor aid agencies and NGOs were in close contact with key ministries, but their activities were concerned with programme development rather than with supporting the formulation of strategic health policy.

The proliferation of programmes uncoupled from any unifying policy framework enabled greater donor control over programme design and management. It also enabled donors to limit the risks associated with project implementation to carefully defined boundaries which conformed to their areas of expertise, while leaving out those services with which they felt less able to cope. For example, the control of malaria, a major cause of morbidity and mortality, remained unaddressed. Interventions thus tended to conform to areas of agency expertise rather than to health needs. Donors also preferred to support development (or capital) costs over recurrent costs, and particular efforts were put into the physical rehabilitation of the health infrastructure, particularly hospitals. Thus there was a strong tendency to focus on generating measurable outputs, rather than supporting the underlying processes which support health systems and health development.

Study of the Ugandan 'post-conflict' situation suggests that donors rushed in with aid for programmes instead of trying to ensure the development of coherent health policy. This is understandable, from the point of view of both donor and recipient, because of the impact of immediate visibility, but in the longer term may have constrained or even distorted future policy. What was learned from the rehabilitation process carried out in Uganda in the mid-1980s? One observer suggested that what was needed was 'to be modest in your objectives and to ensure that priorities are set according to needs'. It seems that donors missed an opportunity to formulate a comprehensive health policy which would have provided the basis for sustainable and equitable health development. (Macrae, J., Zwi, A., and Birungi, H., 1993.)

The position of the ministry of health

So far we have been looking at the government in general. But government is segmented – ministries pursue their own interests, and policies often emerge from relatively specialized policy communities. These policy communities can be rather closed informal structures, with few links to other sectors or ministries. Where does the ministry of health fall in the pattern?

The ministry of health is often described as the Cinderella among ministries. In the hierarchy it will usually come after the ministries of finance, defence, foreign affairs, industry, planning and education. Although the ministry of health, as with education, is a high-expenditure department, largely because of the salaries paid to its workers, it nevertheless has relatively low status in the departmental hierarchy.

> The ministry of finance and planning, full of Western trained economists holds the predominant view of economists that development is a problem of economic welfare first, with social welfare a distant second. 'Investment' is the priority: that is, investment mainly in infrastructure and industry. 'Consumption' is to be deferred for as long as possible and health is seen as consumption (Gerein 1986: 262).

The minister himself or herself may or may not be a member of the executive and because of its relatively low status, the ministry does not always attract the high fliers among politicians.

The extent to which health commands any attention on the government's policy agenda therefore depends to some extent on the skills of the minister to argue for competing claims on the government's budget, and to put across the needs for, and implications of, a new direction of health policy. However, it is unlikely that health issues appear very often on the agenda for meetings of the executive except at times of crisis: and although these may be crises about epidemics such as cholera or AIDS, economic crises are more likely to force discussions about the financing of medicines or high technology, or the introduction of users' fees in previously free health clinics.

For example, in Kenya in 1989 and 1990 economic recession brought a period of intense policy dialogue over the future financing of the health service. The main policy makers were the Ministry of Health, the World Bank, USAID and a consultant supported by the Swedish Development Agency. In August 1989 the results of their discussions went to the Kenyan cabinet, which basically endorsed the proposed system of health financing for the public sector, but made some reductions in proposed fee levels for in-patients (which Kenyan Ministry of Health officials had argued were too high, but which the Bank insisted on), and eliminated out-patient fees at the dispensary level. The new fee system was applied from December, but only a couple of months after its introduction the President intervened, to reduce further the level of fees: from 100 to 20 Kenyan shillings per day at the Kenyatta National Hospital for in-patients (Dahlgren 1990). The reason given was that too many people could not afford the new fees, and utilization of the hospital service had fallen drastically. The President and other government politicians were under considerable pressure from leading newspapers, consumers and professional groups to decrease the fees. The government was also being highly criticized both externally and internally (on human rights grounds and corruption charges), and may have been feeling particularly sensitive to public opinion. The cost to the government was a considerable reduction in fee revenue. Some two years later, however, fees for out-patient services were reintroduced, with revisions, exemption mechanisms and a waiver system for those unable to pay (Mbiti, Mworia and Hussein 1993). Reversals in policy were due, at least in part, to the abrupt introduction of the fees, with insufficient information and education of both the public and professional groups (Mwabo 1993).

The relatively low status of the ministry of health has implications for its relations with other ministries, whose policies also affect people's health. Most ministers become absorbed with and bound by their own policy sectors, rather than being concerned with contributing to collective decision making within government. Departments with responsibilities for water, agriculture and education all have their own goals to pursue and while not unsympathetic to health issues may not be prepared to take on active roles in policy and planning for health. Although many countries set up intersectoral bodies for health in the 1970s (for example, a national health council in Sri Lanka, a national rural development committee in Thailand), there was little evidence a decade later of any systematic effort on the part of government to evaluate the influence on health. Most policies were pursued in relation to economic or sectoral objectives. Thus, the ministry of agriculture was too concerned with revenue and gaining foreign exchange to support any policy that promoted diversification of crops in order to replace tobacco growing, even where the deleterious effects on health and nutrition were pointed out (Gunatilleke 1984).

Another example of departments pursuing their own objectives and constituencies is provided by the differing goals between a ministry of health and a ministry of overseas aid. In Sweden the Department of Health and the Agency for Development Aid (SIDA) both sent representatives to the World Health Organization's Global Programme on

AIDS, but where the Department of Health felt that WHO should be placing much more emphasis on preventive action in eastern Europe, SIDA felt that resources should go to developing countries, especially Africa.

The problems of policy coordination are exacerbated by intersectoral rivalry and territorial jealousy: each ministry is, in the end, arguing its own case for a slice of the government budget against other sector's claims.

The position of advisers

The ministry of health is itself a complex organization, unique in the high status of its professional advisers, but one which, like any other part of government, has to relate to other central departments, to regional health authorities and to outside interests. Let's look at its relationship to these different parts and structures that make up the health policy community.

Medical, dental, nursing and pharmaceutical professionals have official positions in the ministry of health, and provide technical advice to the administrators or bureaucrats within the ministry. In many countries they dominate the ministry as heads of sectors. Potential conflict between high-status professionals and other bureaucrats in the ministry is clearly a possibility. If the minister is a doctor there may be some dissonance between political and professional goals. For example, in his study of Colombia and Iran, Ugalde (1978) showed that physicians dominated the ministries of health (although more had a background in public health in Colombia than in Iran) and that this strongly affected policies because of the extent to which professional, medical values permeated all levels of policy making – including implementation – because the professionals were involved in service provision as well as policy formulation. The predominance of medical professional values led to a tendency to equate health with medicine. This in turn resulted in a clear conflict of interests in one case where it was to the advantage of the doctors that ministry of health resources went to hospital building, equipment and maintenance rather than to building up the primary health care infrastructure because physicians used public hospitals (which had the most advanced technology) for their private patients. In Uganda, in the period of reconstruction of the mid-1980s, after years of political conflict, doctors constituted a significant political pressure group both within and outside government. A number of physicians occupied key positions in government, and the medical school at Makerere had an important and influential position. Although endorsing the principles of primary health care, many of these medical professionals lobbied strongly for the physical rehabilitation of hospitals (Macrae et al. 1993; see Box 5.1).

On the other hand, bureaucrats rather than professionals often retain the upper hand, in spite of the latter's high status. Jeffery (1988) writes that in India almost all commentators agree that the bureaucrats are, in the last resort, dominant in policy making because they control access to the minister. They can also talk as colleagues to the heads of other ministries. Doctors, whose careers are restricted within one ministry, can use their technical skills as a political weapon, claiming that decisions need specialist medical knowledge, but they are in a less powerful position than the bureaucrats within the ministry.

In some countries, the advisers are foreigners. In Africa alone, during the 1980s some 100,000 donor-funded expatriate advisers worked in the public sectors of forty countries at a cost of US$4 billion (Cohen 1992). They are often professional planners or economists, and may play an important and not disinterested part in the policy process. In discussing administrative reform of the ministry of health in Chad, two of the most important actors in designing change were the French advisers, who had invested considerable time and energy in arguing for certain sorts of restructuring within the ministry (Foltz and Foltz 1991). They also brought to the attention of policy makers in the ministry what the World Health Organization's guidelines were on how health ministries should be organized.

However, the impact of advisers on policy is not always apparent. Justice suggests that advisers have little opportunity to learn about the local system and seldom recognize a need for cultural orientation or language training, so that relationships are 'commonly single stranded, job related, and impersonal' (Justice 1986: 42). Cohen (1992) notes that advisers may fulfil several roles: as high-level, neutral advisers, as gap-fillers, gate-keepers, specialists or as condition-precedent advisers – inserted by donors as administrators of projects to ensure proper implementation, the position described by Klitgaard (1991). Some may contribute to 'capacity building', many will leave nothing behind.

Consulting with experts

Consultation may take place through a variety of channels: through established advisory committees (which may include outsiders with special expertise) or through *ad hoc* meetings or working groups set up to advise on specific issues.

For example, in Britain's Department of Health policy on pharmaceuticals is, on the whole, a consultative process which takes place in committees within the department. The first committee, called the Medicines Commission, is charged with advising ministers on all matters of drugs policy. The other policy-making body is the Medicines Division within the Department of Health, which has the day-to-day job of licensing new drugs and overseeing and reviewing their use and benefits. It is composed of five committees which look at various aspects of drugs, the most important being the Committee on the Safety of Medicines. Members of these committees (all from outside the civil service) are appointed by the Secretary of State for Health, and they include many people who are consultants for pharmaceutical companies, or have shares in drug firms. In 1987 five of the twenty members of the Medicines Commission were from the pharmaceutical industry. Many of the clinicians serving on such committees will have received funding from pharmaceutical companies to support research (Collier 1989) and may therefore be influenced to act in favour of the industry.

The sorts of people appointed to such committees are likely to be members of the Association of the British Pharmaceutical Industry, the ABPI. Furthermore, the revolving door *into* the Department of Health works *out* of it too. It is an increasingly common feature of bureaucratic life in Britain that on retirement from the civil service, top bureaucrats join the boards of companies and industries with which they have been consulting as civil servants. Thus, in 1984, the civil servant in the Department of Health in charge of drugs for the National Health Service took on the job of director of the Association of the British Pharmaceutical Industry. There are no legal sanctions governing the transfer of public servants to the private sector after their retirement at the age of 60 or in mid-career, although they are required to apply for permission from the Cabinet Office if the move is within two years of leaving the service. Such appointments are clearly useful to industry, because their incumbents bring with them valuable inside information about the civil service and government: all the more so when they move from the ministry of defence into the arms industry (Pallister and Norton-Taylor 1992). We explore the role of industry as an interest group in the next chapter. What is clear from this example is that, at least in Britain, the pharmaceutical industry is represented at many levels in drugs policy development within the Ministry of Health.

Having said that, it is interesting to note that when the Thatcher government decided in 1984 to introduce a restricted, or limited, list of drugs that general practitioners working in the National Health Service could prescribe, the government acted swiftly without consulting the industry, because they knew that it (and groups within the medical profession) would oppose the policy. What this example suggests is that government will consult often, but if the sense of crisis is strongly perceived (the drugs bill had risen by 79 per cent in real terms over the ten-year period 1974–84 – Bateman 1993) and opposition is anticipated, it may take a knowing risk and ignore pressure groups to pursue a desired policy. The government was determined to introduce the restricted list although, through consultations with the professions, the list was increased from an original thirty products in seven therapeutic categories to 129 preparations before it passed into law in 1985.

Tensions around consultation do not only occur between the ministry and outsiders: there are often tensions and competition between different sections *within* the ministry itself. Ministries of health in many developing countries have established vertical programmes to deal with particular diseases or target groups: diarrhoeal diseases, the vaccine-preventable diseases of childhood, AIDS, maternal and child health. In Ghana, for example, this approach to the provision of public health services has resulted in separate divisions of the ministry; each controlling its own area of intervention, with separate management systems for finances, transport, supervision and in-service training (Cassels and Janovsky 1992). Where such programmes attract funding from external sources, there can be considerable jealousy in protecting such sources, in retaining rather than sharing resources, and in promoting the achievements of such programmes, even where these may be in direct conflict with ministry of health goals to provide integrated health services.

The tendency towards autonomy and independence may be quite strong in the ministry. In Afghanistan, for example, senior officials from other sections resented having to collaborate with the ministry's planning sector, perceiving it as

> a power shift away from the relative autonomy their departments had enjoyed. They preferred fragmentation and the political sleight-of-hand possible where they were individually responsible for their plans, which could be rationalized and slipped through a largely uninformed review process (O'Connor 1980: 289).

Sub-national institutions

While the ministry of health is instrumental in policy identification and formulation, often other bodies are responsible for policy implementation. Although they may play a part in getting certain issues onto the policy agenda or even in reforming existing policy by feeding back information on the effects of policy implementation, experience suggests that this does not occur often. In most countries ministries of health are strongly centralized, with vertical lines of authority, and there are not many opportunities for lower-level authorities to make inputs to policy formulation.

When it comes to policy implementation, however, the central ministry of health is reliant on regional, provincial or district authorities. All governments transfer some responsibility for planning and management from national to subnational levels, or from higher to lower levels of government (Mills et al. 1990). The largest bodies may be at state, regional or provincial level, with the second tier called districts, thana, block, gun, municipality, and so on.

The extent of decentralization differs according to the type of government, and has changed over time. In many developing countries in Africa and South-East Asia, public health services were initiated largely by central government, and local governments have played only a small role. These highly centralized services moved towards strengthening lower levels of health services in the 1980s. In contrast the health services of developed countries were amalgamated into comprehensive national services only over the past fifty years.

Decentralization takes many forms, and is used loosely to mean different things (Mills et al. 1990). Sometimes, contrary to what is usually envisaged, decentralization actually deepens domination of policy formulation and implementation, especially in Latin America (Collins 1989). The four main types of decentralization are usually defined as deconcentration, devolution, delegation and privatization (Rondinelli 1983). They reflect different degrees and approaches to decentralization, which influence the actual degree of discretion enjoyed by local bodies. It is the extent of control at the sub-national level that determines how far local bodies can affect and influence implementation and policy making. This depends on sub-national bodies' ability to raise and control resources and mobilize political support, their capacity to attract and retain competent officials, and the legal framework of rules and regulations within which they work.

The ministry of health usually retains functions of policy formulation, development of health plans, and allocation of resources among other things. There is, however, a huge variation in the functions of regional or provincial authorities in different countries. Some may be similar to a ministry (as in India, for example), others merely an intermediate hierarchical level in a bureaucracy. In particular their control over personnel and finance ranges from very limited to quite extensive. Commonly, regions and provinces have functions relating to regional health planning and programme monitoring, coordination of regional health activities, budgeting and accounting, employment and control of some or all health personnel. Finally the most peripheral administrative level, often referred to as the district, may come under the ministry of health or local government. Districts' functions are usually to organize and run district hospital and primary care services and to manage and control local health budgets, among other things.

As we shall see when we look at implementation, the ministry of health often tends to retain control over policy, legislation and budgets. Lower-level institutions may be able to raise money from local taxation to spend more or less as they wish, but usually, especially in poorer countries, they depend on central governments to allot them a proportion of the total government budget. Many ministries retain tight control over local spending by mandatory demands for services, by setting targets or by preventing local transfer of funds between functions or inputs. The opportunities for policy initiation may be few, in spite of the fact that lower-level institutions are better located to respond to local needs and problems.

Collins (1989) notes that there are many scenarios in which decentralization is a political manoeuvre either to abandon functions (in Pinochet's Chile functions were transferred from central to local government and subsequently privatized), or to cut central government expenditure. Decentralization can also be used to disperse or defuse social and political conflict. Urban protest movements in Colombia in the 1970s and 1980s over the deficient provision of public goods and services, such as water and sanitation, were diffused when the functions and resources for such services were transferred to local authorities. Decentralization may also reinforce access to decision making of local dominant groups. In many rural areas, landowners manipulate politics for their own interests. And finally, decentralization can simply mean strengthening the position of the ruling party or central government at the local level.

In Papua New Guinea decentralization was seen by politicians as a means of achieving greater political control for themselves over bureaucrats (Thomason et al. 1991). When formal authority passed from Australia to Papua New Guinea in 1975, bureaucrats had well developed habits of participating in the policy process, and were able to exercise their power in an already existing administrative structure. Politicians found themselves in an unfamiliar position within the newly created political institutions which had been drawn from an alien tradition. They had neither the experience nor the skills necessary to hold their own against the better educated administrators. Through decentralization, politicians realized that they would enhance their own local political positions. Officials in the Department of Health, on the other hand, resisted decentralization because they saw it would diminish their power and authority. For this reason, among others, after thirteen years of 'complicated and often tortuous' decentralization of health services in Papua New Guinea, the completion of the process was not yet in sight in 1991 (Thomason et al. 1991: 152).

Besides regional authorities, many countries have large *parastatals* which, although government organizations, fall outside the main lines of departmental or ministerial hierarchies. They may have a great deal of autonomy in their day-to-day decision making. Since they function in the economic sphere they often become relatively powerful if they make a substantial contribution to the gross national product of the country. They often have access to foreign finance, may be the largest borrowers from the country's commercial banks, and in this position wield considerable power. Control by the state may be weak, and adherence to government policy may be resisted or marginalized.

For example, the Ministry of Health's attempts to develop a national drugs policy in Tanzania have been hampered by differing goals pursued by different ministries. The National Pharmaceutical Company, a parastatal, has a great deal of autonomy, but is nominally under the Ministry of Trade and Industry, and is guided by principles of profit. The Central Medical Stores, on the other hand, comes under the Ministry of Health, and has as its main goal the provision of inexpensive, safe, effective and generic drugs for the public sector. The National Pharmaceutical Company imports any drugs on which it can make a profit for the private sector, and has strongly resisted attempts to rationalize policy on drugs (Kanji et al. 1989).

The judiciary and the military

While both of these institutions are usually separate from government (although clearly this is not the case in all countries), they may play a direct and indirect role in trying to influence government policy formulation. Most societies have specialized judicial systems – courts of law which determine whether the rules of the society have been transgressed, and if so, whether sanctions should be imposed on the transgressor (Danziger 1991). The interface between the legislature and the judiciary in the interpretation and creation of law is critical. Constitutional jurisdiction covers three main areas: resolving conflicts between state and citizens over basic liberties; ruling on whether specific laws are constitutional; and resolving conflicts between different institutions or levels of government (Hague et al. 1992). The Supreme Court of the USA has offered many striking examples of where it has challenged the laws of individual states: in the 1950s it invoked the fourteenth amendment of the US constitution to enforce black civil liberties, and to make segregation (of schools, for example) illegal. However, the law is not always an impartial force for good: in some communist states (in the Soviet Union under Stalin, for example) it became a major instrument for prohibiting opposition to the state, and in many Third World countries the judiciary has been clearly subordinate to the executive.

Similarly, the military may be an important actor in policy formulation, and in those countries where it disagrees with the sort of policies being pursued by government (Chile is only one example of many), intervention may occur in various forms – ranging from expression of disapproval to takeover of government. Military regimes are likely to be more rigid and less open than others, and may pursue health policies that are seen as authoritarian and repressive. Escudero (1981) argues that health status in Argentina declined significantly under military regimes, although it is difficult to substantiate because of the lack of data. However, he points to 30,000 *desaperacidos* (disappeared) after the 1976 military coup, of whom only 11,500 were accounted for, dead; the destruction of the system of health services run by labour unions after they were taken over by the junta; and an ideology that treated medical care like a commodity, with a huge increase of high technology and drugs imports.

Whatever the strength of the military, it is common that, as a sector, it provides health care for its own personnel and their families. In some countries the military health service is by far the most developed and sophisticated, and medical professionals may be highly influenced by colleagues able to employ the most up-to-date diagnostic and therapeutic technology, and demand it for their own working environments and patients, whatever its appropriateness for the population.

We'll come back to these issues when we look at implementation. What can we conclude from the process of policy in the government arena?

Conclusions

Although most countries have legislatures which ostensibly make policy, their main function is often one of debate and scrutiny. The real control over what gets on to the policy agenda and is formulated into policy generally lies in the hands of the executive, which may be fairly narrowly defined. Thus the bureaucracy may have significant power in policy formulation and implementation, especially where civil servants have careers and stay in place while politicians change.

Within the ministry of health there may be some tension between high-status medical and nursing advisers and civil servants and politicians. But in developing policy, ministries of health will probably have established mechanisms for consultation with a wide variety of professional bodies. Ministries of health will also have to deal with lower-level authorities (regional, state and other bodies) which are usually the implementers of policy. How far such authorities have a say in policy making depends on the extent of decentralization in the political system. In many countries, power is tightly controlled by the centre. When it comes to implementation, however, sub-national authorities may have the power to resist, to block and to delay.

6

Can interest groups influence government policy?

In the last chapter, I suggested that the heart of the public policy process is government: and within government the debate about the policy process revolves around the question of who makes decisions. Is it the politicians – or is it the bureaucrats? In searching for the answer to this question, however, we have to look beyond government, and beyond the ministry of health. Neither politicans nor civil servants operate in an isolated world. They have many contacts outside parliament and their own government departments, and they often consult groups outside government. If they make policies which are strongly disliked by the public or by particular groups they know that they may well be resisted – implementation simply would not occur. The media or political opposition may focus attention on unpopular decisions and weaken government resolve. Or there may be urban riots or student demonstrations. Conversely, there are many groups outside government, referred to as interest or pressure groups, who want to influence government thinking on policy, or on provision of services. They may use many different tactics to press governments into taking their demands or their points of view into account.

Of course, the extent to which such groups can or do influence policy depends on how far you accept that societies are pluralist, with many groups vying for influence in order to put their own preferences. Adherents to this view argue that the sources of power – information, expertise, finances – are distributed non-cumulatively, and that no one group ever controls them all. We have argued that this is probably accurate for many of the routine matters of health policy, although the notion of 'bounded pluralism' does allow that major economic decisions are made by a small ruling elite.

Pluralists usually view interest groups as an important brake on the executive, acting as a healthy conduit between the people and the government. Ideally, in such a system, 'sensible' policies will usually prevail. But a few writers, notably Olson (1982), have argued that interest groups can be seen in a negative way – bending public policy towards their own narrow interests, and actually making the business of government much more difficult. For example, in times of economic retrenchment, trade unions may argue for government subsidies for labour to attract investment, at the same time that government is seeking to reduce subsidies on food. Indeed, Olson argues, somewhat controversially, that in those countries where interest groups are weak and not well organized, economic growth has been fast (South Korea, Thailand, Indonesia) but that as soon as stronger networks of interests begin to form (trade unions, industrial interests, professional groups) economic growth begins to slow down because such groups pursue narrow, sectional interests, and interfere with the mechanisms that lead to growth. Such arguments may have led to the clamp-down on trade unions and professional groups in Britain and other liberal democracies such as South Korea and Taiwan in the 1980s, fitting in well with the call for more reliance on the market and less on government provision.

Clearly there are major differences between countries and over time. In much of the Third World, there is little observable evidence of action from national interest groups putting pressure on government. Trade unions are weak, and commercial or business interests use associational links with relevant officials in government. In these countries, family and kinship ties are enduring, and strong customs of reciprocity mean that politicians or officials are expected to use their position to enhance or protect the situation of members of their families. A minister of health will not be surprised to have a continuous flow of extended family members asking for jobs, financial assistance, advice on illness. A provincial medical director in Zimbabwe once told me that he was happy to be medical head of a province which was a long way from the province where he was born, because of the pressure he would be under from kin were they living in the same area. Thus, in many developing countries, the number of interest groups is small and political systems have often been more autocratic in their decision-making processes – not conferring widely with groups outside government. Citizens have shown their discontent through non-compliance, evasion or disengagement (for example, through migration, smuggling, bartering or informal markets) – more at the stage of policy implementation than formulation.

However, the lack of documented activity of pressure groups does not always reflect reality. The political changes of the past few years have opened up the system, and in some countries there is a great deal of growing activity among civic organizations, residents' associations and trade unions. There are also many examples of existing active groups: the Consumers' Association of Penang in Malaysia has been an important interest group both at national and international levels. The Bombay-based Association for Consumer Action on Safety and Health (ACASH) has, together with other organizations such as the Medico Friends Circle, drafted a Bill of Patients' Rights to protect patients against the relatively unregulated medical profession. ACASH hopes the issue will be widely discussed through different media and ultimately introduced as a Bill to Parliament (Sharma 1993). Many community and professional organizations in São Paulo, Brazil, have used pressure group tactics and advocacy to argue for change in the field of public health (Pedalini et al. 1993).

But even in those situations where interest group activity has been relatively limited, the same cannot be said for non-government organizations (NGOs). There are hundreds of indigenous and international NGOs which have been working in developing countries for many years, and at least some of these groups have been influential in changing public policy. We will look more at these groups later in this chapter.

In the industrialized countries there has been a huge growth in the number of interest groups over the past few decades, so much so that Richardson et al. (1982) talk of an 'overcrowded policy environment' which is leading to difficulties in reaching decisions. They point to the increase in environmental groups as an example of growth in national and local pressure group activity: by 1975 it was estimated that membership of the environmental movement in Britain had reached 2 million; in West Germany there were more participants in environmental groups than in political parties, and in France an average of 25,000 voluntary associations were established annually between 1967 and 1976, compared with 1,000 in the interwar period. This growth has increased the difficulties of decision makers.

> For example, the lead time for large development projects such as road building, power stations and airports has been adversely affected by the need to accommodate the demands of such groups and some projects have had to be abandoned. What might have been a technical decision about, say, road construction in 1950, is now often a hotly debated issue, involving rather wide participation and quite new values in society (Richardson et al. 1982: 7).

So far we have talked about interest groups in general. Let's look a little more closely at different sorts of groups, in order to assess how far they are likely to be able to influence health policy.

The definition of an interest group

Most definitions of interest (or pressure) groups contain the following notions:

—they are voluntary bodies;

—they aim to achieve some desired goals;

—they do so without attempting to infiltrate the process of decision making to the point of adopting formal government roles.

In other words, they are not interested in taking formal political power. If such a stage is reached, the interest group ceases to function and becomes part of the institutional process of government. The Green Parties in Britain and Germany, which started off as ecological and environmental pressure groups, are examples of this, because they later formed political parties, putting up candidates for election to public office. Thus they wanted to be directly involved in policy making from the inside, not merely trying to influence it from the outside. In many Third World countries where single-party systems are giving way to multi-party systems there is a flurry to set up non-governmental organizations which will seek to influence policy. It is easier to get financial assistance to establish an NGO than to start a political party. Many NGOs are having to deny their interest in becoming political parties – although there are suspicions that that is their long-term aim.

Interest groups may have very inauspicious origins – they may start life simply as a group of people concerned about a particular issue. Sometimes several such groups are formed (including researchers, professionals, individuals with particular problems), and may become 'social movements', a sociological concept which tries to capture an element of spontaneity and change that describes people coming to-gether to promote or resist change in the society or groups of which they are a part. For example, Scotch (1989) analyses the growth of the disability rights movement in the United States, which started casually with individual people with disabilities pressing for changes to accom-modate their disabilities (for example better housing, accessible trans-port), and became an institutionalized and articulated structure of several organizations promoting better policies. This example is discussed further on p. 115. As such social movements become institutionalized, many of the groups that make them up become pressure groups.

Lindblom uses a rather broader definition of pressure group activi-ties as

> all interactions through which individuals and private groups not holding government authority seek to influence policy, together with those policy-influencing interactions of government officials that go well beyond the di-rect use of their authority (quoted in Jordan and Richardson 1987: 187).

Essentially Lindblom is using a much broader definition, because he is including parts of the government machine acting as interest groups

– for example, the ministry of health trying to influence the ministry of trade and industry on tobacco policy. This is an unusually broad definition of interest groups, and while it is useful because it acknowledges that parts of government may, at any one time, act as interest groups to influence policy in another part of government, it is more usual to think of interest groups as organized groups which are *outside* government – although as we will see, they may have a very close relationship with government.

So, for our purposes, the main characteristic of interest groups is that they attempt to influence public policy but they do not seek political power.

What sorts of interest groups exist?

The political science literature abounds with a great variation of classifications of interest groups defined by their goals and membership.

For example, Duverger (quoted in Jordan and Richardson 1987) says interest groups are either

— *partial groups* whose main goal is to protect the interests of their membership, and who only attempt to exert political pressure as a secondary aim (for example the Trades Union Congress, the Confederation of British Industry); or
— *exclusive groups* which exist primarily to pressurize on particular issues – peace, abortion, the environment, keeping lorries off village roads, and so on.

As shown in Table 6.1, other authors who differentiate groups by their function and membership use different terms for the same category of pressure group. I usually use sectional and cause groups to differentiate the two although, as we see later in this chapter, the boundaries between such groups are not as rigid as the typologies suggest.

Table 6.1 Types of interest groups by goal and name

Main goal is to protect the interests of their membership; attempt to exert political pressure as a secondary aim; membership is restricted	Partial **Sectional** Interest Producer
Main goal is to promote a particular issue or cause; membership is open to anyone who supports the cause	Exclusive **Cause** Consumer Promotional

SECTIONAL GROUPS   The first group – the partial, interest, producer or sectional group – is a collection of individuals who have a similar productive role within society, and they are able to bargain with government using sanctional pressure. In other words, they are often relatively strong, and if they do not like what government is doing, they are able to challenge policy. For example, trade unions, particularly public sector unions, can persuade their members to withdraw their labour, so inflicting harm on the economy. Obviously this depends on their strength: in many Third World countries trade unions are divided along ideological lines, supporting particular political parties. They are often quite weak: few members pay dues, and there is insufficient funding for training leaders or for communication with members. Their ability to enter into collective bargaining (over wages or broader economic policy, for instance) is therefore relatively limited.

Health professionals are a particularly interesting sectional group, giving the health policy process unique features. Until relatively recently, many argued that medical power was an entrenched part of public health policy. In many European countries physicians were seen to be in dominant, exclusive, monopolistic positions within the health sector, with considerable control over the training and regulation of their own members, and with the ability to subordinate other health professionals to their influence. Nurses and other health workers were referred to as semi-professionals or paraprofessionals, and their organizations as 'bit' players in setting policy. Furthermore, the medical profession was perceived as having high status by the great majority of government policy makers and the public, a legitimacy supported by considerable consensus about the central role of the state in health care.

By the 1980s this picture was changing. There was a significant challenge to the medical profession's privileged status based on its technical knowledge and expertise, and to the 'medical model' which explained ill health and diseases largely in terms of biological factors. The primary health care approach was part of a revolution in health policy which put more emphasis on the value of lay care, and control of factors outside medicine, to improve people's health. As the costs of providing health services rose, so doctors came to be seen as careless in their use of resources, and from the early 1980s many governments began to look for ways of decreasing the power of the medical profession. The example given in the previous chapter of the introduction of a restricted list of pharmaceuticals was just one of many different ways in which the British government flexed its muscles in the 1980s, and took on a much more combative approach to the British Medical Association. Introducing general managers into the National Health

Service was another attempt by government to curb physicians' control over hospital resources. As consensus about the role of the state in health provision has broken down, the medical profession has moved from a privileged position at the centre of health policy making to a considerably more marginalized position.

In many countries of the Third World, professional associations do not seem to have played such a central role in health policy. In Latin America and India, for example, professional medical associations appear to have much less power in general, although many individual doctors have high status within the community and when they are policy makers in the ministry of health, they do, of course, have a major say in health policy. The weakness of professional associations may result from the fact that the profession has not regulated entry into it, so that there is an over-supply of doctors, and less confidence in the overall quality of their training. In Asia and Africa, where the bulk of primary health care has been provided by nurses who greatly outnumber doctors, professional associations are still relatively weak and so far have had little perceptible impact on the policy process. For example, in many countries in Africa the introduction of community health worker programmes was decided entirely by doctors – usually inside the ministry of health – with minimal consultation with nursing associations who were expected to be the trainers, managers and colleagues of these future health workers.

CAUSE GROUPS   The second group – the exclusive, cause, consumer or promotional groups – draw their membership from a wide range of people within society and aim to emphasize or promote concerns that are general, and not specific to the group itself, although this is not always true. For example, a group of disabled people, or sufferers from a particular disease such as AIDS, or a group of women, may form a pressure group to try to influence policy directly related to them. But a British pressure group such as the Campaign for Nuclear Disarmament (CND) will be made up of a broad range of people who may sympathize with any of the political parties in Britain or may be strongly religious or atheists. They join CND because they want to ban the use of nuclear weapons. A Consumer Council, formed to protect the interests of a wide range of consumers, will campaign on a range of issues such as appropriate labelling of pharmaceuticals or safety of food products. The Medical Action Group in the Philippines, the Medico Friends Circle in India, the former National Medical and Dental Association in South Africa have all campaigned on the link between poverty and health. The Society for the Promotion of Area Resource

Centres deals with issues relating to shelter for pavement dwellers in Bombay.

INSIDER AND OUTSIDER GROUPS   These classifications – sectional or cause – are only important inasmuch as they help us to assess how far pressure groups are or are not influential. Another way of looking at pressure groups – instead of defining them by goals or membership – is to assess how far they are recognized or legitimized by government. Grant (1984) suggests that pressure groups fall clearly into two main categories – *insider* and *outsider* groups. The insider groups are accepted as respectable by government policy makers, with whom they often have a close consultative relationship. Government may well turn to such groups for information or even to test ideas for policy changes. They may be invited to join particular government committees and be deeply involved in decision making. Putting their point of view to government may therefore be relatively easy for the insider groups. In the last chapter, we saw how the UK pharmaceuticals industry – the Association of the British Pharmaceutical Industry (ABPI) – has clear insider status with the Department of Health – perhaps not surprisingly since the British government is clearly concerned to promote the pharmaceuticals industry (one of Britain's most successful export sectors), allowing a steady and profitable flow of drugs to reach the market. Of course, at the same time, the Department of Health has to ensure that dangerous, ineffective or expensive drugs do not waste health budgets or harm National Health Service patients. By conferring closely with the pharmaceuticals industry, resolution of what are conflicting goals may be eased.

The ABPI will spend considerable time and energy in preserving its insider status by inviting retiring civil servants to take top positions in the Association, as well as through regular contacts with specific civil servants in the Department of Health. It will organize formal meetings between the industry and top officials – perhaps including the minister – once or twice a year, and will have a series of contacts with members of parliamentary committees to ensure their view is put.

Some NGOs such as Oxfam or Save the Children Fund (UK) sometimes try to influence the government's aid or development policy, and are often perceived as insider groups. The British government, for example, may confer with such groups regarding bilateral agreements with Third World governments, using NGOs as sounding boards, but also as sources of information. Their insider status is confirmed by the British government's joint funding of NGO work in the Third World, which increased from £1m to £28m between 1975 and 1992. Conversely,

Oxfam may pressure government when it disagrees with policy intentions. For example, in 1992 it was announced that the British government was likely to cut the UK overseas aid budget by up to 15 per cent. Oxfam (and other agencies) launched an immediate campaign against such cuts, taking full-page advertisements in main, establishment newspapers showing a waving, grinning Prime Minister under the ironic headline 'Au revoir Africa?' These advertisements were followed up with letters and editorial comments, as well as action by local Oxfam groups, presenting the case at Party conferences, and joining with other agencies to lobby the European Community's Summit meeting in Birmingham. As respected insider groups these agencies were, of course, supporting the Foreign Office's overseas aid programme against its struggle within government to maintain its funding base. The NGOs were useful allies. The campaign was said to have embarrassed government (Oxfam 1992) and, whether or not as a direct effect, the aid budget was not cut in 1992.

Outsider groups are, by definition, not perceived of as legitimate by government policy makers, and may therefore have difficulty in penetrating the policy process. What they do is pursue different tactics. They may decide on direct action – attack whaling ships (as did Greenpeace), demonstrate outside the laboratories using animals for experimental purposes, or dump thousands of bottles on the doorstep of the firm making non-returnable, non-biodegradable bottles. Anti-abortion organizations stand outside clinics that counsel women about unwanted pregnancies, harassing workers and clients; they organize boycotts against pharmaceutical firms producing medicines that induce abortion and in extreme cases use violence against clinic workers. In the USA they were successful in halting the clinical trials of RU486 (an anti-progesterone drug which acts on the endometrium, aborting early pregnancy) for one year. In 1988 when the French government approved the marketing of RU486, the drug company succumbed to pressure from anti-abortion groups to suspend distribution. Two days later the French Minister of Health ordered the company to resume distribution, saying 'From the moment governmental approval for the drug was granted, RU486 became the moral property of women, not just the property of the drug company' (Woodroffe 1992). Such groups may receive considerable media coverage, and possibly evoke some response from a public which is otherwise relatively passive on such issues.

Not all outsider groups use sensational strategies – or they may only use them occasionally. They might, for example, try to persuade individual politicians to take up their cause in the legislature by introducing a bill, or by bringing up the subject of their concern for debate. Most legislatures will have opportunities, albeit limited, for ordinary representatives to raise questions of interest to them or their constituents.

And of course, outsider groups can become insider groups. Simms (1987) describes how the Abortion Law Reform Association, established in Britain in 1936, was 'beyond the pale' until the 1960s, when a number of different policy 'streams' came together giving the Association a professional respectability previously denied, and enabling it to influence government to promote major change in the law on abortion. Similarly, policy studies on AIDS in Britain show clearly that outsider gay groups led the way on policy in the early stages when the disease first became recognized because the government lacked information and knowledge about AIDS and had to turn to them (Strong and Berridge 1990). This is a picture familiar to many other countries too, where HIV activist groups and gay organizations started off as being clear outsider groups. In Zimbabwe, for example, when initially Ministry of Health policy was to keep AIDS a secret, and not to divulge the numbers of people who were HIV-positive or had full-blown AIDS, consultation between the Ministry of Health and outside groups was minimal. By 1990, the growth of AIDS service organizations, including groups of AIDS sufferers who put pressure on government, led to more open discussion of the AIDS problem in Zimbabwe. Many of these groups have been in open conflict with the Ministry of Health, which is in favour of statutory notification of all those who are HIV-positive, but because of their standing and pressure, they have been able to dissuade the Ministry from introducing this particular policy. Many of the AIDS service groups would be considered insider organizations today: representatives sit on the Ministry of Health's National AIDS Control Committee, with direct access to government policy makers.

Often an outsider group becomes an insider group through its delivery of services. By building up expertise in a specific area, outsider groups may become useful to government policy makers, and may become accepted as authoritative – especially if they are working in an area in which government has little knowledge. In many countries the Family Planning Association (FPA) was very much an outsider group for years. In Britain it was only in the mid-1960s that a Minister of Health visited the FPA, thereby conferring a respectability on the Association which had been unthinkable until then. Today the FPA is seen as a legitimate pressure group with insider status, and closely consults with the Department of Health over a series of policies regarding reproductive health. The Bangladesh Rural Advancement Committee (BRAC), a non-government organization set up in 1972 to empower rural communities through a series of activities in health, education and development has, over the years, attained important insider status with the Bangladeshi government through its successful provision of programmes. Because its work has been evaluated and assessed internally, BRAC has a great deal of information about the rural communities with which it works, which further consolidates its position. Finally, through its development programmes, BRAC has an annual operational budget of around US$23 million per year, from funds received largely from abroad (Howes and Sattar 1992). This, too, makes it an important player in the policy field, and when it wishes to pressurize government on a particular point, it is likely to be given a serious hearing.

It is probably fair to say that most groups would prefer insider status to outsider status, and often they will prefer to use persuasion or informal contacts with policy makers, and avoid strategies that are confrontational. They develop a perception of the rules of the game and, on the whole, try to play them. However, this can be difficult for some groups, especially if they are challenging basic societal values. Stedward (1987) gives an excellent example of a *thresholder* group – sometimes on the inside, but often on the outside in the policy process – because of the nature of the group. She describes the first women's refuge centre which was set up in Scotland – as a result of public recognition of the need for women who were victims of domestic violence. Within two years a formal organization was established, and they received a grant from the Scottish office.

From the beginning Women's Aid was conceived of as a pressure group (bringing to the public's attention the problem of violence in the family, and how it affected women and children) as well as a group involved in service delivery – offering a place of refuge for women (and their children) whose husbands were abusing them. Although at one level Women's Aid clearly acquired insider status (not least because it was providing a service the government was not particularly keen to provide itself), on another level, it was not always consulted when policies about women and violence were being drawn up. Stedward suggests that the democratic nature of the organization meant that consultation was difficult and sometimes a lengthy process. Representatives had to report back to the organization, and could not take positions on policy without discussion. Furthermore, the Women's Aid feminist perspective challenged conventional social welfare analysis. While the policy community of professional social workers, police, local authorities and others valued what they did, they often did not accept their feminist analysis of why violence occurred. Womens' Aid was thus a *threshold* group – sometimes accepted as an insider group (especially in terms of service delivery, or implementation of policies) – but often perceived of as an outsider with excessively radical views.

A similar example from Zimbabwe suggests that groups which work in areas which are marginal may always be considered thresholder groups. The Musasa project in Harare, set up to support and provide shelter for women victims of violence – domestic abuse and rape – has achieved high standing among professionals for the work it is doing. Apart from its service work (providing shelter, training, counselling), it has been able to negotiate with the police on how victims of such violence should be treated and has pressured for increasing the length of sentences for those convicted of rape. Government officials may well consult with such an organization on changes in policy, but because of the difficulty of where to set boundaries between state and private behaviour, government will probably always keep some distance from such groups.

PROFESSIONAL LOBBYISTS   As the number of interest groups has increased, so has lobbying. Lobbying is generally thought of in a relatively narrow context: as the attempt by professional lobbyists to influence members of parliament. The lobby is the front hall of the legislative building.

Lobbyists are commercial lobbyists or cause lobbyists. The commercial lobbyists (a growing group in western Europe) are professional persuaders whose main job is to persuade policy makers to take up, subject only to personal reservations, *any* causes (corporate or promotional) that seek professional assistance (including cause groups). They are paid for lobbying. In contrast there are the cause lobbyists, who lobby for a cause and not for cash. They are often said to be more effective than commercial lobbyists because conviction and passion carry weight.

Commercial lobbyists may be multi-client lobbyists or in-house lobbyists. Multi-client lobbyists offer themselves as a guide to parliamentary procedures, contacts, strategies, information sources. Any group can buy their services in order to run a campaign in parliament or to raise concern about a specific policy being discussed. Private hospitals, for example, concerned about the government's policy on the private health sector – say, in relation to attempts to regulate fees charged for private care, or excise duty levied on high-technology equipment – may be relatively ignorant about legislative and political realities. So they may hire a firm of lobbyists who will put their point of view to members of the legislature.

The other group of professional persuaders are the in-house lobbyists. Often large companies will set up special departments which deal specifically with the company's relationship with government. Such a department may

— ensure the company is aware of the political developments which may affect its operations;
— see the company is not pursuing contradictory policies to government;
— ensure company employees in contact with the government are fully briefed.

One of the people in this department may be an in-house lobbyist, whose job is to take MPs out to lunch, and to keep them informed about the company, its goals and what it is doing. They may have a long-term strategy, to build up relationships which they hope they will be able to call on should some policy come up that directly affects the company. The lobbyist will also arrange for MPs to visit the company and see how it works, or invite them to social events. Of course companies will also belong to trade associations or professional associations, which may themselves have their own lobbying department: and occasionally, a company may call in an external consultant to run a particular campaign.

Many companies will try to attract ex-MPs or top civil servants as members of their Boards of Governors, or heads of their public relations (or government) departments, because they have inside knowledge and contacts. The 'revolving door' between parliament or the civil service and commercial companies, trade unions and other organizations is a well-known mechanism for attempting to influence the policy process.

Cause groups are fuelled by conviction for a particular issue, and therefore those lobbying on their behalf are often devoted to the cause, lobbying not because they are paid to lobby but because they are paid to promote the cause. This can make a great deal of difference. Cause group lobbyists may be just as professional as the commercial lobbyists, although not always as rich! In developing countries community-based cause groups are sometimes able to call on professional lawyers, journalists or social workers to help them put their case to the media or to lobby elected representatives (Pedalini et al. 1993) but direct lobbying by professionals is not common in the Third World.

Both commercial lobbyists and cause lobbyists may use similar tactics to try to influence policy. In the UK they seek close relationships with civil servants, because it is in the departments of government that consultation and negotiation over policy may begin. By the time a policy gets to the legislature, and is debated, much will have already been discussed. Although elected representatives may scrutinize and even challenge policy, they are often unable to exert much influence over it, other than suggest small changes, at the stage that it reaches discussion in the legislature. So all lobbyists try to keep in contact with civil servants.

How successfully they can do that will depend to some extent on their perceived legitimacy: are they insider or outsider groups? Some cause groups may not get access to civil servants, in which case they may focus much of their efforts on Parliament. Over time they may shift from outsider to insider status, as occurred with the Abortion Law Reform Association (ALRA) in the UK, when a number of different policy 'streams' came together, making the time right for change, and legitimizing ALRA's role.

As is by now clear, interest groups are part of networks of influence: government may be central to the network, but there may be many interest groups (some with conflicting aims), and all with different levels of authority and power. Interest groups are parts of these networks, with criss-crossing levels of exchange and power.

Networks of influence: policy communities

Governments are affected by many forces that shape their knowledge base, as well as by shifting currents and fashions that turn their attention from old to new problems. These emanate from policy communities, which are networks of individuals from various institutions, disciplines, or professions, and in the health field may be practitioners (health professionals), researchers (academic epidemiologists or parasitologists) or commentators (medical journalists). The health policy community might also include pharmaceutical companies, hospital administrators, any interest groups, and members of government. This would clearly differ from country to country and issue to issue. Examining policies on domestic violence will draw in the police; examining tobacco policy will include the companies. Both these groups may be uninterested in health policy.

The main point about a policy community is that there is a constant exchange of information about activities and ideas, and that some of these reach government policy makers. Policy communities provide a number of different fora in which the early stages of opinion formation and consensus building among experts takes place (scientific meetings, journals, newspapers) although it may take years for ideas to diffuse broadly, especially where they are critical of existing policy. Policy networks are made up of different, perhaps overlapping, policy communities both within and outside government, which may affect government thinking. For example, three main policy networks have been shown to have influenced the development of British social policy in the 1950s. Smith (1991) highlights the role of the Cambridge Keynesians, the Titmuss social administration school, and the Oxford school of industrial relations (see pp. 181–2). In Czechoslovakia in the 1990s there have been heated debates about social policies – what should be retained; what role the state should play – among emergent rival governmental factions (Castle-Kanerova 1992: 91). Similarly, at a wider international level, policy networks of development economists, family planning protagonists and disillusioned health professionals influenced a revolution in thinking about health which resulted in the promotion of primary health care (Walt 1993b).

In order to show that policy communities are by no means consensual networks, Sabatier (1991) sees competing coalitions within networks, which he calls advocacy coalitions. They consist of actors from many public and private organizations who share a set of basic beliefs (perceptions about the nature of a particular problem, its causes, and what sorts of policies would resolve it). Advocacy coalitions seek to manipulate the rules of various government institutions in order to achieve those goals over time. Conflict among coalitions is mediated by 'policy brokers' who are more concerned with system stability than with achieving policy goals.

A useful example of the tobacco policy network in the UK is given in Box 6.1. Read (1992) says that in order to understand government policy on smoking in Britain, it is necessary to examine its immensely complex policy community. He paints a picture of core and peripheral interests, tracing how they interact with government and other bodies.

Box 6.1 The UK tobacco policy network: core and peripheral interests

Policy networks are made up of intricate overlapping communities, some core, others peripheral, with a common focus but very different interests. Looking at the tobacco network in the UK gives an idea of its complexity.

The *main supporter* of the tobacco industry is, of course, the producer network, with its close relationship with government built over many years. At the core of the producer network is the tobacco industry, in the UK composed of four major companies, and their trade association, the Tobacco Advisory Council. The tobacco industry is one of the most profitable of all industrial groups and is growing. In spite of falling domestic consumption of tobacco, profits have continued to climb through diversification and exports.

The Tobacco Advisory Council represents all manufacturers of tobacco, and meets regularly with government – politicians and civil servants – to discuss issues ranging from taxation on cigarettes to attempts to ban advertising. The Tobacco Advisory Council also sends delegations to meet with European Union (EU) officials, to express their view. In 1992, as part of a campaign against the EC proposal to ban cigarette advertising in Europe, the Tobacco Advisory Council took out two whole-page advertisements in major British newspapers saying that 'there is no proof that banning tobacco advertising reduces consumption' (for example the *Observer*, 9 February 1992). Although it has been contested, there is still considerable evidence to suggest a link between bans and reduced tobacco consumption (Department of Health 1992).

The Advertising Association (which looks after the interests of advertisers) defends the tobacco industry in its fight to be able to advertise its wares, because it represents huge amounts of advertising revenue (£100 million per annum). The publishers (newspapers and journals) may also support the tobacco industry for the same reason.

The core government departments (many of which have an economic or revenue interest in the tobacco industry) that meet with tobacco representatives are: HM Customs office (and the Treasury), which receive taxes from tobacco; the Department of Trade and Industry (gives grants and subsidies to industry); the Department of Health (on voluntary agreements regarding the advertisement of cigarettes) and the Department of the Environment (on sports sponsorship).

Besides these core government departments, there are several which are peripheral to the politics of smoking and, because they are often relatively passive in their action, lend support to the industry. For example, the Home Office is responsible for prosecuting small retailers or tobacconists who sell cigarettes to children – but in fact pursues legal action against such retailers only occasionally. The Department of Education is responsible for health education in schools, but spends relatively little on smoking. The Ministry for the Arts gets sponsorship from the tobacco industry for the arts, as does the Ministry of the Environment for sport, leading to an indirect form of advertising. The Department of Employment is concerned about employment opportunities and may subsidize the industry to build new factories.

Besides these government departments are a number of other groups which support the tobacco industry because of their own interests. For example, labour unions representing the tobacco and distributive trades (who sell cigarettes, have vending machines and who are concerned to protect jobs); and the Tobacco Alliance and the Freedom Organization for the Right to Enjoy Smoking Tobacco (FOREST), an ideological group which emphasizes individual freedom as a key value. Both of these pressure groups were formed to put the industry's case against restricting advertising.

The *opponents of the industry*, are, in comparison, rather few and it is more difficult to assign them to core or peripheral positions in policy making.

The Department of Health, in comparison with revenue-linked government departments (trade and industry, customs and excise), is weaker, and the health arguments about the links between smoking and disease do not hold much water against economic arguments about revenue from taxation, sponsorship for the arts and sport, or employment opportunities, even when the economy is buoyant. In Britain in 1971, an inter-departmental government committee which examined the economic implications of a reduction in the consumption of tobacco stressed the economic costs – loss of tax revenue, greater numbers of pensioners alive and collecting pensions, and therefore greater spending power on imported goods, all of which would lead to a deterioration in the balance of payments. The admitted health gains hardly figured in the quantitative analysis.

Outside government, the British Medical Association (BMA) brings professional authority and expertise to the arguments about smoking and ill health. It runs campaigns and lobbies government, has easy access to the Chief Medical Officer and other departments. Action on Smoking and Health (ASH) is a pressure group formed to persuade the government to adopt a political solution to health and smoking. It is respected, works closely with the BMA, and has some access to government departments.

What this case study shows is the complexity of the networks of influence – particularly the close links between government and the tobacco industry. Even if the strong association between smoking and disease has today been clearly established and accepted by the majority of health professionals, the tobacco industry's producer status confers on it huge power and access to government policy makers. In some countries, notably the US, the tobacco industry has even used the execuvtive branch of government to call for an end to trade restrictions in other countries, in order to open new markets for American cigarettes (see Box 7.3).

Interest groups gain access to government policy makers through formal, institutional links or through quite informal and subtle means. For example, Taylor (1984) shows that between 1978 and 1981 British American Tobacco's guests at the Wimbledon Tennis championships included thirty-six civil servants from Customs and Excise, the Treasury, the Department of Trade and Industry. In another example of what has been called the 'revolving door syndrome', Lord Hunter, chairman of the Scientific Independent Committee on Smoking and Health at the Department of Health, resigned to take up a position with one of the four largest tobacco companies in the UK. More recently, ex-Prime Minister Margaret Thatcher was appointed as a consultant to Philip Morris, a major American tobacco company. According to the *Sunday Times*, Philip Morris believed that Mrs Thatcher

> would be particularly helpful in its dealings with Vietnam, China, and South Africa, and in dealing with distribution problems in Russia. The company also wants to tackle restrictions on foreign ownership of tobacco companies in Malaysia and Indonesia and take on the Government's anti-smoking programme in Singapore. Finally, of course, the company will be manoeuvring to prevent tax rises on tobacco in all countries where it operates (Dean 1992: 294).

(Read: 1992)

Policy change may come about because a number of different policy communities initiate action on a particular issue. They may start as social movements consisting of groups that are interrelated, have common identities and interests, and come together to promote a particular cause, but which only form formal pressure groups after some time. Alliances are forged between scientists, the media, members of the general public, and political representatives. New problems are brought to the public's attention, and they can have a major influence on government policy. In the United States the disability rights movement, which comprised a wide variety of individuals and national and local organizations, controlled by and acting on behalf of people with diverse physical and mental impairments, wrought significant changes in policy in the 1970s

(Scotch 1989). The movement began with a few spirited individuals in the mid-1960s, grew into a loosely structured grass-roots movement until the mid-1970s, and formed the American Coalition of Citizens with Disabilities (ACCD) which began to lobby members of Congress in Washington. By the end of the 1970s several major federal laws had been passed which outlawed discrimination against people with disabilities. Another example is given by Fox (1989), of the rise of the Alzheimer's Disease movement (made up of scientists, the National Institute on Ageing, and the pressure group ADRDA – the Alzheimer's Disease and Related Disorders Association), which elevated the disease from one perceived as dreadful but insignificant, to one which was accepted as socially and medically significant, and a leading cause of death in the USA. Increased public awareness led to an increase in research funds made available for the disease.

Non-governmental organizations as interest groups?

Most scholars, whether from the development field or political science, argue that civil society in most of the Third World is weak, and that there is very little influence on public policy making from outside government. Government is portrayed as isolated from its citizens and, on the whole, not accountable to them.

Although this picture is probably broadly true – especially in Africa – it does not acknowlege sufficiently the existence of the myriad NGOs which do exist, or the informal way in which much policy is diffused.

In many parts of the Third World there is a growing number of groups – commonly referred to as non-governmental organizations – which are not recognized as interest groups, and yet which may, among other things, have a clear aim of influencing public policy. This may not be their formal, primary goal but through their activities they seek to change or reform the way the state operates in particular areas, and to force the state to be publicly accountable. Like interest groups everywhere, they do not want to overthrow or replace state structures or even become part of them. They include consumer councils, human rights groups, women's groups, AIDs networks; trades unions and professional groups such as nursing associations or public services associations, the national union of journalists or students; residents' associations or cooperative organizations. The churches may be a strong force, with large, active memberships. Such groups may, through informal and formal contact with each other and with policy makers – bureaucrats and politicians – have significant parts to play in forming and changing attitudes to particular policies. They are a growing force. Sometimes they are self-help groups which have inauspicious beginnings. Edge (1993) describes a group of Palestinian doctors driving around the West Bank to identify local needs: the medical relief committees which resulted have become a mass movement crucial for the provision of health care and decisions about health policy. By the 1990s the Palestinian NGOs were attracting over US$30 million from overseas donors. Such groups are likely to have a major influence on the shape of health policy in the lead up to, and after, Palestinian independence.

Moving from 'doing' to 'influencing'

Just as political scientists have attempted to categorize interest groups by membership and function, or insider versus outsider status, so development scholars have tried to divide the broad spectrum of NGOs into categories. One writer (Constantino-David 1992) cynically, but perhaps informatively, refers to BINGOs (big NGOs), GRINGOs (government-run or inspired NGOs), BONGOs (business-oriented NGOs), and COME 'N GO's (NGOs which are established for opportunistic reasons, and do not last long).

Another way of looking at NGOs is provided by Clark (1991) who uses a dynamic typology, dividing NGOs into six schools, reflecting their historical evolution:

1. Relief and welfare agencies, including missionary societies, providing services routinely and in emergencies;
2. Technical innovation organizations, which promote new or improved approaches to problems (for example, the Intermediate Technology Development Group in the UK);
3. Public service contractors, NGOs contracted by aid agencies to implement parts of official aid programmes because of their special expertise (for example, the US NGO called CARE is entirely funded by the government, and distributes US food aid);
4. Popular development agencies which are northern NGOs and their southern counterparts which focus on self-help and social development (for example, Oxfam, BRAC);
5. Grassroots development organizations, which are locally based, southern NGOs, which may or may not receive funding from popular development agencies (for example, Musasa in Zimbabwe, or TASO – the AIDS Support Organization of Uganda);
6. Advocacy groups and networks, which are groups which do not necessarily have field projects, but which exist primarily to educate

and lobby (for example, Health Action International, which has branches in many countries, and which campaigns on reforms in the marketing of pharmaceuticals).

Historically, non-government organizations in the health sector were apolitical providers of welfare and relief to the poor. They were largely service deliverers, and often provided an essential service in rural areas underserved by government. They were predominantly from the developed world, staffed and run by expatriates. That picture has changed. Many NGOs have moved from a 'doing' role to an 'influencing' role (Clark 1991) taking up causes of injustice and oppression, and challenging governments, as well as delivering services. Clark (1991: 5) gives an example of an NGO in the state of Gujarat, India, called DISHA, which has begun to force acceptance of legislation concerning minimum wages and bonded labour which was being ignored by employers. DISHA has challenged the landlords but has also taken action on behalf of labourers in the High Court, in the state parliament and through the media. Also northern NGOs have become more advocacy oriented, speaking out on behalf of their southern partners. For example, a European-wide group of NGOs has formed to plan common action on the debt crisis in the Third World – arguing for special debt relief measures for the poorest countries in Africa, among other things.

Although it is useful to divide NGOs into categories to distinguish their functions, rigid differentiation is unsatisfactory. Categories often overlap to a considerable degree, or NGOs undertake multiple functions. From the point of view of the policy process, however, what is important to consider is the different ways in which they may influence policy: through working with government; introducing innovative approaches; taking a direct advisory role; or by building networks.

NGOS WORKING WITH GOVERNMENT   Many NGOs work with governments in small projects, providing some resources in terms of personnel or funding. Where there is a receptive environment, NGOs may be able to introduce innovatory ideas, or change attitudes which may over a period lead to others following suit, and may effect an eventual change in policy. For example, Klinmahorm and Ireland (1992) describe a project in Rajanukul hospital for children with learning disabilities in Bangkok, which was supported by Save the Children Fund UK, which over the years has stimulated change in public attitudes and provision of education for these disabled children. The authors point out that a national policy in fact existed, but was far ahead of actual practice within the government sector. For example, policy in support of integrated education (including such children in ordinary schools) had existed since 1957, but little had been achieved.

> Given the educational priorities of the period (principally to extend primary school enrolment rates throughout the country) this is neither surprising nor necessarily a matter for criticism. The implication, however, is that it is not necessary to target changes in official policy in order to achieve the necessary improvements, but to analyse why existing policy has not been implemented in practice (Klinmahorm and Ireland 1992: 68).

In this situation an NGO, working with Thais, was able to stimulate a process whereby policy began to be implemented.

INTRODUCING INNOVATIVE APPROACHES   Because of their smallness, their ability to respond quickly to community demands, their relative lack of bureaucracy and their grassroots or field experience, NGOs are often willing to support or try out innovative ideas. Where these work, and their achievements become known, they can provide models for other communities, or even the public sector, with more appropriate approaches becoming policy. Sanders (1992) describes an example of a village health worker scheme run by the Bondolfi mission hospital in one of Zimbabwe's provinces during the cease-fire period after the liberation war. After independence, the Ministry of Health's policy was firmly in favour of primary health areas, and redressing the imbalances in access to care between urban and rural areas, and Sanders notes that the national village health worker programme launched to help achieve this aim was 'strikingly similar' to the Bondolfi scheme.

A DIRECT ADVISORY ROLE   Since 1987 Save the Children Fund UK has played a direct advisory role in Uganda to the ministry responsible for social welfare, assisting in the drawing up of legislation concerning children. The one piece of legislation set down the standards of care expected by government from organizations (including NGOs) which run children's homes, the procedures for obtaining approval to operate, and the regulatory system which maintains and improves standards over time. The other was to review current legislation on juveniles and recommend changes. Parry-Williams (1992) describes how the beginning of political stability from 1986, and a strong commitment to change and reform on behalf of the government, led to the setting up of the Child Law Review Committee, which included practitioners, administrators, academics and independent professionals. Wide consultation helped to produce a report which was widely accepted, but implementation has not been easy. We discuss this in Chapter 8. Parry-Williams makes the point that NGOs which take on an advisory role within government face a number of difficulties. They have to become trusted and accepted partners of government, but may also face hostility from those who feel threatened by change in existing legislation, or who feel that external NGOs funding such processes are exercising undue influence in national policy making. Other tensions may also occur: the United States government paid disability groups to implement some of the legislation they had been successfully pressing for, while the disability groups were still trying to organize disabled people to keep up the pressure on government. In this way the government may have, to some extent, co-opted the instigators for change and dissipated any opposition that existed.

BUILDING NETWORKS   One of the weaknesses of NGOs (although it is also a strength) is that most are fiercely independent, and preserve their autonomy energetically. Even where they have similar functions, their work may be motivated by very different ideals, and where some NGOs may be happy to work with government, others will be cautious about being seen to be co-opted by government. For all its strengths, however, independence brings its own weaknesses. Many NGOs collect information, are in touch with grassroots feelings and reactions, and their own experience gives them expertise in many areas. In getting together, NGOs can exchange information which may be useful to their own constituencies, as well as give a broader picture than is possible for a small NGO limited to working in a confined area. As a result, NGOs have begun to form networks, building on the legitimacy gained through their grassroots work and experience, in order to have a greater impact at the national level. Constantino-David (1992) describes a process in the Philippines, where by 1988 there were ten major national networks of NGOs, with a combined membership of 1,300 individual NGOs. Some of the networks had links with each other. They grouped and regrouped around sectors (peasants, workers, the urban poor) and issues (women, peace, US military bases, the environment). Such networks relate to, and debate with, each other, exchanging information on technical procedures, coping mechanisms, strategies and tactics; they can advocate, campaign and lobby for change; assess policy change suggested by government; and put alternative policies or views.

Policy takes time to change, even to implement, as we saw from the above example from Thailand. Many different groups may be involved over long periods of time, and it is too simple to assume that NGOs are so busy delivering services that they have no direct influence on the policy process. Even in issues of high politics, NGOs may be involved quite significantly. This chapter ends with an example from Hall (1992) where he shows how the regional power authority in north-east Brazil was forced to make significant policy changes in its building of a new dam and reservoir, which involved the displacement of 40,000 people. Dam construction began in 1978. The regional power authority's policy was to resettle 10,000 of the urban population, giving the 30,000 rural inhabitants (who were legally eligible) cash compensation, but no access to land. Property speculation had begun in the early 1970s, given the expected hydropower scheme, leading to conflicts between peasants and those who wanted to buy land. The local Catholic church was the only organization at community level, and in this period initiated an educational campaign among peasants to warn them of the impending dangers. Later a few small rural unions were formed and, part funded by Oxfam-UK and union workers, the educational campaign expanded to include the muncipalities affected. A more dynamic union federation was established in 1979 and a sustained public campaign began against the regional power authority. By the mid-1980s the issue had been taken up by a US environmental group, a World Bank mission had laid down some basic conditions regarding satisfactory resettlement provisions, a widely publicised occupation of the dam had taken place, and finally the regional power authority was forced to negotiate with the union federation. A comprehensive resettlement plan was drawn up for the entire displaced rural population.

This example is useful for two lessons. First, many different groups were involved in trying to influence the policy of the distant and powerful regional authority: the Catholic church, trade unions, local and international NGOs, and they included the strong arm of the World Bank. Second, the struggle went on over a period of more than fifteen years, and none of the ups and downs, the dashed hopes or steps forward or backward, are recorded here. In other words, influencing policy may be a long process in which there are gains and losses for the interested parties at different times.

Conclusions

In summary, there are many groups outside government which may try to influence government policy on particular issues that interest them, at various stages of the policy process. Several different groups may form alliances and act as social movements to propose or resist policies. These groups differ in the way they are perceived by government, and some are accorded high legitimacy, 'insider' status and are closely conferred with. Sectional groups often fall into this category, because they are powerful, and can employ sanctions if they do not approve of government action. Cause groups, in contrast, may be highly regarded and consulted, but they have less recourse to sanctions, and may have to persuade or embarrass to put their points. They may be perceived as 'outsider' groups, and use tactics (such as demonstrations) to ensure maximum publicity through the media for their actions.

Although the policy environment in many Third World countries has not been conducive to much exchange between government and outside groups, many tend to overlook how many NGOs can, and do, influence government thinking on policy. If opportunities for civil society increase in the 1990s, so the opportunities for exchange may also be increased.

7

The international arena:
who is driving policy?

Up to now we have assumed the primacy of governments over public policy. How fair is this? Over the last fifty years the world has become significantly more interdependent. What difference does this make to policies about health? How far are national policies influenced by the policy process at the international or global level?

Clearly governments are increasingly affected by international policy procedures – the debate in Britain during the early 1990s over how far sovereignty would be threatened by the plans for a federal Europe is just one manifestation of a concern expressed in some quarters that national governments are losing more and more control over policies which should be primarily decided domestically. Many have argued that developing country policies are being decided externally, by financial institutions such as the World Bank. National policy on trade has long been affected by GATT, the EU and other global or regional agreements. Through the huge empire of United Nations' institutions, based on relations between governments, some states put pressure on other states (to provide food in famines, to attack invaders, to reform economic systems, to stop testing immigrants for HIV). Furthermore it is clear that transnational corporations, non-governmental organizations, and pressure groups (human rights organizations such as Amnesty International, for example) may operate in more than one country, and are active players at the international level.

It seems to me, therefore, that confining public policy analysis to the borders of one country gives a highly skewed picture of today's world. In this chapter we explore the policy process at the international level, starting with the United Nations system, focusing on policy making within the World Health Organization. We then go on to explore the role of other actors in the international policy arena, and the extent to which international agencies can affect domestic policy making – a question which is pursued into the next chapter on implementation.

What are international organizations?

There are many definitions of international organizations, sometimes referred to as intergovernmental organizations, or international institutions (Archer 1983). In this book we use a minimal but generally accepted definition of an international organization as one whose *membership, finance and field of operation involves three or more member countries.* If the membership is not based on state or territory – an example would be the Association of Commonwealth Universities – then it is known as a transnational organization. *Multinational* corporations are those businesses established by agreement between a number of countries which operate according to prescribed agreements, while *transnational* corporations are primarily enterprises operating from a home base, across national borders (Judge 1978). International (or intergovernmental) organizations may be global (part of the UN system) or regional (the European Union, the Organization of African Unity, the Arab League).

The United Nations system

The United Nations (UN) was established formally, and with many high hopes, by Charter in October 1945, to coordinate and increase cooperation between countries. There were fifty-one founder states, of which the US played a critical part:

> the United States, being by far the major provider of funds, energy and goodwill, dominated the United Nations' infancy, acting as both good and bad fairy at the christening. A nursery was laid out, toys were provided; siblings were spawned, in the form of affiliated UN agencies in specialized fields (of health, of culture, of agriculture, and so on), and in due course a resemblance to the parents was discerned (Hazzard 1973: 6).

However, the vision of the UN overlooking a peaceful and secure world, supervised by a benevolent concert of great powers, was quickly dispelled. The political life of the UN became a continuous effort to improvise ways to sidestep the mutual hostility of East and West and to find substitutes for the unanimity that was to have been the driving force (Urquhart 1990: 11).

In spite of the Cold War between East and West, the 1950s was the period of unchallenged hegemony for the United States. US supremacy was political, military, economic and financial. Even culturally, the American way of life was communicated around the world through the growing mass media, including cinema, and was what many aspired to emulate. It seems, in retrospect, to have been a period of surprisingly

convergent theories on, for example, the process of economic development: the countries of the Third World were seen as 'infant' versions
of the developed world, and it was assumed that they could move from
traditional to modern states by judicious, large-scale investment. The
policy environment, dominated by the Western industrialized countries,
appeared to be relatively consensual.

By the mid-1960s this had changed considerably. De-colonization led
to many newly independent nations joining the UN institutions –
membership increased substantially in this decade. Economic theories
about development shifted, acknowledging the imbalance in terms of
trade and domination of world markets which, many argued, had led
to the underdevelopment of many Third World countries. The policy
environment opened up more contentious debate, in which the developing countries often challenged the industrialized nations. The
'politicization' of UN agencies increasingly became an issue, sometimes
pitting the minority of countries which provided most of the funding
to the UN against the majority of member states. Many of the newly
independent countries introduced socialist-inclined systems, so that the
Soviet Union and other Eastern Bloc countries were joined by many
Third World countries against Western industrialized capitalist nations.

The agencies of the UN

Six principal organs of the UN were established by the UN Charter:
the General Assembly, the Security Council, the Secretariat, the International Court of Justice, the Trusteeship Council and the Economic
and Social Council (ECOSOC). This last body supervises the work of
numerous commissions, committees and expert bodies in the economic
and social fields, and endeavours to coordinate the efforts of the specialized agencies associated with the UN. The specialized agencies were
originally established as organizations with a mainly functional purpose,
to act as international clearing houses of information in special areas
and to advance international standardization in matters of global concern. After 1950 they all – some more than others – acquired technical
assistance functions mainly in respect of Third World countries (Williams
1987: 14).

The specialized agencies are independent, have their own budgets
and constitutions, and are supposed to cooperate with the UN and with
one another. The specialized agencies were established

> as organizations with a mainly functional purpose to act as international
> clearing houses of information in their speciality and as a means of advanc-
> ing international standardisation in certain subjects of international concern.

After 1950 they all – though some more than others – acquired technical assistance functions mainly in respect of Third World countries (Williams 1987: 14).

The specialized agencies were either created by the General Assembly or were existing agencies which were integrated into the UN system. For example, the World Health Organization developed from the Parisian Office Internationale d'Hygiène Publique (established in 1909) and the health organization of the League of Nations, created in Geneva in 1923 (Brockington 1975: 146).

The four biggest specialized agencies (in terms of staff and finances) are the Food and Agriculture Organization (FAO), the International Labour Organization (ILO), the UN Educational Scientific and Cultural Organization (UNESCO) and the World Health Organization (WHO) – see Table 7.1. The lead agency for health is WHO, but many of the other specialized agencies have an interest in, and affect, health status. The FAO's focus on food and agriculture clearly affects health; the ILO has an interest in occupational health and safety; and UNESCO in health education. Some of the smaller agencies also have health concerns, depending on their constituency. Although not strictly speaking specialized agencies because of differences in funding, constitutions and mandates, there are also other UN agencies which have interests in health: UNHCR's focus is refugees; UNCTAD and the United Nations Industrial Development Organization (UNIDO) are concerned, among other things, with the transfer of technology related to the manufacture of essential pharmaceutical products; UNFPA, established in 1969, has been primarily concerned with promoting family planning programmes. Even WIPO (the World International Property Organization) has been used as a forum for debate by some multinational pharmaceutical companies who argue that, as their intellectual property, brand drugs should be protected from generic drugs' competition. UNICEF's focus is on mothers and children and it has played an important role in health, often as a partner to WHO. Unlike other UN agencies, however, UNICEF does not have member states which contribute to its funding, but depends for its financial base on voluntary contributions from the public (through Christmas card sales and so on) and from other organizations (which may be other UN specialized agencies, governments, foundations and so on).

The World Bank and the International Monetary Fund (IMF)

While the World Bank and IMF are part of the UN system, they have very different mandates and status from other UN bodies. Some view them as so financially powerful that they are in a category of their own.

The World Bank was established in 1946 (along with the IMF and GATT) as one of the pillars of the Bretton Woods institutions, to prevent a return to the instability of the 'beggar-thy-neighbour' economic policies of the 1920s and 1930s. The World Bank was to lend for long-term development, and since the 1980s has focused exclusively on loans to the less developed world. The IMF was to provide finance to rectify short-term balance of payments deficits, and the GATT to discourage restrictions on the free flow of trade and investment.

The 'World Bank' is in fact made up of five closely related institutions. For our purposes, the most important of these are the International Bank for Reconstruction and Development (IBRD) and the International Development Association (IDA), which share the same staff, policy, project and supervision procedures.

The functions of the international financial institutions have changed considerably since their establishment and, from the 1980s, with economic recession and indebtedness, the World Bank and IMF have often acted in concert to gain control of the levers of economic policy in less developed countries by imposing policy conditions for loans or interest repayments on debt. Their power has been considerable. Structural adjustment programmes have been forced by the World Bank and IMF on many Third World countries and, while judged successful in some countries such as Chile and Indonesia, have had little success in Africa, where the entire social fabric has been put at risk from cuts in health and education budgets and diminishing state sectors leading to unemployment (Stewart, Lall and Wangwe 1993). There are some instances of where governments resisted World Bank and IMF strictures (Tanzania and Zambia) for a period, but they had to succumb in the end. There are also some isolated instances where countries have resisted obliquely. For example, in 1983 the Kenyan government agreed reluctantly, under substantial World Bank pressure (supported by the UK's Overseas Development Administration which threatened to withdraw a previously agreed British programme loan), to privatize maize marketing. By 1990 no serious steps had been taken to remove controls on the movement or marketing of maize (Mosley 1991).

Within the Bank, the Anglo-American domination of policy making is generally not questioned. Although voting rights are based on levels of shares (approximately 45 per cent of the shares are held by Japan, USA, Germany, Britain and France), in fact, voting seldom occurs, and it has been argued that most policy is decided by management (the equivalent of the bureaucracy) rather than by shareholders. However, the nationality of staff in the Bank reflects shareholding power, although this is beginning to change to include more staff from countries other than the Western industrialized world (Mosley 1991).

In matters of health the World Bank, at least until the 1990s, focused on poverty alleviation through family planning programmes and improving nutrition. Expenditure on health increased substantially from the late 1970s, until by the 1990s it had reached over US$5 billion annually – more than all the other UN organizations involved in health. Having had a low profile on health, the Bank has increasingly become a major actor in the health sector. At the international level, its *World Development Report*, published in 1993, set the scene for a shift in policy in health, based on economic principles of cost effectiveness. In the straitened economic circumstances of most countries affected by global recession, governments were advised to consider developing only those packages of interventions which could be shown to be cost effective in terms of gains to health.

Box 7.1 Setting the global health agenda? The World Bank's role in health policy

The World Bank has become the major external funder of health sector investment in developing countries. Although only approximately 5 per cent of the institution's resources are devoted to health, it has positioned itself, operationally and intellectually, at the fulcrum of international health development. How did the Bank move to the centre of the international health stage?

The Bank's foray into the health sector began with a concern about population growth at the end of the 1960s, coinciding with a change in leadership at the Bank (Robert McNamara became President) and growing consensus in the development community that population growth constituted one of the principal causes of poverty in the developing world (see Box 4.1). A Population Projects Department was established in 1969, and the Bank's first population loan was made to Jamaica the following year.

However, it was only a decade later, in 1980, that the Bank began direct lending for health services. This was justified on the grounds that the Bank could provide valuable analytical skills and programming experience to country policy development. The Bank also considered that direct involvement in health was necessary to attack poverty and increase the productivity of the poor. In addition it recognized that involvement would 'strengthen ...

opportunities for dialogue on population issues'. As for its role with respect to the other multilateral agencies: it would 'essentially complement the activities of WHO' (World Bank 1980: 61).

The Bank's 1980 *Health Sector Policy Paper* envisioned that Bank-supported health projects would strengthen recipient countries' sectoral and budgeting capacities. Elements to be considered in the projects were to be the standard primary health care interventions elaborated in the Alma Ata Declaration, but it was stressed that family planning would be given high priority because of the interaction between health and population.

In practice, lending for health services strengthened the Bank's overall standing in the health sector. Operationally the changes provided bargaining leverage, legitimacy and an implicit vehicle for population activities as required by the particular country context. Moreover, increased project sponsorship and policy analysis enhanced its credibility as an influential actor.

By the end of the 1980s, the Bank had become the major funder of health sector activities, with annual lending between 1991 and 1993 averaging at US$1.5 billion per annum. Current funding levels place the Bank slightly ahead of WHO and UNICEF. However, comparing Bank funds with those provided by other multilaterals is complicated by two factors: first, Bank finance is loaned, not granted. And second, Bank funds provide direct support to public sector projects, while UNICEF and WHO programme expenditure include a substantial proportion of technical assistance and administrative costs.

However, because of the Bank's prestige among other agencies and donor governments, it can magnify the impact of these funds through a variety of mechanisms. One is by attracting 'co-financing' resources from international and bilateral agencies and 'matching' funds from recipient governments. For example, in 1991, twenty-nine projects were approved in the health sector at a total value of US$3.3 billion, less than half of which was committed by the Bank (World Bank 1991: 152). Other ways the Bank extends its influence are through country-specific health sector analysis, issue-related research and policy dialogue.

The Bank's involvement in international health reached a watershed in 1987. By then the Bank had come under international criticism as a result of its wider structural adjustment policies. It responded by setting up a limited fund aimed to mitigate the adverse social and economic consequences of structural adjustment programmes. At the same time the Bank signalled its intention of becoming a major actor in advocating health sector change. *Financing health care: an agenda for reform*, published in 1987, heralded a new and proactive stance to national health policies. In essence it called for a diminished role for the state and increased reliance on the market to finance and deliver health care. Its publication at the height of structural adjustment orthodoxy provided health sector reformers in the Bank with the opportunity to inject health finance policy into the framework of conditionality in structural adjustment dialogue. Subsequent policy documents proposed the prioritization of specific diseases and programmes based on cost-effectiveness criteria. In 1993 the Bank's *World Development Report: Investing in Health* brought these policies together in a comprehensive approach combining health sector financing and delivery. An editorial in the *Lancet* (1993: 63) suggested that *Investing in Health* marked a shift in leadership on international health from WHO to the World Bank, although this was disputed in a later letter by the Executive Director of UNICEF (Grant 1993).

Whatever observers think about who is leading health policy development, there is no doubt that the Bank has been able to assume a central role in the health arena. This rapid and forceful entry is related to a number of considerations of international political economy. Many of the international organizations involved in health have had to confront problems whose solutions were less obvious or visible than past more technical efforts. For example, credibility gained through the smallpox eradication programme was not possible to replicate in fighting AIDS. The promotion of Health for All by the Year 2000 through primary health care led to competition between WHO and UNICEF, and both organizations became embroiled in politics (see Box 7.2). In contrast the Bank remained aloof to such problems. The Bank's image among major donors as apolitical, neutral and successful made it a choice candidate for an expanded mandate in the sector.

There has been a major realignment of actors in the international health policy arena over the past two decades. The Bank has assumed a more central role as a major financier and as an authoritative source of policy ideas. These changes raise a number of fundamental questions. How should the mandate for health be shared among those UN agencies currently involved? How will the Bank's involvement influence pluralism in agenda setting? What are the potential positive and negative implications for having a Bank at the fulcrum of health policy development? The answers to these questions require further analysis of the relationship between international and national policy makers in health.

Source: Buse 1993, 1994.

The World Bank is considered by most international actors to be a 'model' multilateral institution, although it is coming under unprecedented scrutiny and criticism from scholars all over the world. Although it has few health professionals within it, it has nevertheless played an increasingly important role in international health at the global level, as witnessed by the perceived policy relevance of its 1993 *World Development Report*. At the country level, the World Bank is increasingly taking a coordinating role among other agencies: for example, in Bangladesh, it chairs a consortium of donors in an attempt to coordinate external inputs to health policy in that country. Because of its high status among multilateral organizations, some have argued that the World Bank is taking over leadership in health from WHO.

International meetings

The international policy arena also consists of many *ad hoc* forums, or special global conferences which may affect policy direction. The UN's Earth Summit held in Rio de Janeiro in 1992 or the once-a-decade global meeting on population (held in Bucharest in 1974, Mexico in 1984 and Cairo in 1994) are a few examples. Such meetings are inclusive, huge, and have representatives from developing and developed states, international agencies, and many different non-governmental organizations. How much they achieve is open to question. One commentator mused whether the Rio meeting was merely a nine-day media extravaganza that would change little. He noted that there was a major gap in expectations and demands between North and South:

> For the north, the purpose of the trip was to secure an international level playing field for the environment. If we are to wreck it, let's all do it at the same speed. For them, the mission was to hamper free trade and constrain the market as little as possible; to secure some palliatives on climate and biodiversity for the satisfaction of the green lobby; generally spend nothing and all would be OK.
>
> But the south had come to negotiate a very complex bill of goods – or so they thought. The organizer, Maurice Strong had encouraged the poorer world to see Rio as a watershed in north–south relations. If the north wanted

to safeguard the planet (arguably having endangered it), they would have to pay the south to protect their forests and forgo cheap and dirty technology, and help on poverty and population (Sandbrook 1993: 29).

While international meetings and global conferences are high-profile media events attended by large numbers of different interests, there are also international meetings which are lower in profile, exclusive and which are conducted with a minimum of publicity. The Group of Seven industrial countries (called the G7) is one example. The G7 represents the closest approximation to governance of the global economy: its members represent 12 per cent of the world's population and comprise the USA, the UK, Japan, Canada, France, Italy and Germany. Russia has made strong applications to join. The deliberations of the G7 countries affect economic and trade policy well beyond their own frontiers (although they are clearly concerned about protecting their own economic interests). The same countries are included in the Geneva Group, established in 1964 as an attempt to bring the budgets of the UN organizations under control. As Williams writes:

> The date is significant. It was the year UNCTAD was founded and the developed countries were beginning to show concern at what they regarded as a developing country attempt to 'gang up' on them in various institutions within the UN system (Williams 1987: 87).

The Geneva group continues to meet regularly, and discusses policy issues that go well beyond UN budgets. For example, they met to discuss the highly contentious election process of the Director-General of WHO in 1993, and the policy implications of major dissension for this highly respected technical agency.

If the influence of the developing countries is muted by the G7 and Geneva Group concerns with 'high politics' (economic and political global control), and dominated by the North in global meetings such as the Earth Summit, what chance is there of affecting routine policy, politics-as-usual, within other international organizations? Let's now turn to WHO.

Making policy in WHO

Although the different specialized agencies have their own constitutions they have similar structures. They are universal in membership and perceived as neutral. Any country may join as a member, as long as it makes a financial contribution based on the UN formula of population size and gross national product. The main policy-making bodies of each organization are an assembly, an executive body and a secretariat. Let's take a close look at WHO, the relationship between member states and its Executive Board and Secretariat. Who is driving policy?

Member states' representatives (usually a delegation from the ministry of health) meet every year at the World Health Assembly for two weeks in May. This is when policy is decided through a series of recommendations and mandates to be implemented by member states or the Secretariat. In the national context the Assembly nearly parallels a legislature. Because they meet only two weeks a year, the actual influence of member states at the World Health Assembly is relatively curtailed.

Between the Assembly and the Secretariat is the Executive Board, consisting of about thirty representatives who are elected by the Assembly for a period of three years. It meets twice a year, before and after the Assembly, considers progress on past policy and decides what should be included on the agenda for the next Assembly. The Executive Board is most like the Cabinet or equivalent in the national context, although with much less power. The representative acting as chairperson does not have the same status or influence as the prime minister or president, given the sovereignty of member states.

The Secretariat is composed of the Director-General and WHO staff, both technical and administrative. Notably, UN institutions are extremely gender-biased. In only two bodies, UNHCR and UNFPA, is the head a woman and, in general, women are under-represented in professional posts. The Secretariat is the only part of the organization that is continuous, working on day-to-day, routine matters. It is equivalent, in the national context, to the civil service or bureaucracy. The headquarters of WHO is in Geneva, where about one-fifth of its 5,000 staff are based. The other staff work in six regional offices and numerous country offices worldwide.

What is the policy relationship between these different actors in WHO? Member states *are* the organization – it is their financial contributions which underpin WHO. How much say do they have in what reaches the policy agenda?

The Secretariat: how impartial is it?

The Secretariat is the heart of any international organization. Like any national government's civil service, it carries out the policies decided by the governing bodies – in this case the World Health Assembly and the Executive Board. International civil servants are purportedly administrators or professionals who may, among other things, advise on the best, or most rational, policy choices and options but are not themselves supposed to take positions. We have already seen that this ideal description does not occur in practice at the national level. Is it more likely at the international level, where civil servants are even more distanced from their political masters – the member states which decided policy?

Unsurprisingly, civil servants in the secretariats of international organizations are by no means the impartial, neutral actors they are supposed to be. Originally it was believed that civil servants appointed within the UN system would be accountable to the UN, no matter what their nationality. However, it was clear from the beginning that many of those employed in the UN system were subject to scrutiny and pressure from their own governments. The effects of the Cold War and the anti-communist McCarthy era in the USA put paid to the concept of an impartial international civil service.

> The Soviet Union ... imposed its own appointees for the Soviet quota without any pretense about whom they were actually working for. The United States ... imposed on its many nationals in the secretariat a loyalty-screening procedure that caused great hardship for a number of American secretariat members, as well as much distress among their colleagues (Urquhart 1990).

American national security screening of applicants to the UN system continued until it was challenged in 1983, and it was only finally withdrawn in 1986 (Hazzard 1989: 74). Richard Hoggart, who worked at UNESCO for several years in the 1970s, suggests that many governments expected 'loyalty and leaks' from their nationals working in international organizations and noted that:

> The pressures on some Secretariat members can be so constant that they cease to feel like pressures and become an accepted aspect of the job. Many Secretariat members are simply required, by their Delegations, always to have in mind the interests of their countries, to tell all and to act in the way they are told (Hoggart 1978: 115).

Many countries have embassies, delegations or missions in the capital cities of the world which keep in close contact with nationals working in international organizations (especially if they are in key positions). They will also be in touch with important corporate business interests. Links may be social or formal. Such delegations or missions are also likely to be in close touch with civil servants and politicians in their own countries, briefing them as well as being briefed.

Even if international civil servants are open to external pressures from their own governments, how far are these pressures likely to affect their role in policy making? This may depend on which agency is being examined. For example, McLaren (1980) looked at the secretariat in five different agencies (Intergovernmental Maritime Consultative Organization – IMCO; International Civil Aviation Organization – ICAO; International Telecommunication Union – ITU; Universal Postal Union – UPU and the World Meteorological Organization – WMO), and found that the role of the secretariat in policy making was minimal.

However, McLaren suggested that under certain conditions the civil service might have a greater policy effect. First, the number of professional staff in the organization was critical. In the five agencies he looked at, there were few professionals in the secretariat – while the member state representatives were often technical experts. In WHO the number of professionals is much larger, giving them authority within the organization which encourages a significant contribution to policy. Their relationship to member state representatives (who are often themselves professional experts) is more collegial.

Second, in the agencies McLaren looked at, the secretariat officials had very little experience in implementation, which gave them little expertise to propose changes in current policy or new policies. This again is untrue of WHO, where because of their technical or professional expertise, many Secretariat members will have been involved in the implementation of policies at country level, although they may well not have kept in touch with changes.

Much of WHO's authority is derived from its professional core of medical doctors. Not only does the medical profession have high status among other professions, but it serves as an internationally cohesive group. Doctors have common professional bonds, and common global standards. Given the nature of medical training many of those involved in WHO have led at least a portion of their professional life in similar, if not the same, institutions. Meetings of the World Health Assembly and regional committees are structured to emphasize a professional atmosphere. The Secretariat in WHO thus plays a critical role in policy making, partly because of its technical expertise (Cox and Jacobson 1973). Others have testified to the legitimacy conveyed by the general perception of WHO as a technical and professional organization, based on its reputation of policy derived from scientific consensus (Sikkink 1986; Mingst 1990).

The role of the executive director

In spite of the high status of WHO's Secretariat, many have argued that most of WHO's power is vested in the Director-General rather than in the civil servants who make up the Secretariat.

As the only elected member of the Secretariat, the Director-General formally appoints everyone else, at least at the top decision-making levels. Given the infrequent meetings of the Assembly and Executive Board the Director-General has to translate policy and put into practice the tasks assigned to him by the Assembly – many of which may be politically sensitive. He may slow down the implementation of policy, or hasten it; he may interpret it radically or conservatively. The majority of staff in the Secretariat are likely to support him, and he is likely to be treated with great deference.

Clearly the power potentially held by the Director-General is circumscribed to some extent: he has to balance, and satisfy, different forces within the organization, and outside. Precisely because he has been elected, often through a series of accommodations among member states, he may be limited in how much he can impose on the organization. He cannot simply hire and fire staff – there will be many national considerations to take into account, and pressure will be exercised by civil servants within the organization as well as by national delegations and NGOs. However, he can move people around the organization, and into dead-end jobs if he wants change. This may be done quite peremptorily. In the late 1980s it was said that people learned about their change in position when the telephone directory was updated every three months, and they were no longer entered in the same post or office. There are many sub-systems within the organization and the Director-General may have a complicated balancing act to perform.

There have only been four Directors-General of WHO, all of whom were doctors: Brock Chisholm (Canada) 1948–53; Marcelino Gomes Candau (Brazil) 1953–73; Halfdan Mahler (Denmark) 1973–88; and Hiroshi Nakajima (Japan) from 1988. Because of their long association in the organization and their control over the budget, it would seem the Directors-General of WHO have a position of great strength. However, over the past decade the extent of this influence has shifted: two trends are discernible.

One, changes in the financing of the organization have limited the powers of the Director-General, and put more power in the hands of the richer member states. Two, a more politicized milieu within WHO has led to some loss of leadership in the health field, with other agencies such as the World Bank providing a greater input to health policy.

Changes in financing in WHO

Over the years the funding base of WHO has changed from a predominantly regular budget to increasing reliance on extra-budgetary or voluntary funding. The regular budget – made up of member states' contributions – started at about US$6 million in 1950, and from 1960 was supplemented by modest voluntary donations which came from other multilateral agencies or donors. By the beginning of the 1990s, voluntary contributions had overtaken the regular budget by approximately US$21 million.

Thus, by the early 1990s about 54 per cent (as opposed to 25 per cent in 1971) of WHO's budget came from extra-budgetary sources, such as other multilateral organizations (the World Bank, UNDP, etc.) and donor governments (the USA and European – including the Scandinavian – countries, are among the major donors). Extra-budgetary funds are largely given for particular programmes including the Global Programme on AIDS, research into tropical diseases, human reproduction, control of diarrhoeal diseases, and essential drugs. As is shown in Table 7.1 other UN specialized agencies also rely to some degree on extra-budgetary funding.

Table 7.1 Budgets of the UN's four largest specialized agencies

Agency	Regular budget 1990–91 (US$)	Extra budget* 1990–91 (US$)	%**
FAO	569m	775m	58
ILO	330m	115m	26
UNESCO	379m	176m	32
WHO	654m	770m	54

* Voluntary contributions
** Extra-budgetary funds as a percentage of the total budget
Source: The Nordic UN Project, 1991.

The main question raised about the growth in voluntary funds is how far they put influence over policy into the hands of those giving the funds, removing it from WHO's governing bodies. Thus a handful of countries may be making decisions about where the organization's effort and funds should be spent, by supporting specific programmes and not others, by making *ad hoc* decisions, rather than developing strategic policies over the longer term, or by supporting fashionable (and changing) priorities rather than developing country needs or preferences.

Some (Taylor 1991; Walt 1993a) have claimed that extra-budgetary funding has undermined the working of the WHO regional structure. The six regional offices of WHO are unique in the UN system, and have made WHO the most structurally decentralized of the specialized agencies. Regional offices have significant discretionary power over the allocation of the regular budget, and are responsible for formulating and implementing the annual budget and determining programme priorities. The regional offices vary to a great extent in their capacity and effectiveness, and there is often some tension between programme staff at WHO headquarters and staff in the regional offices. The programmes which are financed largely from extra-budgetary sources often use donor concern with effective management and outcomes as an excuse to bypass those regional offices which are considered inefficient or bureaucratic. This can undermine coordination and integration of policy at both regional and country levels.

The regular budget to WHO country offices, which are usually small and poorly funded, is mostly spent on *ad hoc* financing of fellowships or study tours, workshops and miscellaneous supplies and equipment. There is seldom any attempt by the WHO country office, in spite of a direct and close relationship with the ministry of health (the WHO office is often housed within the ministry) to assist in any strategic planning for the health sector or programming the allocation of scarce resources. At the same time, however, the strong extra-budgetary programmes – diarrhoeal disease control, AIDS, essential drugs – may provide countries' ministries of health with significant resources as well as advice and assistance ranging from policy to operational guidance, but they seldom confer with either the WHO regional or country office.

A changing political milieu in WHO

In its early years, WHO was stable and pragmatic, largely disease-oriented and dominated by medical professionals. However, by the mid-1970s it was increasingly evident that the disease approach to health policy was problematic, and that new approaches to health and health care were needed. A variety of alternative, and innovative, health policies had by then been introduced in a number of developing countries and were being widely disseminated in this period. For example, the Chinese experiments in health care stimulated new health paradigms. What really caught people's imagination was the extent to which it seemed possible to mobilize the population to deal with major diseases such as schistosomiasis, as well as to train the so-called 'barefoot doctors' to provide rudimentary preventive care and treatment. Other countries – Tanzania, Vietnam and Cuba – also inspired a generation of health professionals, and by the mid-1970s many of these national governmental and non-governmental schemes were sufficiently well known to be included in a WHO study of alternative methods of meeting basic health needs (Djukanovic and Mach 1975).

The 1970s were a period of radical thinking in many other sectors as well: Ivan Illich (1971, 1973, 1975) challenged organized religion, compulsory education, and health institutions, pointing to the social myths perpetuated in the progressively mechanized and less human societies of the industrialized world. Development theorists like Dudley Seers (1977) criticized the use of traditional measures of development – GNP per capita, for example – and argued for a way of measuring growth through the attainment of basic needs, which included access to health services. Within the health sector many ideas were challenged, and the emphasis within WHO changed from a concentration on disease to a much broader focus on the socio-economic causes of illness. In mid-1975, the new Director-General – Halfdan Mahler – launched the drive to Health For All By The Year 2000, and a few years later the Primary Health Care approach, as the key to reaching health for all (Walt 1990).

However, with this broader, developmental focus came new dangers, and WHO became a much more politicized organization. Halfdan Mahler, as Director-General from 1974 to 1986, orchestrated major change within WHO and encouraged its member states to make a radical review of their health policies. In a number of areas this meant that WHO was sometimes forced to hold the reins amidst a number of competing, and powerful, interest groups. Change in policy direction also led WHO into much greater conflict than before (Walt 1993a). The example in Box 7.2 illustrates this.

Box 7.2 International consumerism in action: interest groups working at the international level

Non-governmental organizations had always had some association with WHO, but in the late 1970s this was extended to enhance collaboration. By the early 1980s NGOs were using a number of measures, both formal and informal, to increase contact with WHO.

In 1981 WHO was put under great pressure from a number of strong NGOs, some member states, and at least one other multi-lateral organization – UNICEF – to pass an international code to regulate the marketing (among other things) of baby foods and brand medicines in developing countries. Although WHO is not a supranational body – that is, it has no jurisdiction over individual states or methods of sanction – many feel that it carries moral and professional international weight which is a help to ministries of health arguing a particular policy position in their own countries. This can be especially helpful where influential industrial interests may act as countervailing forces (Sikkink 1986).

The baby food story (Chetley 1986) started in the mid-1970s and by the end of the decade sufficient public pressure and concern had built up to persuade WHO and UNICEF to hold an international meeting on infant formula foods. It was attended by a large information network of activists concerned about the ill effects of baby foods on the children of the Third World, and also by industry interests, who formed the International Council of Infant Food Industries. From this meeting came the idea of an International Code, to regulate the marketing practices and promotion of infant foods.

While this battle was being fought, a similar conflict was unfolding in relation to essential drugs. WHO introduced an Action Programme on Essential Drugs in 1978. Its aim was to help countries develop more rational drugs policies through a number of means: a limited list of drugs was just one method. From the beginning, the pharmaceutical industry was extremely negative about the concept of essential drugs, and put pressure on WHO to restrict its meaning (Walt and Harnmeijer 1992).

WHO faced ferocious opposition from industrial sources. The infant milk market was dominated by about thirty companies: about one-third were primarily pharmaceutical producers, the rest concentrated on agribusiness or food products. Twelve of these companies controlled the bulk of the world market – US$3.3 billion of sales in 1983, with Nestlé accounting for nearly one-third of world sales (Chetley 1986). The pharmaceutical market is similarly dominated by a few very large multinational companies, with eleven out of the eighteen largest being American. Their annual turnover is massive: in the mid-1980s Bayer's annual turnover alone was US$14 billion.

From the 1980s on, a number of consumer groups started to campaign for changes in transnational marketing practices in the Third World. Lively campaigns and considerable media coverage challenged the somewhat remote transnational companies and a period of intense confrontation began. This was played out in many different settings including WHO: the World Health Assembly of 1981 was besieged by groups such as the Infant Baby Food Action Network, and also Health Action International, supporting WHO's essential drugs programme. They used innovative techniques to get over their messages to delegates from member states. Industry was also present, actively lobbying delegates. Finally an international code was passed in 1981 at the World Health Assembly by 118 votes to one – the sole opposing vote coming from the United States, which objected to what it perceived as interference in global trade and marketing practices.

Subsequent World Health Assemblies were transformed from being relatively sedate forums for information exchange and policy directing, to ones with active lobbying and negotiation of specific policy decisions. WHO was often pulled one way by committed radical consumer groups, and the other by a conservative industry concerned to protect free trade in the global market.

The increasingly politicized arena in which WHO found itself is not peculiar to this particular organization. In the 1950s and 1960s UN agencies in general were dominated by Western views of what were appropriate technical roles and activities. By the 1970s these were increasingly challenged by developing countries, which argued for much broader agendas and introduced more overt conflict into the agencies.

Thus many of the other multilateral organizations have experienced significantly more rancorous political manoeuvrings than has WHO, with strong resistance to challenge. The US, for example, delayed its appropriation of funds to the ILO throughout the 1970s because of disagreements over the role of the USSR within the organization, and withdrew from the organization between 1978 and 1980 because observer status had been granted to the Palestine Liberation Organization. The American departure had considerable repercussions on day-to-day operations, and a number of fairly draconian cuts had to be initiated (Hushang 1982). Similar threats of withdrawal were made by the US to WHO in 1990, when there was a move at the World Health Assembly to recommend the Palestine Liberation Organization for full membership of the organization. Both the UK and US withdrew from UNESCO in the late 1980s for a variety of reasons, not least of which was its challenge to Western ideology (Harrod 1988).

In the final analysis, however, the effect on policy was that US pressure failed to overrule the decisions of the World Health Assembly: the international code on breastmilk substitutes was overwhelmingly supported, and implemented by many developing countries, and the development of essential drugs policies has continued to be strongly supported by member states. WHO's moral leverage won the day.

So far we have centred on WHO as the policy leader in international health. Initially it was the main, and, because of its technical expertise, authoritative actor in a fairly small policy arena. As developing countries became members of the organization, and as its funding basis changed, and as a wider network of interests became involved in health policy, so WHO's position came under fire. Let's now turn to the role of other policy communities in health.

The influence of member states

We have already noted that the rich, industrialized countries have significant influence over policy both inside and outside the UN agencies, as members of the G7 or as important funders of extra-budgetary programmes. In WHO at least, the Director-General and his secretariat are to some extent in the thrall of those funding 54 per cent of the budget. This is likely to be the case in other agencies with large extra-budgetary funds. Furthermore, most of the industrialized countries look increasingly to the World Bank for policy guidance on development and aid-related issues, and over the past decade have embraced the World Bank's proposals for market-driven economies. To all intents and purposes, then, there is a coalition of Western industrialized interests based on common concerns, funds, personnel and technical expertise, and this is played out in the policy arenas of international agencies. Because Western industrialized countries are also bilateral funders of programmes in less developed countries – making government-to-government agreements on support for projects and programmes – those countries' representatives to the UN agencies may be careful not to offend or challenge the richer nations.

This does not mean, however, that there is always consensus around strategy or that dissension is not voiced. There were major arguments between WHO and UNICEF in the early 1980s about how primary health care should be delivered, with WHO accusing UNICEF of dictating what policies developing countries should be following (Walt 1993a). The United States was not able to overturn the passing of the International Code on Breastmilk Substitutes, in spite of its powerful position. And in 1993 when the USA and twelve European nations took the unprecedented step of declaring their opposition to the re-election of the incumbent Director-General at WHO, they were outvoted.

Lacking financial power, developing countries play only a limited part in policy making in the international arena. They can use formal channels to vote for or against policies. During the 1970s the voting strength of the Third World countries enabled them to challenge policy within many agencies, leading to the era of the 'new orders' – the New International Economic Order of UNCTAD, the new World Information and Communication Order of UNESCO, the Health for All programme of the WHO. However, while these programmes challenged current ideology within the agencies and the powerful nations, they changed very little. Informally, developing countries may raise issues for the policy agenda. The introduction of WHO's action programme on essential drugs was said by Mahler, the Director-General at the time, to have been initiated by Third World policy makers complaining about the high and rising costs of pharmaceuticals. However, taking the policy initiative is relatively rare, and many of the Third World challenges to policy in the 1970s were strongly resisted by the more economically powerful members of the UN.

Less developed member countries face many obstacles in the policy process. First, the sheer volume of meetings, committees, sub-committees and conferences held by the United Nations and the specialized agencies can run into hundreds annually. For developing countries, which often lack administrative and technical personnel and resources, releasing national policy makers to go to international meetings and workshops can be a major cost. Against this, at the individual level, attending such meetings is often prized, putting policy makers in touch with others, taking them away from routine problems at home, with the additional rewards of a trip overseas, per diems and the glamour that often attends international meetings. They provide opportunities for employment procurement and recruitment, and may also confer status:

> Kathmandu officials place great importance on high-level conferences because they are a visible activity that extends legitimacy to programs (Justice 1986: 78).

Such meetings may be diversionary, however, with representatives accomplishing little. Delegations meeting in plenary at the World Health Assembly once a year (and in some agencies less often) are unlikely to question past policy or future initiatives. For less developed countries, with weaker infrastructures at home, briefing before the Assembly is probably not very satisfactory. The country's permanent delegations, when they exist, are themselves hampered by having to represent their country at meetings of very disparate organizations such as WHO, the ILO, UNCTAD and UNHCR among others, and may not be well informed about issues on the policy agenda. Furthermore, they may be embarrassed or unwilling to oppose donors who provide their countries with technical assistance. In the final analysis, delegations know they can ignore resolutions once they go home.

The industrialized countries, on the other hand, are usually better prepared for such meetings than the less developed countries. Internal machinery or interdepartmental arrangements elaborated over the years ensure both the production of briefing materials and some measure of consistency in the analysis of problems and subsequent expressions of policy (Williams 1987: 121). A number of delegations may form a 'policy community' with a high degree of cohesion – in order to promote a particular set of policies. Both the Scandinavian countries and the forty-eight countries of the Commonwealth, for example, meet before World Health Assemblies to put forward a unified position on particular issues.

For both developed and developing countries, involvement in policy will depend to some extent on how far the international organization is valued: some have more salience than others (Cox and Jacobson 1973). Because of the WHO's high-status professionals, the agency has been seen as highly technical and competent. The World Bank also commands great respect for its economic expertise. On the other hand, UNESCO is not perceived as a central institution, and the UK and USA used their sanction of withdrawing from the agency when they felt that UNESCO had become too 'politicized'.

This was an example of where ideological congruity with and degree of interest in the international organization on the part of the UK and USA were so low that the final sanction – withdrawal of membership – was utilized. A similar strategy was used in the ILO, when the USA left the organization for two years (1978–80) in protest over what was seen as a violation of function. A second-line sanction is to withhold contributions to the budget. In WHO, the USA has deliberately withheld its financial contribution at times because of policies they disapproved of (such as the essential drugs programme).

How far international agencies affect policy within the industrialized or powerful countries is consistent with their perceived salience by national policy makers, but is probably relatively limited. It also depends on the issue. Some issues are jealously guarded as sovereign, and international organizations are unlikely to have much influence on domestic policy. Although lip-service may be paid to a suggested policy, governments can easily resist implementation. The primary health care approach promoted by WHO and UNICEF in 1978 was adopted enthusiastically in the Third World but was treated much more cautiously in the industrialized world. WHO played a critical role in the late 1980s as the magnitude of the AIDS epidemic unfolded, by stressing the value of liberal against authoritarian policy reactions. This had effect in some countries, where testing of students and visitors for HIV infection was stopped, but a great deal of mandatory HIV testing continues to be employed in spite of WHO policy recommendations against it (WHO 1991). Against this, however, must be balanced the symbolic significance given to international organizations. Although perceived importance is often greater than actual, governments continue to support international organizations for the opportunity they provide to present and lobby for high fundamental principles (world peace and security), as well as quite practical matters (how to encourage family planning programmes).

In sum, the United Nations' formal structure states that policy is made by member states. The reality of day-to-day policy making does not reflect this ideal. In WHO the Secretariat and Director-General exercise some influence on what issues get on to the policy agenda, and how fast they move, but they are not immune to pressures put on them by representatives of both developing and developed countries. Notably they ignore the industrialized countries at their peril. The main formal policy weapon of developing country members lies in their voting power, but this is a much weaker tool than the industrialized countries' potential for withdrawing budgetary contributions. On 'high-politics' questions of value for money, cost-effectiveness of programmes and health sector reform, the industrialized countries form a significant, narrow coalition of interests. On the politics-as-usual questions – the day-to-day health policy or health service delivery questions – there may be greater room for manoeuvre, with more differentiation between countries, and more inputs from other groups such as NGOs, although 'high-politics' may well shape the outcomes of the 'low-politics' policies.

International policy networks

Clearly many groups believe that their presence at the international level is useful. One of the distinguishing characteristics of the past fifteen years has been the increase of interest group participation in public policy processes at the international level. Pressure groups in the international arena are usually referred to generally as non-governmental organizations (NGOs) or international non-governmental organizations (INGOs), although many are clearly sectional, promotional or cause groups. Consultation with NGOs was allowed for in the UN charter, and most registered NGOs have the right to receive UN documents, attend meetings of ECOSOC and its subsidiary bodies and to circulate their own written statements. Category I NGOs can also initiate agenda items and introduce them. Willetts (1993) notes that NGO participation at

ECOSOC meetings has declined, no doubt because the Council involves speechmaking rather than decision making, and there is little opportunity to exercise real influence.

Participation may have declined in the formal UN committees, but intensity of interaction and demand for action have increased in other venues: the World Bank created a mechanism for NGOs relatively recently, NGOs have been extremely active at the specialized global conferences, and many other international organizations have needed to accommodate to a new growth in lobbying by NGOs.

International sectional groups

Sectional groups such as the Confederation of British Industry (CBI) or the Trades Union Congress (TUC) have since their establishment sent representatives to relevant meetings of international organizations such as the International Labour Office or the EU. They are also members of world bodies – the International Organization of Employers and the International Confederation of Free Trade Unions. These bodies will themselves represent their members' interests at meetings of international organizations.

Sectional groups may play an active part throughout the policy process. For example, when pharmaceuticals were on the agenda of the executive board of WHO in the late 1980s, the president of the International Federation of Pharmaceutical Manufacturers' Associations not only attended the meetings of the Executive Board, but was allowed to make an intervention. Representatives from the pharmaceutical industry participated in the deliberations of WHO's expert committee set up to devise a list of essential drugs in 1977 (Kanji et al. 1992), and sought meetings with the Director-General to put their case against an extended list of 'essential' drugs.

Transnational corporations (TNCs) may have significant potential influence on health policy. During the 1970s and 1980s the activities and operations of TNCs – particularly their marketing and production strategies – became increasingly complex. There was an accelerated trend toward global marketing, while production was decentralized and shifted to the country with the cheapest labour costs for each production activity. The labour-intensive low-technology activities were located in the Third World, where there was a pool of unskilled workers, while technology-intensive operations were concentrated in the industrialized countries. The TNCs cooperated with the transnational banks to integrate production worldwide.

Economic power (the largest hundred transnationals control up to 50 per cent of all cross-frontier activities and dominate world trade) confers political leverage. Transnational corporations are able to influence national policy quite considerably, but they have also used their leverage at the international level to frustrate efforts to establish binding codes of conduct called for by the UN, ILO, WHO or the OECD (Allen 1993), to ensure their representation on committees discussing policy changes, and to take opportunities to put their case. The large transnational companies trading in tobacco and alcohol have had significant effects on less developed countries' policies in these areas, often with deleterious consequences for the long-term health of their people. They use many tactics to persuade governments to open their markets, as Box 7.3 shows.

Box 7.3 'We've been itching to get at them': the power of the transnational tobacco industry

The tobacco industry is unique in its extent of concentration in the hands of a few transnational companies with headquarters in the USA or UK. Up to 95 per cent of world leaf tobacco is controlled by six transnational corporations. The largest private-sector corporation produces 550 billion cigarettes per year (British American Tobacco – BAT), while the next two – Philip Morris and RJ Reynolds – produce 400 billion and 280 billion respectively (Stebbins 1991). As consumption of tobacco in the industrialized world has decreased by about 2 per cent per annum over the past decade, so transnational corporations have been looking for alternative markets. Their targets are the Third World and eastern Europe. One tobacco company spokesman said: 'Until recently perhaps 40% of the world's smokers were locked behind ideological walls. We've been itching to get at them – and we're much relieved and excited that this 40% is now open to us. That's where our growth will come from' (Macalister 1992). Indeed the major transnational corporations have been courting the ex-Soviet bloc countries. As formerly state-owned enterprises have been privatized, so the transnationals have established new factories and bought old ones. Where the tobacco-growing lobby has resisted privatization (in Poland for example) transnationals are helping state enterprises to modernize and eventually hope to take them over. China, which is still dominated by its state monopoly – the China National Tobacco Corporation – is another country the transnationals are hoping to penetrate. Half the increase in worldwide tobacco use between 1975 and 1985 occurred in China.

Transnationals use many different approaches to put pressure on governments. They often lobby their own governments in the USA or UK to assist them in countries where tobacco import controls have been enforced to protect national industries. For example, between 1986 and 1990 the US threatened to impose trade sanctions on the cigarette markets of Japan, Taiwan, Korea and Thailand, among others, unless they removed their trade barriers on tobacco. Section 301 of the revised Omnibus Trade and Competitiveness Act of 1988 provides for retaliatory restrictions against a country's imports to the US if American access to their markets is limited. In the mid-1980s the Japanese were threatened with having to pay tariffs on export goods to the US. Mackay (1990) quotes a letter sent from Senator Jesse Helms to the Japanese Prime Minister of the day, Yashiro Nakasone, expressing concern that American cigarettes only claimed 2 per cent of the Japanese market. After a number of similar tactics, the Japanese government succumbed to American pressure, and by 1992 Western cigarette brands had cornered 20 per cent of the Japanese market.

Multinationals also use aggressive marketing tactics to advertise their products. The pervasiveness of advertising and associated promotion of smoking in the less developed world is in stark contrast to controls in the industrialized world, where advertising in the cinema, television and radio is often forbidden. Even if advertising is regulated, transnational corporations often flaunt the rules. Mackay (1990) notes that Shanghai Television showed an advertisement for Marlboro, with the familiar cowboy, music and slogan, but no actual cigarette. Chinese teachers from Shanghai reported that everyone knew it was an advertisement for cigarettes. Other methods of advertising are also used: free cigarettes are given away on the streets, and a wide range of events, from sporting activities to concerts or dancing contests, receive sponsorship, which is visually acknowledged. Even in remote villages brightly coloured posters associate attractive lifestyles with particular brands of cigarette.

The multinational corporations often overwhelm countries which do not have a clear tobacco policy in place, or one in which there are major tensions between revenue from tobacco sales (in some developing countries this may be up to 15 per cent of total government revenue (Stebbins 1991), or tobacco exports (in 1988 tobacco export earnings reached 60 per cent of Malawi's total export earnings from all commodities (Chapman and Wai Leng 1990). Even where governments recognize the hazards of smoking, and the potential future morbidity and mortality burden, they are not always willing to restrict maximum tar levels, control advertising, or prohibit smoking in public places or sales of tobacco to minors. Reluctance to develop firm policy may be due to a pressure on scarce resources, a weak administrative infrastructure or a wish to avoid the ire of the transnational corporations.

The promotional activities of the multinational corporations parallel increasing concerns about the adverse effects of tobacco consumption on health. Consumer networks and organizations such as the International Organization of Consumers Unions (IOCU) and AGHAST (Action Groups to Halt Advertising and Sponsorship by Tobacco) continue to lobby on this issue, and even the World Bank articulated a policy on tobacco in 1992. Among other points, the World Bank policy states that it does not lend directly for, invest in, or guarantee investments or loans for tobacco production, processing or marketing (World Bank 1993a: 89). However, the anti-smoking lobby is pitted against powerful transnational interests which have considerably more leverage with governments at home and abroad.

International cause groups

It is the growth of cause groups that has challenged the international policy sphere, however, and upset established conventions. In the case of the essential drugs concept, WHO was forced by the actions of consumer groups to take a more radical line than many in the Organization approved (Hardon 1992). As we saw in the case of the International Code on Breastmilk Substitutes (Box 7.2) industry was galvanized into action by the activities of cause groups, which have pressed their claims at the international level.

This heralded an era of much more active, and professional, lobbying and campaigning by NGOs at the international level. Agencies such as Oxfam have been involved in education campaigns aiming to inform the public and put pressure on governments and international organizations to consider rational drugs policies, the effects of structural adjustment policies, and proposals for alternative ways of dealing with debt. Through such action they have become more expert, more professional, and command more respect for their links with grass-roots views, expressed through quite extensive information networks.

With committed staff and a relative lack of bureaucracy, many NGOs are able to respond with speed and greater flexibility than governments. By forming coalitions with other NGOs, from both the north and the south, and working at the international level to rally support for specific issues, interest groups can increase pressure on national governments who may be seen to be deviant if they reject a widely accepted UN resolution, especially if other friendly governments have accepted the resolution. The UN system is strengthened by the action of pressure groups if they rally support domestically, or publicize UN decisions.

NGO action may be behind-the-scenes pressure, or public pressure. One of the most flamboyant examples of successful public campaigning on a global scale was a result of a television film by Michael Buerk on the Ethiopian famine in 1984–5. The film so moved an Irish rock star, Bob Geldof, that with money raised through a rock record 'Do they know it's Christmas?' followed by rock concerts, he established the Band Aid Trust to help provide famine relief to the starving. Two 'Live Aid' concerts in London and Philadelphia were televised throughout the world in 1985, and raised £50 million. Band Aid drew on the charities with experience to distribute those funds to Africa, and then disbanded. In an interview in 1991, Geldof suggested that Band Aid had been useful because it had taken an item which was nowhere on the political agenda (famine relief) and put it squarely at the top. However, he did not want to continue putting a bandaid on a gaping wound and so closed down the organization. Jacques quotes Geldof as saying:

> The creation of an institution is anathema to me. Band Aid could simply have continued, but I didn't want the name to be meaningless and simply a repository for money, it would cease to be a political lobby. It was never political, but by its size it could influence change (Jacques 1991: 27).

International organizations exerting pressure

Lacking sanctions, international organizations may act as pressure groups in their own right. Although they may be discreet in their lobbying, they can play an important role in long-term consciousness-raising and policy dialogue, encouraging countries to take a stand on policy. WHO has taken a consistent, if low-profile, position on smoking and health, producing numerous reports enumerating not only the dangers but also the potential actions which could be taken by governments. International meetings keep up a steady information flow, and keep the issue on the policy agenda. Similarly, the EU has been fairly radical in lobbying for changes in policies on smoking in Europe, setting maximum tar limits for cigarettes, improving health warnings, banning advertising on television, proposing minimum tax levels to raise prices. In the end, however, even if a resolution is passed banning advertising on smoking and tobacco (as at the sixth world conference on smoking and tobacco) WHO has no authority to effect such restrictions, and although the EU has more recourse to legal or fiscal sanctions, countries can delay or resist implementation of policies. On the other hand, national governments may come under significant pressure from domestic and international groups to respond and adhere to international guidelines and policy recommendations.

Sovereign states or interdependent world?

Even if national policy makers retain major authority over their policy environments, this chapter throws some doubts on the common assumption in policy analysis that nation states are completely in control of their public policy-making processes: that they are the sovereign equal of each other; that governments possess exclusive control over the totality of their defined territory and the citizens residing in that territory, and that all groups wishing to influence policy interact only through recognized national governments. This statecentric view ignores the existence and importance of many important changes in the world over the past four decades. Let's look at these trends.

One of the most important has been the growth in the number of intergovernmental organizations. The member states of many such organizations, especially those that have joined to form some sort of regional common market, such as the EU, have relinquished some sovereignty to permit the executive bodies decision-making and enforcement powers in specified areas. The need to coordinate and consult has become a requirement in many instances. There are also far more actors in the contemporary system than fifty years ago, and with changes in east and central Europe the number of members of the UN (179 in 1992) is well over three times as many as the fifty-one founding members.

The number of NGOs has increased too, and as communications and travel have become more accessible, their activities have made transnational contacts easy. Transnational corporations have penetrated far into the Third World and many governments would have to concede that there has been a loss of national sovereignty due to the internationalization of economic interests. Clearly all these different actors have varying levels of influence. Further, the clout of the UN should not be overestimated.

The total budget turnover of the UN agencies is relatively modest.

Official development aid is disbursed (as loans and grants) to recipient countries from two main multilateral sources: the multilateral development banks and the agencies of the UN system. In the early 1990s the World Bank (IBRD and IDA) disbursed US$12.9 billion to countries (World Bank 1993b: 65), while the specialized agencies (WHO, UNICEF, UNDP, etc.) altogether provided about US$3.8 billion (World Bank 1990: 129). The percentage of aid available for the health sector stagnated in absolute terms and declined as a share of total aid in the 1980s. By the end of the decade barely 6 per cent of total aid went to health (UNDP 1992).

Bilateral aid, on the other hand, is much greater. The USA alone provided US$11.3 billion, Japan US$10.9 billion in 1991 (World Bank 1993a: 274). While bilateral aid is criticized because it is given on political, strategic, and commercial grounds – only 25 per cent of overseas development aid goes to the ten poorest countries which represent three-quarters of the world's poorest people (UNDP 1992: 45) – for individual countries it may be much more significant than anything coming from the multilateral agencies. Similarly, the TNCs play with high financial stakes in countries and have huge turnovers. The operating revenues of the American company Philip Morris is larger than the gross national product of Egypt and twice that of Ireland.

Furthermore the UN system is in financial difficulties arising from non-payment of assessed contributions, with deficits increasing sharply in the 1980s, and crippling accumulated arrears. In 1992 the USA owed the UN around US$250 million for peacekeeping and US$555 million for the regular budget (*The Economist* 1992). In 1991 the rate of collection of contributions to the effective working budget amounted to just over 81 per cent, leaving over US$55 million unpaid. Fifty member states made no contribution. The break-up of the USSR has also had a major impact on budgets.

The crisis in financing is by no means due only to economic recession. Some disappointment in the UN development system has been expressed since its inception, but nothing like the crescendo of dissatisfaction of the last decade. It is expressed as a lack of political support, especially by the USA, and as criticism of the bureaucracy and incapacity to deliver, as well as of the 'free-wheeling lifestyles, power, prestige and corruption of the "lords of poverty" who disburse aid' (Hancock 1989). There have been increasing calls for reform of the system (Saksena 1993).

So in the industrialized world, the UN may not be very influential – although it seems that most industrialized aid-giving countries take their cue from the World Bank's policy framework for the Third World.

To some extent the UN is more important to the Third World than the industrialized world because of aid flows, even if these are considerably less than bilateral aid. Multilateral agencies are less caught up with ideological and political aspects of aid giving than are the bilaterals. Also, developing countries are able to carry out diplomatic relations through the UN where they would not be able to maintain embassies worldwide. The UN continues to be accorded great prestige by most countries, although there are complaints about excessive bureaucracy or technocratic approaches. Conditionality attached to assistance from the World Bank has also been strongly criticized, although many countries have accepted the need for economic reform. In the end, however, the multilateral agencies are not supranational bodies: governments control domestic policy, and although the sanctions at the disposal of the development banks are significant, governments have occasionally found ways of getting the loans they need while resisting measures they do not want to implement, as we saw in the case of Kenya and grain marketing mentioned earlier.

Conclusions

It is probably more useful to see the international world as one in which many ideas and policies are current; some of them for a long time. Ideas that may be resisted over time may come to be accepted. Many of the Third World policy makers who attended the Population Conference in Bucharest in 1974 roundly rejected the notion of population control through the introduction of family planning programmes. At the related conference in Mexico some ten years later, attitudes had changed significantly (see Box 4.1).

The UN system provides an important channel, through meetings large and small, expert committees, research reports and publications, for dialogue on many different issues. As we have suggested, some of the agencies act as pressure groups themselves for particular policies. In this teeming international milieu, policies may well be driven by an elite of Western industrialized donors.

As at the national level, it seems that the picture of policy making at the international level is one in which the important economic decisions are clearly controlled by a small elite, led by the World Bank and the IMF. For 'politics-as-usual' policies – sectoral or micro policies – there is room for manoeuvre, however, and NGOs or developing country policy makers may challenge existing positions. To have any effect they probably have to have a number of the more powerful, richer countries on their side.

8

Implementation: do those who implement decide?

We know by now that the policy process is interactive: many networks of groups exist which may try to influence policy formulation. Can we assume that once a policy decision has been made, it will be implemented as intended?

Theoretical models

Top-down approaches

As we saw in Chapter 3, the early theoretical models perceive policy making as linear, with a clear division between policy formulation and policy execution. Most of these models perceive policy formulation as avowedly political, concerned with value judgements, with what government feels it *ought* to be doing. Implementation, on the other hand, is perceived as managerial or administrative. In a top-down model, it is assumed that policy formulation occurs within national government or, at the international level, between donors and national policy makers. Once devised it is a largely technical process to be implemented by administrative agencies at the national or sub-national levels. In the case of health policy, decisions by politicians and bureaucrats within the ministry of health are communicated to planners in the health planning unit (they may or may not have been involved in policy formulation), who operationalize policies by designing appropriate programmes, with guidelines, rules, and monitoring systems. These are then transferred to local health authorities (at the provincial or district level) or to health care institutions (hospitals, health centres) to be put into practice.

Such approaches were often derived from an ideal model of 'perfect implementation'. Hogwood and Gunn (1984) drew up ten preconditions which would have to be achieved if policies were to be implemented so as to achieve their objectives. The model is useful as a checklist against which to score the likelihood of any policy being successfully executed, although the chances of attaining all ten preconditions are negligible. A 'perfect implementation model' suggests that:

1. *The circumstances external to the agency do not impose crippling constraints.* Clearly external events may not be in the control of the implementers of policy: a drought may mean that subsidies on bread cannot be withdrawn because of resulting hardship; wars prevent the introduction of health measures to protect workers.

2. *Adequate time and sufficient resources are available.* A lack of resources, whether they are of personnel, equipment or finances, affects implementation. If public health inspectors are few, and have many tasks, adding another (such as surveying latrines to see they are using anti-malarial polystyrene balls) will make enforcement of public hygiene less, and not more, vigorous.

3. *The required combination of resources is available.* Improving immunization coverage means having the trained health workers, vaccines and cold chain systems and children in place. If any one of those is missing, implementation will be partial. One government report drew attention to the implementation process during India's immunization programme, saying that major failures had occurred because substandard or expired vaccines were given to thousands of infants (Nandan 1993).

4. *Policy is based on a valid theory of cause and effect.* If policies are bad policies, they can fail. Every policy is based on a theory (although it may not be explicit) of cause and effect, and if this is wrong, the policy will be unsuccessful. Preventing the transmission of AIDS by introducing mandatory premarital testing, for example, is unlikely to have much effect on the prevalence of AIDS and may have unintended consequences. In Illinois state in the USA residents travelled to neighbouring states to avoid the test (Brandeau et al 1993).

5. *The relationship between cause and effect is direct*, and there are few, if any, intervening links. Any implementation process is a long one, and involves a complex series of events and linkages any of which may derail policy. Promised famine relief arriving late in an afflicted country may be further delayed by bureaucratic systems, corruption in the port, transportation dependent on state and private sectors which are not coordinated. Hence distribution is too late and untargeted.

6. *Dependency relationships are minimal.* There may be many participants involved in implementation: the ministry of health may have to negotiate with insurance or social security agencies, professional

organizations, and others, all of which depend to some extent on the others. Government policy may be against HIV testing for insurance, but insurance companies set their own rules.

7. *There is an understanding of, and agreement on, objectives.* Policy objectives are often quite vague, and different actors may have different conceptions of what constitutes implementation. Introducing community health workers (to expand primary health services) was seen by some clinic nurses in Botswana as a useful way of getting 'an extra pair of hands' rather than a way of improving outreach services to the community (Walt 1990).

8. *Tasks are fully specified in correct sequence.* If policies are to be executed uniformly, all tasks to be carried out by different organizations or people have to be clearly differentiated. Policy failure occurs through confusion or duplication.

9. *Communication and coordination must be perfect.* Since stories about breakdowns in communication and the difficulties of coordination are legion, it is difficult to see how this would ever be achieved, although it might be aspired to.

10. *Those in authority can demand and obtain perfect compliance.* Except for those military governments which have used coercion to enforce policies, it is difficult to see how any authority will be able to attain complete compliance where implementers or target groups are radically opposed. Passivity or neutrality may result in compliance, but resistance through smuggling or illegal activities may also occur.

Bottom-up approaches

In contrast to the linear view of the policy process and the model of 'perfect' implementation, the bottom-up view is that implementers often play an important part in policy implementation, not merely as managers of policy percolated downwards, but as active participants in an extremely complex process that informs policy upwards too. Thus implementers may change the way a policy is implemented, or even re-define the objectives of the policy because they are closer to the problem and the local situation. Rather than seeing implementation as a stage in the sequential transmission of policy from formulation to implementation, it should be seen as a much more interactive process, and just as policy formulation may be characterized by bargaining, so may implementation be characterized by negotiation and conflict. An example illustrates this.

De Roo and Marse (1990) describe how Dutch health policy makers at central level were challenged by the actions of health care institutions, resulting in an overturning of policy. In the Netherlands the central government controls the introduction of high technology by means of a licensing system. In 1984 the official health policy was to wait some years before initiating a heart transplantation programme, because policy makers argued that the operation was still in an experimental stage. Heart transplants were therefore not covered by health insurance and no funds were available for investments in facilities and equipment.

The heart surgeons thought otherwise, however. In June 1984 a secret, and successful, transplantation took place, with two hospitals collaborating. There was a great deal of media coverage, public opinion was favourable, and the Heart-Patient Society announced it was prepared to give financial aid for the operation. Politicians felt they had to respond quickly, and in September the central government changed its policy, and granted licences to three hospitals.

This was a situation where the main policy makers involved in the formal policy process were in favour of delaying the introduction of a new technological innovation. But outside this process were three interest groups which had opposite views: the heart surgeons who had acquired transplantation skills, the managers of the hospitals they were working in (who wanted to maximize opportunities for medical interventions and profits), and the Heart-Patient Society. It is not clear from this case how far consultation had occurred during the formulation stage of the government's policy on heart transplants, but because the medical profession has great power over the implementation of health policy, they are often in a position to strongly influence the policy process.

This case makes an interesting contrast to Britain, where the Department of Health kept a firm hand on heart transplantation policy development, and apparently pursued a more rational process. It first commissioned an interdisciplinary cost-benefit study of the transplantation programme at the hospitals which had pioneered the operation. Following this report, the Chief Medical Officer orchestrated a consensus of the professions to back cautious expansion. Consultation with the Royal College of Surgeons led to four transplant centres being sanctioned (Klein 1990).

In sum, given how interest groups may influence policy (Chapter 6) and having seen that there are, at least potentially, a multitude of opportunities for participation in policy, I clearly reject the notion of a policy process that is linear, or where policy formulation is separate from implementation. If there are clusters of public and private actors involved in formulating and influencing the outcome of policy, then there are other, or the same, clusters involved in implementation. Some may be the supposed beneficiaries of the policy. Policy making is interactive, with formulation and implementation two elements in a continuous loop, and both as political as the other.

Implementation in practice

International influence: power without responsibility?

International agencies engaged in policy dialogue with national policy makers often seem to assume a separation between policy formulation and implementation. We have already met examples where external donor agencies assumed that once policy was decided by government, it would be implemented. The Kenyan case (where maize marketing was not privatized as had been promised) in the last chapter is a case in point. It seems that donors often underemphasize the practical consequences of adopting particular policies, whereas this is precisely what preoccupies national policy makers. Further, the validity of conditions demanded as part of aid is sometimes questioned on the basis that foreign negotiators are insufficiently informed by local understanding and knowledge. A leaked 1992 World Bank report on *Effective implementation: key to development impact* contained criticisms from national policy makers on the 'psychological pressure' they felt to take loans that ended up with conditions that the country had no way of honouring, and a contract that could not be implemented. They argued that Bank staff appeared more driven by pressure to lend than a desire for successful implementation (Chatterjee 1992).

However, although donors are less concerned with implementation than they should be, their decisions about aid affect policy execution in a number of ways. For example, policies may be decided by one ministry on behalf of another (implementing) ministry. There are many countries where the government has accepted aid to build a new central hospital, against the ministry of health's objections to the long-term recurrent expenditure implications. Alternatively, ministries and donors may not anticipate problems down the line. Fiedler (1988) gives an example of the Ministry of Health (MOH) in El Salvador receiving loans from the Inter-American Development Bank (IDB) to expand the health infrastructure. From 1980 to 1985 the IDB channelled almost US$30 million into new construction. However, there was no concomitant closing of old facilities or improvement of the existing, dilapidated health facilities, so the surge in need to maintain the new and expanding structures, meant that the Ministry of Health's budget for building maintenance and repair was squeezed. Thus Fiedler concludes that the IDB was a victim of the MOH's recurrent crisis (because facility construction depreciated prematurely due to inadequate maintenance and repair) but also a cause of the crisis.

Problems with the implementation of aid fall on the shoulders of both international agencies and national governments. In an analysis of a large health sector reform programme in Niger, supported by USAID, Foltz (1992) shows that implementation moved more slowly at every stage than had ever been envisaged. Although the grant was signed in 1986, implementation did not begin until over a year later. What had been anticipated would be a programme of reform over five years, with regular tranches of money as each part of the reform was implemented successfully, actually took much longer (only two out of six sets of reforms had been implemented by 1991) with many hiccups on the way. There were many reasons for this delay. First, there was growing instability in the economic and political environment which led to severe fiscal crisis in 1990–91 – even civil servants were not receiving salaries – and considerable uncertainty as democratic elections were introduced. Second, the USAID grant was extremely complex. 'Few officials in USAID and even fewer in the Ministry could follow it knowledgeably.' Third, insufficient people were assigned to administer the grant, there were many changes in personnel, and there was a general underestimation of the complexity of managing a policy reform programme. One full-time staff person was insufficient to monitor and facilitate activities as well as oversee the grant's complex fiscal disbursement system.

Many other well-known defects in the aid system produce obstacles to implementation of projects and programmes. There may be many foreign donors working in a country. The proliferation of aid-supported projects often results in demands on the recipient country for separate accounting systems, evaluations, visits by missions, tying up policy makers' time with duplicatory efforts that impede actual implementation. Similarly, competition and bureaucratic demands on donors can lead to poor thinking through of the potential complexities of project implementation (Clift 1988). An example comes from Somalia in the late 1970s, when the country was deluged with refugees from Ethiopia. WHO, UNICEF and UNHCR were all trying to help, but from different mandates and perspectives:

> their roles in refugee health care were clearly confusing to the Government of Somalia and it was difficult for them to know which UN agency should be approached for assistance in providing health relief. Furthermore, during the emergency period, the poorly defined and overlapping roles in health relief among the UN agencies led to significant delays in planning and implementing health activities for the refugees by the government (Godfrey 1990: 114).

A general conclusion from studies on policy reform in particular is that donors complicate decision making, and that power is asymmetric. This depends on the level of aid. In a study of Swedish aid negotiations, research suggested that, in countries heavily dependent on external resources, negotiations were often dominated by recipient submissiveness and donor assertiveness. Thus even where the relationship between donor and country nationals was cordial and integrative (such as Tanzania), there were substantial elements of coercion and donor intransigence. In those countries (such as India) where aid was a small part of the gross national product, national negotiators were often tough and uncompromising (Elgstrom 1992).

Central–local relations: who pays the piper calls the tune?

Almost all governments transfer authority or disperse some power in public planning, management and decision making from national to sub-national levels, or from higher to lower levels of government (Mills et al. 1990). In practice any system of decentralization varies enormously between countries: at one end of the spectrum the centre exercises very tight control over lower levels of the administrative system through legislative and financing mechanisms. At the other end lower-level authorities may have considerable discretion in the interpretation of central policy. Implementation of policy is clearly affected by the prevailing system.

Budgetary control is usually jealously guarded by the centre, in order to impose, if necessary, national policy and preserve power at the central level. Implementation is clearly affected by where the funds come from to carry out policy, and who controls them. In Papua New Guinea, for example, 58 per cent of public sector expenditure for health goes to the provinces, but 88.5 per cent of this is provided as conditional grants or funding of salaries by the national government. Provinces had total control over only 11.5 per cent, raised from untied grants and internally generated resources (Thomason et al. 1991).

The ability of the centre to pay for a particular part of public expenditure is a powerful inducement for lower-level authorities to follow central policy proposals. Thus in a federal system, the national government may exercise some control over even relatively autonomous states, by providing financial support for particular programmes. Indeed, attempts to reclassify funding from federal to state level are likely to be met with considerable protest. On the other hand, states may be quite reluctant to accept financing as an inducement to introduce a particular policy if it is time-bound or conditional, because of recurrent expenditure implications. Jeffery (1986) gives the example of the Indian federal government's attempt to get the states to introduce community health worker programmes in the late 1970s. Three states (Tamil Nadu, Kerala and Kashmir) refused on the basis of having alternative ways of meeting the health needs of the rural population, but also because they did not want to be landed with a cadre of workers who would be politically difficult to get rid of if the federal government withdrew funding. In fact, the federal government later made moves to transfer some of the costs of the community health worker scheme to state budgets, but was unable to enforce its policy.

Similar controls have been exercised in Mexico, in spite of attempts to devolve authority. Thus the federal Ministry of Health gave direct grants or subsidies to lower-level health authorities, in order to retain central control, justifying this as a means of avoiding both federal and state-level bureaucracy, and increasing the effectiveness of implementation of national policies at the field level (Gonzalez-Block et al. 1989). The state governments did not press for financial devolution because of their own financial insufficiencies, and the implications of greater responsibility if they gained it.

Another example of centre–local conflict comes from Zimbabwe. In August 1993 the Bulawayo City Council was accused by a senior government minister of defying government policies. He argued that the local authority was 'dilly-dallying' over the implementation of suburban upgrading and the granting of home ownership status to particular residents. The government minister noted that Z$150,000 had been allocated for the initial stage of this project, and threatened to call upon the Ministry of Public Construction and National Housing to take over from the Bulawayo City Council if implementation was delayed further (*Daily Gazette* 1993).

Lack of resources also makes local-level authorities vulnerable to policies which may not be cost effective, but which bring other rewards. Waddington (1992) describes how scarcity of resources affected decisions about immunization campaigns at the district level in Ghana. Although it was more effective to deliver immunizations through routine health service delivery, mass campaigns were favoured because they supplemented local resources. Not only did donors provide vehicles for mass campaigns, but they also supplied daily allowances, torches, wellington boots and raincoats, providing extra income and perks for staff.

Complex decentralized structures can also impede rather than facilitate implementation. Gilson (1992) illustrates the tension between District Medical Officers (DMOs) in Tanzania, who have responsibility for the daily operation of primary health facilities and district hospitals (supervision and supplies), but who do not have the power to make key resource decisions. This lies with the District Executive Director (DED) for 70–80 per cent of funds received from the centre for health services in the district, and with the District Administrative Officer (DAO) for funds allocated to the district hospital.

> In 1991 district supervision visits to rural health units could not be made because the DED refused to use 'his' funds to pay for the allowances of district staff employed by central government (and so funded through the DAO's office), whilst the DAO claimed that 'his' allocation was already overspent. ... the DMO had no power to counteract either claim or to ensure that supervision was undertaken (Gilson 1992: 220).

However, in some countries there may be several sources of financing for health programmes at the local level, and the ministry of health may not be in control of health policy. Fiedler suggests that in Ecuador the Ministry of Health's 'theatre of operations' is relatively narrow, because budgetary devices are used to make particular health programmes autonomous. This is accomplished by legally mandating funds to be channelled directly to the local level, bypassing the Ministry of Health. Provincial health budgets, for example, are approved by the Ministry of Finance, while the budgets of the malaria eradication service are approved by the National Congress. The Ministry of Health does not have the authority to approve or contest the budgets of either the provincial health authorities or the malaria eradication service. Implementation of national policy is considerably undermined: '... as goes the power of the purse, so goes the ability to manage – to co-ordinate, direct and control' (Fiedler 1991: 39).

Implementation of policy is therefore heavily dependent on the extent to which the centre can expect lower-level authorities to follow its guidelines. In many countries this control is safeguarded by the centre through financing mechanisms, although this is less true in Latin America where ministries of health often have low status and are weak in comparison with social security or health insurance authorities. But funding mechanisms cannot, by themselves, ensure implementation of policy. If the centre wants to be sure that policy is implemented, legislation may be necessary.

Using *legislative control* is probably relatively rare in the health sector for day-to-day policies (although it clearly plays an important part in the regulation of professions and the private sector). Legislation carries most authority but regulations or rules, publicized as central policy through letters or circulars, can also carry substantial weight. When the policy to introduce nurse practitioners in Jamaica was decided in the

1970s, it was recognized that legislation would be necessary, but in the event, the policy was implemented without legislation. Cumper (1986) shows how this left nursing practitioners in a difficult position, because pharmacists would not accept their prescriptions without a doctor's counter-signature. The pharmacists argued that the legal right to prescribe had not been established, even though the medical profession and policy makers in the Ministry of Health had agreed to it.

Laws may be mandatory or permissive, either requiring local authorities to act, or giving them the opportunity to do so. Even if laws are statutory, they are not always enforced vigorously, and local authorities may delay implementation of policy for considerable time. When central government is not fully committed to a policy, sub-national authorities may follow suit:

> the reasons why some policies are not implemented is that no one ever expected them to be. Acts are passed or ministerial speeches made to satisfy some party pressure or some awkward interest group, but civil servants know that they need not strain themselves too hard to achieve results. The policy is symbolic (Korman and Glennester 1985: 7).

However, most local authorities are reluctant to break the law: they may be taken to court, and can incur expensive fines, cuts in budgets, or other financial penalties.

The legal process can be a long one, and for that reason, will not always be an attractive way to communicate policy from the centre to lower-level authorities. It is also not sufficient to ensure policy will be implemented as desired. Parry-Williams (1992) describes the attempt to change the law regarding children's homes in Uganda (Chapter 6, p. 118). The new law set down the standards of care expected by government from organizations running children's homes, the procedures for obtaining approval to operate and the regulatory system to maintain and improve standards over time. It took eighteen months to go from committee stage to becoming law, and the actual implementation involved different groups which had only been peripherally involved (if at all) in policy formulation and the drawing up of the legislation.

Parry-Williams points out that if the law is implemented in the way its supporters wish, many other actions need to be taken. Regular inspection of homes will require district probation and social welfare officers, district public health inspectors and medical officers to accept new responsibilities (with no additional remuneration). Training and familiarization meetings for district and children's homes staff will be a prerequisite for implementing the new law, and 'vigilance and persuasiveness' will be required if positive changes are to be consolidated.

Sometimes central government uses legislation to curtail the power of lower-level authorities. A common example is to limit the use of funds. It is only recently that moves to decentralize authority in the health sector have led to central governments allowing local hospitals or large health centres more discretion over finances raised through charges to patients. Where all monies collected previously had to be remitted to the ministry of health, recently some health facilities or district health offices have been allowed to keep a proportion of fees raised to be used to improve services as they see fit.

At the same time, because most policy is couched in fairly general terms, it is left to those implementing to decide precisely how to carry it out. Lower-level authorities often have considerable discretion because they have expertise in the performance of assigned tasks. Also, the implementation process is relatively invisible, little noticed by the public or reported by the press. Implementing agencies doing the day-to-day work of government are closest to citizens affected by the policies, and therefore sometimes more sensitive to the range of responses than is central government. Grindle and Thomas (1991) give the example of how, in the 1980s, the World Bank said that it would not support water projects that subsidized consumers, and wanted the Indian government to introduce water charges. Near unanimous opposition at various levels of government on the part of those who would have to implement such charges (because they perceived the introduction of user fees to be unenforceable) led to the World Bank's policy stand being rejected.

Another example comes from Britain: partly because central government wanted to insulate itself from the small, but highly vocal and active anti-fluoridation lobby, the British Department of Health's dental policy from the 1950s was to encourage local authorities to improve children's dental health by introducing fluoridation (adding fluoride to the water supply). Although central government did not legislate to give local authorities the power to add fluoride to the water supply, local authorities were assured that the government would indemnify any local authority in the face of legal action taken against it. Very few local authorities then introduced fluoridation because of the uncertainty about being taken to court by the anti-fluoridation lobby, and fear of major local grass-roots action against them (Walt 1976). Finally a bill was passed in 1990, giving local authorities the legal right to add fluoride to water supplies, as long as a thorough consultative process was pursued. Some three years later implementation was stalled as local authority after local authority rejected the policy. Although in the 1990s there were arguments against the addition of fluoride that had not existed in the 1950s (for example, fluoride toothpaste was readily available and used by the majority of the population), there were also political reasons why the policy may have been rejected. In the 1990s many local authorities were dominated by parties in opposition to the central government party. The combination of local opposition to fluoridation and 'cocking a snook' at central government left many local authorities unwilling to pursue a centrally initiated policy.

Of course, governments often have it in their power to force compliance without legislation. Morgan (1993) refers to the malaria control programme in Costa Rica which entailed house-to-house spraying of DDT. This was extremely unpopular with rural dwellers, who objected to the unsightly residue left on their house walls. Yet if people refused to have their houses sprayed they were fined. Anti-malaria workers were badly received in many communities, but central government was relatively insulated from the negative response of communities and had sufficient power in relation to local authorities to insist on implementation. Obviously some regimes are more coercive than others. Military regimes determined to implement policy, even at great hardship to citizens, may meet little resistance because of the fear of reprisals. People will select the issues on which to challenge government. If the risks are too high and the gains likely to be limited, opposition groups may choose to delay their challenges or concentrate on other issues.

Even changing the rules can involve a number of different groups of people. A new Ministry of Health policy allowing all mothers to stay with their sick babies in hospital was introduced in Mozambique in the late 1970s, after years during which the Portuguese regime had insisted on the separation of mothers and babies, not even allowing visiting. The policy required hospital administrators to work out where the mothers would stay, what facilities they would use, and what resources to allocate for their food. It also required health workers to accept more crowded wards, and mothers to be separated from the rest of their family. A doctor working in Mozambique during the period in which the change was implemented writes of the conflicts between mothers, health workers and administrators:

> At the end of 1978 when residence for the mothers had really become a fait accompli the hospital directorate announced that all the mothers had to go. The ward council met and expressed unanimous disagreement with the decision and regret that there had been no prior discussion. All the workers stood firm on this even when individually questioned. The mothers eventually decided the issue by picking up their children and belongings, forcing a compromise to be reached (Dick 1984: 51).

Similarly, a change in government policy requiring local health authorities to establish family planning clinics, or to improve food hygiene in markets, may involve many different departments and professionals within the local authority, as well as other groups. For example the church, women's groups, private family planning clinics, private doctors and nurses and pharmacists may all have reactions (positive or negative) to a government family planning clinic. Market stallholders, street cleaners and food distributors may have different responses to new regulations on food hygiene. All these groups may affect implementation, as will those directly responsible for action: the administrators, the nurses and doctors, and the hygiene or sanitary inspectors.

Implementation of policy is therefore in the hands of many different groups, all of whom may also be involved in policy formulation. Where there is resistance to policy, groups at different levels will use different tactics to change policy in those regimes where such pressure is allowable. Policy formulation, even in the form of a legal statute, is not a sufficient condition for implementation. It is necessary to mobilize sufficient power to execute a policy, and this depends a great deal on the policy environment.

Finally, while funding mechanisms, legislation and rules may strengthen the centre's control of the implementation of policy at lower levels of government, other factors also come into play at the micro-level which can affect the implementation of policy.

For example, there may be significant cultural differences and disjunctions of loyalty between government officials working in national offices, and government officials working at the local level. Justice notes the irony of Nepalese government officials, who frequently said that foreigners did not understand local conditions, and yet who

> because of their urban backgrounds and career positions in the Kathmandu administration, are also removed from the reality of rural conditions. Most officials rarely make field visits and do not see that information collected during such visits would be relevant to their planning procedure, which emphasizes quantitative data and targets (Justice 1986: 123).

Aitken (1992), also describing Nepal, talks of a two-culture scenario in the Ministry of Health. The explicit culture is one which promotes the Ministry as existing to improve the health of the population, through the provision of preventive and curative health services. The purpose of the health staff is to provide these services. The implicit culture is different, however, and is centred around the view that the Ministry of Health exists to distribute and account for funds, and to provide staff, directly or indirectly, with an income. Therefore the main duty of the staff is to provide reports showing how funds have been distributed and justifying their expenditure against the Ministry's targets. Aitken argues there is considerable complicity between the two cultures, so that the language of the official culture is used to justify decisions which satisfy the implicit culture. It helps to explain why some policies emanating from the Ministry of Health may be implemented (for example, in-service training for district staff) yet fail to accomplish their objectives (better quality care).

Bureaucrats at the local level may have different loyalties from national level bureaucrats. Agrarian land reform in Peru which the military government tried to introduce in the 1960s and 1970s failed for many reasons, not least among which was the disagreement within and between the government and the local bureaucrats (who were responsible for implementing the programme) about the specific content of the programme. McClintock suggests that in fact

> policy was only really 'made' in each region, enterprise or community when it became clear which officials – those with a technocratic, a statist, a radically redistributive, or even an opportunistic bent – would emerge on top of the bureaucratic heap in that area (McClintock 1980: 94).

Education reform (introducing new examinations for seven- and fourteen-year-olds) in Britain was blatantly and publicly repudiated by local education authorities and teachers, who simply refused to implement the tests in 1993, the year in which they were supposed to start, because there were violent disagreements about the validity, as well as the timing, of the introduction of testing.

Constraints on implementation, even where local officials are willing to execute a policy or programme, are legion. Gadomski et al. (1990) use a five-component model to explore some of the difficulties in implementation. It is useful to compare this approach with Hogwood and Gunn's 'perfect' implementation model on p. 154. Gadomski et al. suggest that implementation may face problems at these five different stages.

INPUTS   The interface of technology with field conditions can precipitate problems: for example, temperature sensitivity of vaccines and failures in the cold chain, lack of kerosene to keep refrigerators working. Technologies may lose their efficacy – resistance to anti-malarial drugs is an example. Technologies are only as effective as those who deliver them: mistakes, inaccuracies, or wrong timing (immunizing at the wrong age) can all lead to poor execution.

PROCESS   The implementation process involves the interaction between the community and the health service, as well as between provider and recipient. Poor-quality care or information, rudeness, lack of communication alongside human resource problems of incentives, motivation, support and supervision, can all intervene to make successful implementation of services break down, or lead to lost opportunities for intervention.

OUTPUTS Rather than counting the direct outputs (numbers of immunizations or oral rehydration solutions given), outputs that count the effective use by the recipient are a better test of usefulness. But effective use often requires behavioural changes, and these can be extremely difficult to initiate and maintain. Mothers may know how to make and use oral rehydration solutions, but they also have to recognize the conditions under which such solutions will be helpful, and have the ingredients, time and motivation to feed sick children with the solution. They have to recognize the need to continue to take children (not just babies) for immunization.

OUTCOME Effective coverage means reaching those most in need of the intervention or those at high risk. Often these are the very groups most difficult to find, because of where they live, or for socio-economic or cultural reasons. Poor families may find difficulty finding the time or transport costs to get to a clinic.

IMPACT At the end of the line of implementation, there remain many constraints, including biological constraints, that attenuate the impact interventions can have in reducing mortality. There are multiple, competing causes of death, and health interventions may only tackle some of these. Immunization may simply delay the death of a fragile child who succumbs not to an infectious disease, but to a combination of diarrhoeal disease and malnutrition.

And finally, implementation may be resisted at the organizational level, depending on the source of the impetus for change or reform. Martin (1992) suggests a framework of four dimensions that describe the process of implementing change within organizations (and might be applied to ministries of health). The first is the rational-empirical dimension, which is, unsurprisingly, a linear, sequential logical problem-solving approach. The second is designated as a 'social systems' approach, which emphasizes human interrelationships and interpersonal aspects of change. It stresses the importance of understanding the implications of change and of full consultation with all interests within the organization and in sub-units of the organization. The third dimension is power-politics, and is determined by the relative power of the competing interested parties affected by change, and less by any rational problem solving or participative approach to change. The final dimension – which Martin calls values-vision – has been under-emphasized, but deserves more attention. This dimension includes an appeal to new vision, based on explicit values. It offers a new perspective of purpose and commitment and may affirm a new or renewed mission and value base.

Depending on what dimension of change is employed, different actors will be important. In the rational-empirical model, where problem solving is the driving force, technical or professional experts, researchers and people in positions of formal authority will be foremost. In the social-systems model, skilled facilitators, communicators and representatives will use the ability to unite and encourage consensual action. In the power-politics model lobbyists and negotiators will join with those who are seen to have power; and finally, in the values-vision model the leaders of change will be people with moral force, with a sense of commitment, accepted or new leaders, and charismatic personalities. Implementation of change will thus also depend to some extent on the culture of the organization or institution.

Does the type of policy affect implementation?

Major policy decisions (macro or systemic policies), which attempt to introduce changes in social or economic relationships and behaviour, may be difficult to implement because of the stiff resistance they meet, perhaps because particular interests are threatened. Regimes may be toppled if major changes introduced are strongly resented by important elites.

Even with micro or sectoral policies, most governments will be fairly cautious about introducing policies if they anticipate strong reaction. But they may use a series of tactics to dissipate reaction, such as putting the onus on local authorities to implement the policy, in the hope that any negative responses remain localized. Certain characteristics of policy may make implementation easier or more difficult (Cleaves 1980). Some of these characteristics have been discussed earlier in this chapter under 'perfect' implementation.

If the policy has relatively *simple technical features*, then clearly it is easier to introduce than one which is complex. If knowledge and technology already exist, no one has to be trained to use new technical equipment, no new resources have to be allocated and equipment does not have to be bought. In the case of fluoridation, mentioned above, there were fairly complex techniques of adding fluoride to water, and perceived dangers if too much fluoride was added. This added strength to those who argued about the dangers of fluoridation, and further paralysed implementation.

If a new policy requires only a *marginal change* from the status quo, the risks of error are less great, the amount of information needed is smaller and capital and other costs are lower. As Lindblom has said, incremental changes are much easier to get agreement on than are major leaps unless under specific crisis situations. Clearly the introduction of a health insurance system to raise revenue for the health system is a much larger step than increasing existing consultation fees.

If the policy is to be *implemented by one actor*, and does not depend on collaboration or coordination with officials from other sectors or NGOs then, again, the implementers have more control of execution. In the case of legislative change on children's homes in Uganda, at least two ministries were involved – the Ministry of Relief and Social Rehabilitation and the Ministry of Health – plus other national bodies such as the National Council of Voluntary Social Services, the Child Care Agencies Forum (representing children's homes) and a foreign NGO, Save the Children Fund (UK). Where the ministry of health is solely in charge of implementation it is likely to run more smoothly, although this is by no means a sufficient condition for successful implementation.

The same is true if the *goals of the policy are clearly stated* and if there is *one major objective*. In the population field there has sometimes been considerable confusion over the goals which cover women's reproductive rights and/or health, the rights not to have unwanted children, controlling the population today for the sake of the next generation, and so on. Yishai (1993) examines the formulation and implementation of abortion policy in Israel, showing how abortion policies failed because of the incompatibility of the policy goals: curbing birth rates among the Arab population and encouraging fertility among the Jewish population.

And finally, the more quickly a policy can be introduced, the more likely is uncertainty to be reduced to a minimum. *Short duration* of actual implementation means it is less likely to encounter organized resistance, for new actors to enter the scene, for leadership changes, and for the policy to become distorted.

This last factor was a major feature in the successful implementation of a radical drugs policy introduced in Bangladesh in 1982, as is described in Box 8.1. Rapid implementation of policy meant that interest groups were somewhat taken by surprise, and had little time to organize their opposition to the policy.

Box 8.1 The banning of 1,600 drugs: achieving change through rapid implementation

When Lieutenant-General and Army Chief of Staff H.M. Ershad seized power in a military coup in Bangladesh in 1982, he used the opportunity presented by a new political environment to introduce a radical change in drugs policy. Within four weeks of the coup he established an expert committee of eight members to confront the problems in the production, distribution and consumption of pharmaceutical products. Less than three months later the Bangladesh (Control) Ordinance of 1982 was issued as a Declaration by Ershad, based on a set of sixteen guidelines that would regulate the pharmaceutical sector. The main aim of the Ordinance was to halve the 'wastage of foreign exchange through the production and/or importation of unnecessary drugs or drugs of marginal value' (Reich 1994). The drugs policy was to be applied to both private and public sectors and created a restricted national formulary of 150 essential drugs plus 100 supplementary drugs for specialized use. Over 1,600 products deemed 'useless, ineffective or harmful' were banned.

Policy formulation on essential drugs was internally initiated by a group of concerned physicians and others close to the new president. Among them was a well-known physician, Zefrullah Chowdhury, who had established the Gonoshasthaya Kendra (GK) health care project soon after independence in 1971. Among other activities started by GK was a factory manufacturing essential drugs. Production began in 1981 and by 1986 GK Pharmaceuticals Ltd had over 300 workers and was producing over twenty pharmaceutical products. As a member of the expert committee Chowdhury was later accused of promoting the interests of GK Pharmaceuticals in the committee. Perhaps more important than who was on the committee was who was *not*. The Bangladesh Medical Association (BMA) was represented by one member of its pharmaceuticals subcommittee, but the General-Secretary of the BMA was not officially consulted because of his connections with a transnational pharmaceutical corporation (Chowdhury, quoted in Reich 1993). The pharmaceuticals industry was not represented. It was argued that its presence would delay and distort the process of policy development. While this had the advantage of expediting policy formulation in the short term, it meant that implementation was likely to face difficulties in the long term.

Reaction and antagonism to the Ordinance was immediate. The body representing domestic and transnational drugs companies, the Bangladesh Aushad Shilpa Samity (BASS) started an advertising campaign against the national drugs policy, calling it a 'conspiracy against the nation's drug industry' (Chetley 1992: 17). Ambassadors from the US, France, the UK, Germany and the Netherlands complained to the President about the restriction on free trade (Wolffers 1992: 94). Since 80 per cent of aid to Bangladesh came from these sources these visits to voice opposition to the policy could not be ignored by the government (Reich 1993). The World Bank also expressed concern over what was perceived as the restrictive nature of the policy. In April 1992, Abid Hassan, the head of the Industry and Energy Unit of the Bank, sent a letter to the Bangladeshi government strongly recommending that they consider lifting price controls, import restrictions and regulation of foreign companies. This advice, however, ran counter to another unit within the Bank, the Population and Health Unit, which had been supportive of the national drugs policy and was in favour of rational legislation on drugs. Hassan was forced to soften the tone of his recommendations. The World Bank has since then clarified its policy on pharmaceuticals, recognizing the need for a reduction of waste and inefficiency (World Bank 1993). Other agencies such as WHO publicly supported the policy, and a number of international NGOs also publicized the Bangladesh policy as courageous and progressive, thus reinforcing the government's credibility.

As it stood, the policy promoted domestic production so national drug companies flourished. Their own anxieties were placated once they saw implementation working in their favour. Local production of drugs increased, and by 1986 80 per cent of essential drugs were manufactured locally as opposed to 30 per cent in 1981. The value of production increased. Prices of some essential drugs dropped by up to 75 per cent. By 1986 national drugs companies had retracted their initial criticisms, and openly supported national policy. BASS conceded that the Drug Control Ordinance had benefited 'not only the pharmaceutical industry but the public at large' (Chetley 1992: 36).

The gains were not universal, however. Internal logistical problems impeded implementation. Banned and illegal drugs were smuggled into the country, and the resulting black market in drugs was difficult to control. Quality control of manufactured drugs was also a problem. In 1992 there were only thirty-five inspectors in the

Drug Administration to monitor quality, and they could not keep up with the expansion of the national industry. In the mid-1980s Ershad made some concessions to industry in formal amendments to the drugs policy, permitting the return of some banned products, for example (Reich 1993).

In 1990 President Ershad attempted to introduce new health reforms as a first step towards a national health system. Although the policy passed unanimously through parliament, it was strongly rejected by the BMA, and a 72-hour strike by doctors was among several measures used to express discontent. GK's office in Dhaka was set on fire, probably because it was identified with the drugs Ordinance as well as with the new health policy (Wolffers 1992: 93). Partly as a result of the strike, partly because of economic upheaval and instability, Ershad was forced to resign. The new government which took office after parliamentary elections in 1991 established a new committee to review the national drugs policy. Politicians, the Bangladesh Medical Association, representatives of the drugs industry, dispensers and pharmacists were all represented on the committee. The national drugs policy continued to be tolerated, but in 1993 it was not clear what changes would be made.

The implementation of drugs policy in Bangladesh highlights the importance of timing for policy formulation and implementation. Ershad was able to introduce a radical change in pharmaceutical policy at the beginning of his regime, a time of some optimism and open-mindedness. He had the support of specific groups within the country, who had strong international links. By acting quickly Ershad avoided the build-up of resistance, and because some of industry benefited, hostility was tempered. Some eight years later he was unable to introduce another radical shift in health policy, and indeed, the attempt at least partly led to his removal from office (Reich 1994).

In their analysis of policy reform, Grindle and Thomas (1991) draw attention to the *impact* of a policy and its *visibility*. Thus, if the cost or burden of reform is felt strongly by the public, or by strong interest groups, they suggest that opposition will emerge during implementation. Reforms that impose broadly dispersed costs directly on the public also frequently generate benefits that are not widely understood or appreciated. The removal of subsidies on basic foods – maize or bread, for example – is an obvious policy which has often met great resistance from populations over the last decade. People do not recognize the supposed benefits of removing subsidies in order to stimulate the market: they respond to the negative effect on their household budget.

The visibility of the reform may affect public reaction too. If a policy change does not require major administrative resources or high technical skills to sustain it, it is more likely to be implemented. The more 'self-implementing' the reforms are, the more likely they are to be executed painlessly. Devaluation does not require new techniques or administrative procedures, nor usually does raising existing hospital charges. However, reforms which can be introduced quickly may have a broadly felt and immediate impact and if the reform is perceived by the public to be in their interests (for example, increased consumer rights) they may mobilize support for the government. If it is perceived to be negative, and has a rapid impact, there may be a violent response (riots or demonstrations). The legitimacy of the regime may have an important effect on how far the state can keep such demonstrations of opposition to policy in check.

When, however, policy reform is largely determined by, and absorbed within, the government arena, it is administrators, policy makers and officials who might gain or lose by reform. The benefits to the population are long-term and may not be clearly visible. For example, the reorganization of primary health services will lead to greater accessibility to care in the long, but not short, term. Thus the public may benefit over the long term from the reorganization of a ministry or the creation of a PHC system, but the direct impact is originally borne by officials, health managers and professionals who have to change old habits and institutional rules and relinquish accustomed forms of security, control and responsibility. If opposition arises in the bureaucracy, implementation may be delayed or even arrested. Administrators are likely to understand the costs long before the public recognizes the benefits, and unless policy makers (politicians) can mobilize some countervailing support for the policy in the public arena, it is unlikely that the policy will be implemented as intended.

A strategy for implementation

Up to now we have been fairly discursive about the implementation of policy. What seems clear from the analyses of policy is that most attention is focused on the formulation of policy – on policy dialogue between international and national policy makers, and between bureaucrats and politicians at national levels. There appears to be an assumption that fate or managers will carry out the desired changes in policy, and that there is little reason for a specific strategy for implementation. Analysts argue that

> in many cases, reforms have been attempted when the administrative or political resources to implement them did not exist. The result has generally been misallocated resources, wasted political capital, and frustration on the part of both those who support the reform and those who oppose it (Grindle and Thomas 1991: 149).

From her case studies of health reform in Niger and Nigeria, Foltz (1992) concludes that one of the weaknesses in implementation was due to the fact that national policy makers did not appear to engage in much policy analysis before the policies were introduced. The implication is that had there been greater analysis of the policy environment, to assess whether the conditions for successful implementation existed, many later mistakes could have been avoided. Policy change calls for political, financial, managerial and technical resources (Grindle and Thomas 1991) and although not all policies will call for all these, a task for policy makers is to assess the availability of resources, and then to consider how they can be mobilized. Let's examine how policy makers might analyse each of these areas in order to assess how far it will be necessary to mobilize resources to ensure more effective implementation.

Political resources

A number of questions help to decide what political resources exist, and whether more need to be mobilized. Policy makers may ask, for example:

— How legitimate is the regime? How stable is it? If there is broad-based support, the public is not likely to rise up in opposition on one single policy change, even if it has a negative and visible impact.
— Is this a single, one-off policy change, or part of many different (and unpopular) changes? The question here is, is this the policy that 'breaks the camel's back'. Or is there sufficient time (before the next election, for example) for the government to persuade or replenish its political bases of support?
— How autonomous is the government? If the government depends on one or two powerful interest groups, then the question of whether those interests are affected by any policy change becomes very important – especially if that interest group is the military. Coalition governments may contain many small parties, which may be able to exercise undue influence under certain conditions.
— Is there a consensus among elites in favour of policy change? How

far do elites share the government's perception of the problem? Can the government rely on the support of the elite groups in society – ranging from the military to the church? If elite opposition is muted, then implementation is more likely.

Governments can therefore anticipate what political support or resistance there may be to policies. The importance of potential support or opposition depends primarily on three factors: location, organization and socio-economic status, including literacy. If supporters have easy geographical access to policy makers and opinion makers such as the media, their power to influence policy and implementation is greater than if they are dispersed. Urban residents are almost always taken into account in policy change – because they are so close to policy makers. They can be mobilized more easily than rural populations both in support of, and in opposition to, policy change.

Groups organized around common interests will be quick to react to policy change if it threatens their self-interest. They may also mobilize other groups. Large landowners in the Philippines, although relatively few and rural, were sufficiently well organized to oppose land reform, and the government never dared to alienate them by trying to introduce land policy changes. Anti-abortion groups were extremely successful in affecting US government policy in the 1980s, although for ideological reasons rather than overt self-interest.

The extent to which information about policy change is understood and used depends, to some extent, on levels of literacy and education. They help determine the capacity to get information quickly, as well as the capacity to use it to wield influence. Those who can read, and can get information about policy changes, are more likely to be able to judge whether change will affect their interests, and then to do something about it. They may also be in a position to mobilize opposition or establish links with the media.

Policy makers need to be able to assess the impact policy change may have, and to mobilize those political forces in favour of reform, as well as to counteract those that are likely to pose a significant threat. It may be necessary to delay implementation of a reform while government introduces an education process, or even a media campaign, to explain and persuade the population of the need for change.

Financial, managerial and technical resources

In addition to political resources, policy makers may have to mobilize financial, managerial and technical resources in order to sustain policy implementation.

FINANCIAL RESOURCES   It may be impossible to guarantee policy implementation without financial resources, and for some policies these may be easier to find than for other policies. For example, anything to do with liberal-based policy reform – say reform in the health sector – is likely to attract some external, donor funding in the ideological climate of the 1990s. In the 1980s, UNICEF and USAID were happy to support programmes that promoted the GOBI interventions, but were less likely to support others, such as health education or income support schemes. However, in post-conflict Uganda donors were less interested in comprehensive health system reform and more in reconstruction of physical health services. Both central government and donors fear conditions where embezzlement of funds or corruption at a local level leads to resources disappearing. In situations of uncertainty or instability finances may be very limited. In Uganda communities and health workers emphasized that low salaries had a significant effect on the quality and accessibility of health centres, as health workers were often absent from their posts in search of alternative sources of income (Macrae et al. 1993).

MANAGERIAL RESOURCES   Control of budget, personnel appointments, control of support services, are important aspects of bureaucratic power. Where policies are introduced, and bring with them extra resources (from internal or external sources), bureaucrats may be very supportive because of the increase in managerial resources gained by the new policy, but they may also jealously guard such resources. As we saw earlier in this chapter, Ghanaian health managers were happy to support mass campaigns because of the extra resources they brought. Management and administrative skills are also an important resource, and where these are lacking, implementation may be slow or distorted.

TECHNICAL RESOURCES   The capacity for technical analysis is an important resource, and its availability can be assessed by the officials considering introducing a reform. Obviously there are many forms of technical capacity needed for evaluating a policy change. Probably the most difficult to obtain is a capacity for policy analysis. Often it consists of policy makers' knowledge of what is feasible. Introducing health insurance systems, or the ministry of health taking on a regulatory role where this has hardly existed, needs basic technical and administrative systems and information which may be in very short supply or even completely lacking. Considerable effort may have to go into training, absorbing or collecting information, working with consultants or advisers, in order to gain the technical competence to execute new policies.

Reviewing resources – political, financial, managerial and technical – provides policy makers with a systematic way to assess what is available and what is not, to support the implementation process. Analysis of the relevant resources also provides a means of assessing the opposition. However, the context of change is also important. If policy change is internal, then there may be sufficient support from groups involved in formulation, to carry the policy through to implementation. If however, policy change is imposed, the process of formulation and implementation may be very different.

Conclusions

To sum up this chapter on implementation, two main issues are clear. First, implementation cannot be seen as part of a linear or sequential policy process, in which political dialogue takes place at the policy formulation stage, and implementation is undertaken by administrators or managers. It is a complex, interactive process, in which implementers themselves may affect the way policy is executed, and are active in formulating change and innovation. However, experience suggests that in the real world there is all too often a major separation between policy formulation and implementation, with little focus on the realities of putting policy into practice.

Second, to avoid the gap between formulation of policy and implementation, all policy makers should be engaged in policy analysis that includes a strategy for implementation: taking into account anticipated objections from the public and the government bureaucracy, as well as the financial, management and technical aspects of the policy.

9

Evaluation and research: feeding into policy?

Evaluation is both the end of the policy process (is the policy effective?) and the beginning (what should be changed?). In order to help make decisions, policy makers depend on information from many sources, and in this chapter we explore how far evaluation and research feed into policy. What is the relationship between policy making and information? Do policy makers change policies, or introduce new policies because their attention is drawn to evaluation reports or research? Do they ignore findings that challenge current policy? Do they commission research because they lack information, or because they want backing for predetermined positions?

We also explore briefly the nature of the relationship between evaluators and researchers in policy formation. Are there actions researchers should take to see that research is disseminated to policy makers? Or, as scientists, should researchers maintain an objective, neutral position, communicating research results to peer group review, but going no further? What role do the mass media play in dissemination of research and evaluations?

Information from research and evaluations

In this chapter we are concerned largely with research and evaluations which may potentially affect policy through introducing new ideas and new techniques or suggesting modifications or reforms to existing policies. However, distinguishing between evaluation and research is not always easy.

Research is generally understood as a systematic process for generating new knowledge. One definition suggests that research uses the scientific method to discover facts and their interrelationships and then applies this new knowledge in practical settings (Commission on Health Research for Development 1990: vii). Health research may therefore focus on parasitology or human behaviour, be conducted in scientific laboratories or rural villages, and use tools from many different disciplines, from the biological and molecular sciences as well as from the social sciences. For example, health research may include:

— pure or basic research which may take place in a laboratory (development of a vaccine);
— epidemiological research based on case control methods (which seeks to establish whether there is an association between breastfeeding and HIV transmission);
— anthropological research to assess the cultural feasibility of introducing new nutritional habits (increasing vitamin A intake through more consumption of fruit and vegetables);
— economic research to assess the costs of one policy option over another (which achieves greater efficiency: a fixed rural health facility or a mobile, outreach service?).

In the hierarchy that dominates Western scientific models, basic physical and biological sciences occupy the top positions. The social sciences (including health services research) are relegated to a lower position, and indigenous, unsystematized or unprofessional knowledge (herbal or homoeopathic remedies, for example) disappear off the hierarchical ladder altogether. Policy makers in particular are attracted to scientific certainty, and demonstrable relationships. They have in the past subjected social and economic research to a fairly strong barrage of criticism for being too academic and theoretical, and of too little practical use. Whether this is fair or not, social scientists have hit back at their critics, and today are less often called in as a last resort, to explain why projects have failed. They have also made real attempts to adapt their methods to give more rapid answers to problems. In 1992 a whole issue of the journal *Health Policy and Planning* was devoted to rapid assessment methods in the control of tropical diseases. Focusing largely on speeding up social science research particularly as a tool for evaluation, rapid rural appraisal has been defined as

> a strategy for appraising a particular situation in the most cost-effective manner possible with appropriate levels of timeliness, accuracy, and relevance (Heywood quoted in Manderson and Aaby 1992: 49).

The distinction between research and evaluation is not always clear, and some prefer to use 'evaluative research' (Black 1992). Evaluations use research methods and may take as long as research projects to undertake. For example, a collaborative evaluation undertaken by Imo State in Nigeria, WHO, UNICEF, and the London School of Hygiene and Tropical Medicine, of the impact on health of improved hygiene and health services in a poor rural area, used a quasi-experimental study design, and took place over three years (Imo State Evaluation Team 1989).

However, many evaluations are relatively short, often take place halfway through, or at the end of, a particular programme, and are ostensibly to ascertain whether the programme met its goals or whether change is needed. Evaluation is defined as:

> any scientifically based activity undertaken to assess the operation and impact of public policies and the action programmes introduced to implement those policies (Rossi and Wright 1979: 197).

Evaluations are usually seen as policy-relevant – providing policy makers and managers with direct feedback on the value of the particular policy or programme. Research is sometimes, but not always, perceived as policy-relevant. Evaluation is usually distinguished from *audit* and *monitoring*. Audit examines or reviews to what extent a situation, process or performance conforms to predetermined standards or criteria, whereas monitoring is concerned with the continuous overseeing of the implementation of an activity to ensure that inputs, schedules, targets and other actions required are proceeding according to plan (UNICEF 1984).

However, both audit and monitoring may be used to inform policy, and indeed, monitoring can be described as policy-relevant research, seeking to grasp a changing picture, and to assess what impact policies are having. Thus standard statistical information such as the crude birth rate may be used by government as a highly simplified measure of the success or failure of a family planning programme.

How do research and evaluation affect policy?

How does information from research or evaluation filter through to policy makers? And do they take any notice of it when it does? Two schools of thought are apparent. Pointing to the social sciences in particular, the pessimists argue that there are few empirical examples that show a direct link between research results and policy. Looking at health services research, two researchers conclude:

> In the United States, as in the United Kingdom, the relationship between research findings, however conclusive, and organizational and policy change is a tenuous one. There is certainly no automatic translation of research into policy (Hunter and Pollitt 1992: 168).

The optimists reject this view as hidebound and too narrow a conceptualization of how policy is made. They argue that new information and knowledge percolate through the political environment, and become part of policy makers' thinking, not in a clear linear fashion (this particular piece of research led to this particular policy), but in a much more diffused fashion.

The pattern of influence can be likened to water falling on limestone: the water is absorbed, but there is no knowing what route it takes through the different strata of stone, or where it will come out (Thomas quoted in Bulmer 1986). Those who argue that few links are discernible between research and policy are still wedded to linear explanatory models. Weiss (1977) calls these either knowledge-driven or problem-solving:

— knowledge-driven model: basic research – applied research – development – policy application;
— problem-solving model: problem exists – research provides empirical evidence – suggests policy action.

Weiss suggests that both of these models derive from an ideal model of the natural sciences. They describe a rational process based on hypotheses, testing, and disinterested results. In this model of science, researchers are free of political bias, pursuing knowledge for knowledge's sake, not influenced by the sources of their funding or concerned about what to do with uncomfortable results. This ideal model of the natural sciences is familiar to the classical model of rational policy making which we have criticized in earlier chapters, as one which many people aspire to, but which, in the real world of policy making, is unusual. In the same way, the research–policy nexus is extremely complex, and cannot be seen as a simple, linear model as described above.

Weiss suggests that it is more useful to use the notion of *enlightenment* to describe the way research influences policy: this draws on the idea of many different, overlapping policy networks, feeding into a dynamic (although murky) process of information exchange and challenge. For Weiss, research concepts and ideas permeate into the policy process, providing a backdrop of ideas and orientation that feed into policy. This is a much more fluid notion of the way knowledge accumulates and infiltrates thinking. Thus research may well be recognized as raising new questions, shedding new light, using new techniques and concepts, but it also has a cumulative effect rather than an immediate and direct influence on public policy.

Smith (1991) illustrates the concept of enlightenment in relation to the UK during the 1960s. He identifies three networks of influence in the social sciences that clearly affected public policy: the Cambridge group of Keynesians, the Titmuss school of social administration, and the Oxford school of industrial relations. Each worked on problems of central importance to government: the management of the economy, the imperfect working of the welfare state, and the role of the trade unions. Each of the different schools had a major impact on government policy at the time, key researchers acting as advisers to government ministers. For example, the London School of Economics and Political Science, through key researchers such as Richard Titmuss, Brian Abel-Smith and others, influenced many aspects of the social welfare policies of successive Labour governments.

Disseminating information

Just as researchers are not necessarily only scientists and academics (research may also be undertaken by government officials, NGOs, and sometimes communities), so policy networks are made up of many different groups. Walker (1981) talks of communities of policy experts who may be civil servants, academics, publishers or editors of professional journals, journalists, elected officials or members of parliament, and lobbyists, among others. Through a common concern with policy issues, they constantly exchange information about activities and ideas, doing this in part to win approval or recognition from other members of the policy community. On the whole, ideas that conform to currently established professional consensus will be rewarded with esteem and recognition.

So, in looking for ways in which to judge whether research affects policy, it is important to look at the networks of influence, over time, and how they are communicating. How do policy makers find out about research, for example? Do they commission it and pay for it? Or do they respond to it? The process of dissemination can be described as deliberate or diffused. In the first case, policy makers actively seek out information from researchers. They may tender for research to answer a particular problem; or to protect a specific position which is under threat; or to show concern ('we've commissioned research on that subject … we're waiting for results'). In the second case, policy makers become aware of, and attend to, information derived from research. This may be through professional or scientific meetings or participation in grant-giving bodies, or through publications, evaluations and so on. The process may be very diffuse – researchers do not necessarily publicize their findings through the mass media, and it may take time for results reported in scientific, peer-reviewed journals to find their way into the policy environment. For example, the positive relationship between women's education and child health in the Third World took years to percolate from reported research to the consciousness of policy makers at the international and national levels.

In order to assess how far policy is affected by research, Weiss (1991) suggests it is important to ask how research is disseminated and to define the form it comes in: as data and findings; as ideas and criticism; or as briefs and arguments for action. Each form has its underlying image, strengths and weaknesses, and there may be certain conditions in which one form is more useful than another. For example, *research as data* is the most technocratic, and is common in the biomedical field, where researchers provide statistics and surveys to inform policy. Such data are not unbiased in either collection or source, and will be affected like all other actions of researchers by the social constructs of the world they live and work in. Although policy makers and researchers may share the same view of normality and reality, there is no guarantee that policy makers will act when faced with such data. They may respond to acute problems, such as cholera epidemics, but neglect statistics that show persistent inequities in mortality and morbidity between social classes.

Information as ideas and criticism is more fluid: ideas come and go, policy makers choose and remember such information selectively. This illustrates the way the enlightenment model works – with ideas seeping through in known and unknown ways to policy makers. Research may alter the way issues are defined and understood, but it may be difficult to pinpoint direct links to policy.

Finally, *information as argument* is altogether more adversarial, more political, with researchers taking the role of advocates, and putting specific options to policy makers. Research-as-argument may have advantages to policy makers, by saving time, by clearly stating interests. Thus, interest groups may produce research to support the case they are trying to make. For example, in the 1960s in the UK, interest groups sponsored research into the negative effects on women's health of illegal abortions. Many groups the world over are undertaking research on environmental risks. As long as the research is methodologically sound, and is perceived to be of high quality, policy makers may well turn to such groups because they have information and ideas on what options for change exist. Table 9.1 gives an indication of the forms of research, and the conditions under which it may be used.

According to Table 9.1, research may be used depending on what sort of questions the research addresses (its characteristics), what sort of images it has and who it is done by, and the prevailing political context into which it is introduced. So research which is primarily addressing a clearly defined, and relatively specific problem (for example, the value of screening for breast cancer) will be used if it is a recognizable problem on the policy agenda. Much evaluation research may come into this category, even if it is not data-dependent, if it is clearly defined, and posed to address specific programme concerns. If the research has not been identified as something policy makers should concern themselves with, researchers may take on the role of advocacy, but this is relatively unusual in the case of research based on data and undertaken in academic institutions.

Table 9.1 Conditions under which research may be used

Characteristics of research	Underlying images	Conditions when useful
Data (apparently objective)	Technocratic (e.g. vaccination or screening); short-term; academic	Consensus situations; clear problem exists; alternatives feasible
Ideas (diffused)	Enlightenment; long-term; policy networks	Uncertainty exists; pluralism of discussion and action; multiple alternatives
Argument (social impact)	Political; adversarial; interest groups and policy networks	Conflict is high; research taken up selectively

Source: Adapted from Weiss 1991.

In the case of research as ideas, the field is more open. Research may be sponsored or undertaken as part of strategic planning or new analysis, rather than posing a direct question about a particular problem. Those involved cover a wide spectrum of public and private bodies, and the way the research is presented, disseminated and discussed will vary. An open, pluralistic system in which policy networks communicate and overlap with each other is essential.

Research used as argument requires taking an aggressive approach to dissemination and use of results: how far it influences policy makers will depend on the political and ideological climate of the day, the extent to which the research is seen as qualitatively legitimate, and the lobbying and dissemination skills of the researchers. Many interest groups have employed people to undertake research, and may use such research both to protect and to demonstrate a particular position. One observer suggests that the researchers who undertook a study on the inequalities of health in Britain in the 1970s (most of whose recommendations were rejected by the Conservative government of the day) provide an example of policy research transformed into policy advocacy, with the researchers seeking to impose their own values and goals on a policy community implacably opposed to those values. 'The moral of the inequalities report is therefore that partisan research will appeal only to a partisan audience' (Klein 1990: 519).

Objective scientists or interested parties?

Let's look more closely at the relationship between policy makers, researchers and the mass media, and the ways they interact. On the one hand, researchers may start with naive assumptions about policy makers, believing that they *want* to act on new information, or react to good ideas emanating from research (Higgins 1980). This is clearly not always the case. In many countries policy makers faced with clear evidence on the relationship between lung cancer and tobacco are still reluctant to regulate advertising and marketing of cigarettes.

On the other hand, some researchers argue that they should not have any direct links with policy makers, that they should remain objective and neutral, and disseminate their results only within the scientific community. Such scientists view the world in which they work as derived from an ideal model of the natural sciences. Thus they describe their research as following a rational process, which includes notions of hypotheses, testing, disinterest and truth. The natural outcome of such an ideal model is that scientists are free of political bias. In a journal interview in 1991, overviewing the life work on lung cancer and cigarette smoking of the British scientist, Sir Richard Doll, the interviewer noted that the crucial research results were published in September 1950, but that it was not until 1957 that any Minister of Health took it seriously. He went on to ask whether Sir Richard was disappointed that the policy makers acted so slowly. Sir Richard replied that he felt that the research worker's job was to obtain the results, to report them, and to comment on them if asked to, but to leave it to other people to act on them. However, at the end of the interview he was asked again:

> But what do you think now about that story, the impact of your paper, the 40 year gap, the continuing mortality? Would you still take the line that the scientist must keep away from over involvement? Or do you feel a need to make that work have its public health bite? (*British Journal of Addiction* 1991: 376).

Doll replied that he was now, in 1992, much more prepared to take an active part, but that he would not necessarily advise a young scientist to become an activist on first obtaining some socially interesting results.

Other researchers may argue that they have a public duty to disseminate as broadly as possible the results from research which may have implications for people's behaviour. They may become advocates for particular policies which take account of their own research results, and may become involved in heated scientific and professional debates. For example, pressure from drug companies, the media and affected persons contributed to the release of zidovudine, popularly known as AZT, as a therapy for AIDS before the completion of clinical trials (Nelkin 1991). Subsequent research suggested that AZT might not be as effective as had been thought, although demand for it continued at the same time as pressure grew once more for running a controlled trial. Debates may be carried out in scientific journals, and be picked up in the mass media, which follow research and new knowledge reported in professional or scientific publications. Research then becomes disseminated much more broadly, and runs the risk of being oversimplified or made to appear more contentious than it really is. Dunwoody and Peters (1992) argue that there is growing evidence that scientists increasingly use the mass media to alert their specialized colleagues to new work, so that the mass media become channels of communication between science and society but also conduits of information within science. They use the mass media because they can derive a number of benefits from mass media visibility, among them personal satisfaction, and recognition from the public, employers and peers.

The role of the media may therefore be important as a way of informing both the scientific community, but also the public and policy makers. We have already seen, in Chapter 4, that the media can play a useful 'alerting role' between researchers and policy makers, getting issues on to the policy agenda (or colluding to keep issues off). But how far they have longer-term influence on policy or public opinion is unclear. There is a confused array of evidence on how powerful an effect they have in the longer term. Media content may influence beliefs and attitudes under certain circumstances, but media coverage is itself influenced by the activities of various sources of information, as well as by the response and reaction of audiences or readers. It is known in health education that interpersonal communication may carry much more weight than even respected and legitimate sources of scientific information, in getting people to change their smoking behaviour for example.

The different institutions of the mass media have varying reputations of reliability, independence and autonomy, and the public are often aware of uneven coverage or disproportionate focus on some issues, inaccurate information, or even exaggerated claims. The media are not homogeneous or uncritical of their colleagues. For example, the editor of the *British Medical Journal* was angry with what he called the 'unholy alliance' between journalists and scientists in 1992, which led to a story in a UK Sunday newspaper promising a 'miracle cure' for asthma within five years. He also criticized another story which employed hyperbole about the use of acyclovir in the treatment of AIDS. The newspaper quoted a well-known scientist as saying that the drug had removed the automatic death sentence carried by HIV, and that AIDS could be as treatable as diabetes by the end of the decade (Smith 1992: 730). There are several other examples, especially in the AIDS field, of similar poor reporting (Dean 1992: 1286). The relationship between researchers or evaluation experts and the media is often fraught with claims and counterclaims of inaccurate reporting by, and poor levels of scientific knowledge among, journalists, and inability to explain or talk simple language on the part of researchers.

However, in a review of the relationship between mass media coverage of technological and environmental risks in Germany and the USA, Dunwoody and Peters (1992) caution against the tendency to regard media information as aberrant, and suggest that perceptions of media bias may themselves be biased. They are mindful of the multi-dimensional space within which journalists work, and argue that journalists must be sensitive to a host of constituencies, not least of which is the audience, which includes policy makers.

Funders of research may also be biased in their presentation of research results, because of pressures to demonstrate that they are spending public money wisely. Desowitz (1991), for example, is scathing of USAID's support for malaria research, and accuses the agency of making promissory statements in press releases in the mid-1980s about the imminent availability of a malaria vaccine for human beings, when in fact most scientists were extremely cautious and not optimistic about early breakthroughs. Funders of research are also biased about what sort of research they are prepared to fund, and are subject to changes in fashion and ideology as well as to political pressures.

Impediments to the use of research

There are many other factors which may intervene in the process of translating information into policy, or prevent its being taken seriously (Greenberg 1992). Policy makers are only likely to use research results they find palatable, viable, persuasive or gratifying. Research can seldom attract either unambiguous support or provide unambiguous results.

Political factors

Politics is also often a problem when it comes to the use of results of evaluations and research. For example, who initiates the evaluation may determine how far it is likely to be used by policy makers. In the Third World, many evaluations focus on accountability to donors who are supporting a particular programme. They are often a condition of support, and are more for external than internal consumption. A donor supporting a diarrhoeal disease control programme, for example, will need to satisfy its own constituency made up of economists and other sector professionals concerned with aid; politicians concerned with justifying public expenditure on aid; and the public concerned that their contributions of money have helped the poor. Donors may also want independent advice on weaknesses and strengths, whether the particular programme should continue to receive support, or whether funds should be withdrawn. However, they are seldom neutral about programmes, and may make it clear to evaluators what they expect, more or less, to come out of the evaluation. If that is not what they get, they are likely to ignore the results and not hire the same evaluators again!

Evaluations may also be used to settle conflicts within a programme, legitimizing change by calling in external professional evaluators. Their results may also be used as tools, to persuade others that the programme is worthwhile, and should continue to be supported, or that changes need to be made.

Box 9.1 Assessing WHO programmes: using evaluation as a policy tool

Two evaluations of programmes in WHO were undertaken by donors funding the programmes for reasons which were never made explicit, in the hope that the evaluations could be used as tools for change. The first was an evaluation of the Action Programme on Essential Drugs. This had existed for almost ten years when a new Director-General of WHO took over in 1988. Always an extremely controversial programme, which had been heavily criticized by the pharmaceutical companies, it had enjoyed the strong support and protection of the previous Director-General, Mahler, and the donor agencies which had provided the US$20 million extra-budgetary support for the programme. With the appointment of a new Director-General, the donors were concerned that the new incumbent had a more compromising attitude to the pharmaceuticals industry, and would not give the programme the same support it had had.

By the time the evaluation was organized, terms of reference agreed, evaluators chosen and methods of work decided, circumstances had changed in WHO. The former, direct link between the programme and the Director-General was removed, and a more formal, hierarchical management structure imposed. Programme staff were not as free to make decisions about their work, and had to report to a new Head of Division. Several staff, including the Programme Director, resigned and posts were not filled quickly. The evaluation report was published one year after these changes. The donors used the report to remind the WHO Secretariat of the importance of continued support for the Action Programme, but it was rather a blunt instrument given the assurance from the Director-General that the programme was highly thought of, and the concept of essential drugs would continue to receive his total support in spite of its having been demoted in status.

The second example is a review of the Global Programme on AIDS. This programme had expanded greatly in its short existence from 1986 to 1990. Two staff multiplied to 400 in four years, and extra-budgetary funds increased from US$1 million to US$100 million over the same period. This investment, coupled with an intense commitment to fight AIDS, led to a frenetic level of activity. However, donors were, by the fourth year, highly critical of certain aspects of the programme: its management, slow disbursement of funds and lack of transparency in accounting, among other things. They therefore called for a review.

Again, it took time to put together a review team and settle the terms of reference, by which time many changes had occurred in the programme. A new director replaced the former amidst ill-feeling and within a short period introduced many changes in management and accountability. The review therefore took place during a year of great change, and by the time it was completed some of its recommendations were already being implemented. The main finding of the review was to call attention to the importance of AIDS as a global responsibility, emphasizing the need for greater coordination and collaboration between the different international organizations working in AIDS. This recommendation was seriously considered by the Management Committee and a new, inter-organizational structure was introduced in 1994.

Where evaluations are ostensibly for the managers of a particular programme, it is often doubted that outside evaluators can understand as much about it as those running it. In a study in the USA, where the investigators went back to a number of programmes which had been evaluated some years before, they asked them whether the evaluation had had any impact. In other words, had the recommendations been utilized? Briefly, although many programme managers at first often denied that the evaluation had been of value, or even utilized after-wards, they often changed their minds in the course of interviews, re-membering the process of the evaluation as being useful in all sorts of ways – but not for telling them anything they didn't already know. One person said:

> If there's a surprising finding it should be rare. I mean, *everybody's missed this insight except this great evaluator? Nonsense!* (Patton et al. 1977: 154).

How far an evaluation is likely to be effective depends on the context of the evaluation: who has asked for it and why it is wanted; how far those involved in the programme are involved in the evaluation; the validity and acceptability of the evaluation report; and so on. Most often an evaluation will either be ignored or lead to incremental changes in the policy as it exists. It is relatively rare for an evaluation to lead to the termination of a policy or programme (Hogwood and Gunn 1984) for a series of reasons, ranging from an intellectual reluctance to confront the issues that lead to the demise of a programme (or organization); a reluctance to admit past mistakes; distaste for dismantling institutions with staff, premises, and existing relationships; anti-termination coalitions of significant groups within and outside the programme; legal obstacles and the high costs of alternative policies. Even if attempts are made to close a programme, managers may procrastinate or delay phasing out, searching for alternative sources of support or funding.

Problems of conceptual confusion and uncertainty

Particularly in the case of evaluations, interpreting results may be problematic because the original policies are often characterized by vague goals, strong promises, and weak effects. Findings may therefore be undermined because they cannot show programmes achieving what they set out to do, and policy makers may be unclear on what to make of them.

Programme goals are often complex, and not necessarily specified in advance. There may be no clear consensus on what the goals are. For example, in large-scale programmes which try to address difficult and long-standing problems (poverty, illiteracy, unemployment, poor health) the expectation of large and rapid improvements is not justified. Yet often policies are introduced with strong promises that they will change the nature of the problem. But we know that often the measurable or demonstrated effects are quite weak – and certainly do not show over the usually short period within which most evaluations take place. Demonstrating any effect on health is particularly difficult.

The extent to which research delivers unambiguous results is problematic. In her examination of environmental policy Jasanoff (1993) notes a number of conceptual problems. One is that science does not always lead to the same explanation for the same observed phenomenon, and when people reach scientific conclusions about the reasons for a particular natural phenomenon their explanations are not always the same. She gives the case of the US public health experts who introduced legislation to reduce levels of lead in the environment because of its damage to children's learning behaviour. It was more than ten years after the US reductions in lead that Britain began to phase out lead additives in petrol. The scientific reasons for doing so, however, were not based on the damage lead caused to children's health (which were considered uncertain and were scientifically controversial) but on the fact that it was highly toxic, even at low levels, and that alternatives to many current uses of lead could be found.

Scientific uncertainty can thus lead to distortion and lack of clarity in policy making. Competing interests may mobilize resources in an attempt to influence the public and policy makers. Where policy makers have to act on the basis of discretion, rather than certain knowledge, they may be more reluctant to take a firm stand. For example, the lack of a food policy in many countries in Europe is partly due to scientific disagreement about the role of fats in diet.

Conception of risk

Individual conceptions of risk may also impede the influence of science on health policies. Greenberg (1992) points out that the pyschological meaning attached to different hazards often mitigates against known public health research. Using the USA as his example, he points to the imbalance in people's perceptions of risk from environmental hazards caused by factories, landfills, nuclear power stations, and those risks to health caused by tobacco, alcohol and poor nutrition. Americans are much more fearful of the former than the latter, in spite of the fact that far more people are at risk of illness and death from the latter. The mass media, from where the American public gets a great deal of its information about public health, reinforce this imbalance by skewing risk information. For example, a study of all nightly network news broadcasts by three major television companies over a two-year period had fifteen stories about asbestos and fifty-seven about tobacco, but over a hundred stories on the Mexico City earthquake and Bhopal chemical disaster, and 482 about airplane accidents. While about 250 Americans were killed in the air crashes, some 800,000 died from smoking-related illnesses.

Reluctance to take risks is also important in relation to public health measures affecting large numbers of people. Policy makers and scientists may take different roles. On the one hand, policy makers may be willing to act more quickly than scientists who demand high standards of reliability and validity of results. On the other hand, policy makers are sometimes unwilling to act even where scientists believe the evidence is clear, and risks of action few. In the case of vitamin A supplementation (see Box 9.2), policy makers were impatient to act on the results of the first trials suggesting that vitamin A supplementation decreased mortality in young children, whereas scientists wanted clearer evidence.

Box 9.2 Vitamin A supplementation: policy attendant on research?

Vitamin A supplementation has long been known to be effective in both the prevention and treatment of xerophthalmia, an eye condition which is one of the commonest causes of blindess among young children in developing countries (Mamdani and Ross 1989). Physicians had also observed that children with xerophthalmia had high rates of diarrhoea, pneumonia, measles and other infectious diseases, and had high mortality rates.

In 1983, a report was published in the *Lancet* of a large cohort study of children up to the age of six in Indonesia (Sommer et al. 1983). The findings suggested that children with night blindness or Bitot's spot (the mildest forms of xerophthalmia) had a greatly increased chance of dying over the next three months than did children without xerophthalmia, even after controlling for other factors such an anthropometric status. The same group of investigators went on to conduct a randomized controlled trial to determine whether supplementing young children aged 1–6 years old would decrease their mortality. They showed that the mortality rate of children who received vitamin A supplementation was 34 per cent lower than that of the children who had not received vitamin A.

The study was received with great excitement: it seemed that a relatively inexpensive intervention could prevent large numbers of children dying, and international agencies such as UNICEF and USAID were eager to add vitamin A to the selected interventions (oral rehydration solutions to prevent diarrhoea, immunizations against the common childhood diseases) that made up the programmes they supported in many Third World countries.

The scientific community was more cautious, however. Researchers were critical of methods used in the Indonesian trial: it was not double-blind, and so bias could have occurred, and there were baseline differences between control and treatment villages for example. Scientists urged policy makers in the large agencies not to rush into introducing vitamin A supplementation to existing programmes, but to carry out further, carefully designed studies to determine whether the effect on mortality was as dramatic as the Indonesian studies had suggested. The debate at the time could be characterized as one between those who wanted a magic bullet to solve the problems of childhood mortality in developing countries, even without conclusive evidence, and those who called for further evidence before scarce funds were diverted to programmes to improve children's vitamin A status.

The debate was carried out in the public domain, and most policy makers suspended their decisions until the results of further studies were available. From the mid-1980s, a number of large scientific studies were initiated in Brazil, Ghana, Haiti, India, Indonesia, Nepal and Sudan to test whether vitamin A supplementation of young children reduced their mortality or morbidity. However, programme managers were impatient to implement what many believed to be a foregone conclusion, and the number of vitamin A programmes greatly increased during the late 1980s and early 1990s, often with financial support from either USAID or UNICEF. By 1993 the results of almost all the trials had confirmed that vitamin A supplementation reduced childhood mortality, though the effects on morbidity were less clear. A formal meta-analysis of the eight major mortality trials showed an overall reduction of 23 per cent in mortality (Beaton et al. 1992). Researchers concluded that 'improving the vitamin A intake of young children in populations where xerophthalmia exists, even at relatively low prevalence, should be a high priority for health and agricultural services' (Ghana VAST Study Team 1993: 7).

With the establishment of a clear relationship between vitamin

A supplementation and mortality, and with indications that supplementation might also reduce the severity of many childhood illnesses, the next question focused on implementation. How should the vitamin A status of young children be improved? Through linking vitamin A supplementation to existing immunization programmes, through a new vertical vitamin A programme? Through the fortification of centrally processed foodstuffs? Or through changed dietary and agricultural practices?

Policy discussions took place at the international level in order to establish common approaches to delivery of vitamin A. Those involved in the policy process included academics who had been involved in trials and studies of the impact of vitamin A on mortality and morbidity; policy makers from organizations such as UNICEF who were keen to introduce vitamin A supplementation linked to immunization programmes; managers from programmes within WHO such as the Nutrition Unit; the diarrhoeal disease control and acute respiratory infections programme (CDD/ARI) and the expanded programme of immunizations (EPI) who were expected to provide policy guidance both to national governments and the international donor community; the major manufacturers of vitamin A supplements (primarily Hoffman-La Roche); and finally, national policy makers concerned about the financial implications of adding vitamin A supplementation to existing health programmes.

These groups all had different interests and immediate controversy occurred over whether vitamin A supplementation should be administered as part of EPI or not. The advantage was that immunization programmes had proved their efficacy, and because vitamin A was inexpensive, adding it to the existing programme of vaccines would make them more cost-effective. Given the World Bank's emphasis on cost-effectiveness as a criterion for choosing what policies to implement in health services (World Bank 1993a), vitamin A supplementation was an attractive addition to the EPI. The other main point in favour was that vitamin A would be delivered through an already existing system – supported by both UNICEF and WHO. Immunization programmes with reasonable coverage provide up to six contacts with mother and child in the child's first year of life: adding vitamin A to a well-established programme would be feasible and easily implemented.

However, there were many opponents to this mode of delivery, partly on the grounds that there was no direct evidence to suggest that vitamin A supplementation of children under the age of six months was either safe or effective. Only two of the previous vitamin A supplementation trials had included young infants, and neither of these had shown any mortality reduction in this age group (West et al. 1993; Daulaire et al. 1992). Since most of the contacts with the immunization programme were of children under six months, it was argued there were real dangers that vitamin A supplementation would occur at an inappropriate age. If so, attention and resources would be diverted from programmes, whether through supplementation, fortification or dietary change, targeted at older infants and children where clear mortality benefits had been demonstrated. The CDD/ARI programme within WHO urged a more cautious approach than was being advocated by their colleagues in the Nutrition and EPI programmes, and by UNICEF.

As this example shows, the research–policy nexus is a complex one: the scientific community and policy makers in international organizations may have different interests and views regarding scientific certainty and long-term solutions. Vitamin A supplementation is a 'magic bullet' approach to deficiency. More sustainable action would focus on dietary modification and nutrition, on eating habits and customs. However, both scientists and international policy makers tend to eschew looking for such solutions. Research on interventions in nutrition and food habits is much more difficult to undertake and the effects more difficult to measure, and therefore funds are difficult to secure. The interventions themselves demand a level of collaboration between sectors which is often difficult to achieve and sustain. Health benefits are likely to accrue more slowly, and therefore are more difficult to demonstrate and defend to voters or donors, than vitamin A supplementation programmes. On the other hand, supplementation programmes do not tackle the root causes of vitamin A deficiency, but merely treat the symptoms.

The policy debate over the most appropriate balance between interventions through food fortification, dietary modification and supplementation is set to continue well into the next millennium and reflects other similar debates in the health field, over the advantages and disadvantages, both in terms of cost-effectiveness and political expediency, of high-profile, short-term interventions over lower-profile, long-term interventions.

Public health research may suffer because governments are lobbied by powerful groups more attracted to basic science or science which depends on high technology and apparently diminishes risks. Research which recommends investment in preventive public health (to decrease the incidence of low birth weights, or transmission of AIDS) is less easy for policy makers to respond to than research which recommends the replacement of CT scanning imaging by nuclear magnetic resonance because of its zero radiation rating. Investment in public health research is less visible and has only long-term results; research resulting in high technology can be visited, photographed, and may have immediate diagnostic advantages.

Ideological influences

Ideology, 'a set of assumptions and ideas about social behaviour and social systems' (Evans and Newnham 1992: 135), also informs the extent to which policy makers are influenced by research, what type of research is funded, or which research ideas and evaluation findings are noted or acted upon. In the 1960s World Bank policy was driven by a concern with poverty. In the 1980s the World Bank's policy was framed within an ethos of efficiency and economic reform. In the UK and USA of the 1980s Thatcher and Reagan's 'conviction politics' excluded issues about needs, inequalities and poverty from the policy agenda, however convincing the research findings. At certain periods policy may be driven by ideology and not by research: the introduction of reforms to the National Health Service in the UK was based on extrapolating from macroeconomic assumptions and not from research. One of the hallmarks of the Thatcher administration was its repudiation of a consensual policy process, and there was no attempt when introducing the reforms of the late 1980s to be informed by evidence or commissioned research (Klein 1990). Similarly, Reagan's policy change on abortion was ideological rather than the result of research.

Of course research can also be driven by ideology. How far do researchers, who rely largely on public or private funds to finance their research, recognize or adapt to the current ideological ethos? Fox (1990: 483) has argued that research in the USA adapted to current ideology through a new approach to research – what he calls the *economizing model*. This model perceives health as a sector of the economy, and uses the discipline of economics to describe health in terms of commodities, consumption, externalities, incentives and disincentives. The economizing model is based on neo-liberal economics (or monetarism), advocating a return to free-market principles. Previous (Keynesian) economic models which advocated a direct role for government in the economy lost favour. For the health sector, which was previously thought of in terms of the public sector, it meant a switch to treating health like a private commodity for individual consumption, and thus subject to market forces.

Fox argues that in the USA over the past decade policy makers and researchers have increasingly come to share core social values about American society. Core values are strongly held normative views of how the world should be, and tend to change only very slowly. They are ideological packages which define the preference of private over public provision, individualism over collectivism. In the 1980s, he suggests, researchers were increasingly comfortable with the core values which dominate the economizing model: a belief in the rights, liberties and welfare of individuals over and above any concept of collective (or public) interest. Furthermore, policy makers and grant-making bodies shared these values.

> Many researchers in this country have behaved as economizers because they view that model as leading most effectively to grants, contracts, publications, jobs, tenure, and influence on policy (1990: 488).

Interestingly, Fox observes that *who* is doing health policy research has changed, as have those commissioning it. No longer is health policy research dominated by the universities (with, he hints, different core values), but by private-sector groups such as the Rand Corporation, interest groups and private industry. The interactive relationship in the USA is probably facilitated by the relatively strong leverage that can be applied through the mechanism of providing government research funds, contractual arrangements, targets on particular areas, and providing basic salaries for researchers in the public and private sectors.

Wagner and Wollman (1986) comparing European governments, argue that given the worsening economic crisis of the mid-1980s, all governments were interested in efficiency and effectiveness and were therefore interested in research that addressed such issues directly. They too observed an 'economic-based approach' to policy analysis, although this has been broadened by inputs from sociology and political science. They argue, like Fox, that much depends on the ideology of governments, and that the change from liberal to conservative governments in Europe oriented attention towards economics – or value-for-money questions in public health as elsewhere.

Researchers are clearly not immune to ideology or 'fashion', and are aware that funders (who may be government policy makers) are interested in certain types of research and not others. Research spending on health is relatively parsimonious. About US$30 billion is devoted worldwide to health research, of which US$1.6 billion is spent on the problems of developing countries which account for 93 per cent of the years of potential life lost. Compare this with the US$4.8 billion spent on research and development of drugs by the ten largest pharmaceutical companies (Commission on Health Research for Development 1990). And patronage is concentrated in most countries – researchers depend heavily on governments for funding. In some countries, such as the United States, private foundations are important supporters of research, and in some developing countries bilateral and multilateral aid agencies provide research funds. These institutions may define what is considered worthwhile research, and researchers dependent on funds from such bodies are likely to propose work that is congruent with funding bodies' ideas.

Perceptions of the usefulness of research

Policy makers are often critical of research for, *inter alia*, taking too long, not being sufficiently applicable, or not addressing primary concerns. There is little doubt that one of the results of the ascendancy of issues about economic efficiency and effectiveness, plus past criticism of much social science research, has been an attempt by many researchers to make their research more useful. Social scientists themselves have been highly critical of early efforts at research. Higgins (1980) suggests that much of the social science research in the UK in the 1960s and 1970s was neither useful nor sufficiently informative for policy makers to use. Social science research was accused of being obvious, common sense, describing unique, and therefore ungeneralizable, situations, and naive.

While some of the criticisms were well founded, much social science research has, in fact, fitted clearly into the enlightenment model of research–policy diffusion. Goffman's studies on mental hospitals informed a whole generation of policies about coping with people in institutions (Goffman 1962). Modernization theorists influenced decades of development policies. Challenges to dominant medical models that dismissed indigenous and lay care changed health policies in the 1970s. The women's movement from the 1960s, among other influences, has clearly affected policies regarding gender and reproductive rights in many countries.

In reviewing the input of sociologists and anthropologists to development projects, Cernea (1991) identifies where they have made a positive contribution. He argues that social scientists act as an important antidote to Western ethnocentrism and technological projects because they have a central interest in putting people first. The value of their input has been recognized because, where once they were called in to explain why development projects had failed in implementation, they have been increasingly asked to do initial research which may highlight the likely effect of social factors on development projects. He gives as examples some World Bank projects evaluated some years after funding had ceased, where it was found that in thirty out of fifty-seven, attention to traditional cultural and local socio-economic conditions had paid off tangibly in economic terms. Projects failed, not due to insufficient funding, but because social and cultural factors had been underestimated or ignored (1991: 14).

Timing and communication factors

Another impediment to research and evaluation findings being used by policy making can be their timing, and the way results are communicated. The research process may be a long one, and even applied, commissioned research may be too protracted for policy makers who are being pressurized to act on a specific issue (Sharpe 1977).

There may be a trade-off between the timeliness and the quality of the research. Studies that are timely in terms of decision-making processes can be dismissed if methodological inadequacies are apparent. However, the quality of the research is not a necessary or sufficient condition for policy makers to take notice of research.

> there have been instances where research of doubtful quality has been used to support foregone policy conclusions and where reliable but politically unacceptable research has been dismissed and discredited (Higgins 1980).

During the Gulf Crisis of 1991, the Jordanian government used some rather exaggerated research undertaken on the children in Jordan, to make a point about the extent of their suffering. Many scientists have been sceptical of the validity of some research on child deaths averted by recourse to oral rehydration solutions.

Communicability will also affect the extent to which policy makers use research. Dramatic, clear-cut, tangible results that answer directly the questions of interest to decision makers are likely to get broader coverage than research that is more opaque. But, however clear the dissemination of results is, if it questions or challenges the status quo, or proposes structural change, policy makers may ignore it.

Perceived quality of the research or evaluation report, and the standing of the institution from which it emanates, will also affect the attention it receives from policy makers. Sharpe (1977) and others (Bulmer 1986) have recorded a lack of confidence in social scientists in Europe (which contrasted with the higher status accorded the social sciences in the USA) which also undermined the chances of research being taken seriously by policy makers. This may well have changed. Certainly in the health field, there has been a huge growth in the number of economists, sociologists and anthropologists employed in research and evaluation of programmes, witness to the acknowledgement that their methods and approaches help to understand complex behaviour and relationships in health. They have helped to draw policy makers' attention to neglected issues such as maternal mortality. Modest achievements from research have been recorded. For example, a five-year programme of collaborative research between American scientists from the Centers for Disease Control and Prevention (CDC) and African researchers led to changes in health programmes. The programme identified malaria as a cause of low birth-weight babies in women's first and second pregnancies. Low birth-weight is strongly associated with risk of death in the neonatal period and after. A series of studies demonstrated that use of an effective antimalarial drug would reduce peripheral blood and placental parasite infection, and reduce the frequency of low birth-weight infants. This helped to identify what the best regimen of prophylaxis would be. As a result, malaria policy was changed to prevention in pregnancy, using sulfadoxine-pyrimethamine as the preferred drug. Other studies resulted in changes in policy regarding optimum timing for giving measles vaccine or running polio vaccine campaigns (Foster 1993).

The picture, then, of whether research influences policy is a complex one, and there are no clear answers. The role and potential contribution of research varies according to the nature of the policy environment and the stages of the policy process, among other things. If there is a basic consensual policy environment, as Klein (1990) describes with regard to the NHS in the UK to the end of the 1980s, there may be little call for research. Where major change takes place, or is imposed, research appears to be more useful because so much is unknown and therefore contested. It seems to me that policies of macro or 'high' and micro or 'low' politics come into play again. Research that is system-oriented, that introduces new paradigms, new ways of thinking, will be ignored unless it fits with policy makers' ideology, in which case it may play an enlightenment role. For example, Enthoven's work on managed markets found resonance in the reform environment of the late 1980s (Enthoven 1985). However, research on routine health services may well feed directly into policy changes, as we have seen from the malaria and immunization examples from Africa.

Conclusions

To sum up, although considerable scepticism has been expressed about the extent to which research and evaluations have been used to inform policy – partly because critics used a linear model and looked for direct examples of research influencing policy – I argue that policy is affected by research. However, the process of influence must be seen not directly, but as a process of enlightenment – many research ideas filtering through to policy makers. Other factors affect how far research is taken up at any particular time. For example, the process of use will also be affected by the nature and intimacy of the links between policy makers and researchers, and the role the media play in research dissemination. Use of research will also depend on timing and mode of communication.

There are also many impediments to research or evaluations being taken seriously and used by policy makers: these include political factors or ideological factors, conceptual confusion and uncertainty about research results, uncertainty about the usefulness of research, timing and communicability. Research and evaluation may not be centre-stage in the policy process, but they certainly play a part, albeit often off-stage.

10

Power and process in shaping change

This book has laid out an introductory conceptual framework for analysis which I hope provides a springboard for action to influence policy, or a starting point for further reading and research. It is a deliberately simple framework, designed to give order and pattern to a complex but familiar world. It provides a map through the maze.

However, I do not want to end without acknowledging that simple frameworks can be deceptive. Power and process in policy making are concepts which are more 'intricate, intuitive and involuntary' (Klein 1990) than they perhaps appear. But they must also be recognized for being more ordered and deliberate than is always apparent. Power is seductive and process can be manipulated. They are enormously complex. Since this last chapter is merely the first stepping stone into policy, I want to end with a snapshot, taken from above, showing the pattern of the maze, and to explore the intricacies and nuances of some of the theories and models used in my analytical framework.

Shaping change: power

Throughout the book I have used the concept of 'bounded pluralism'. I have argued that while high-politics or systemic policies may well be formulated and imposed by policy elites (which to all intents and purposes may be seen as a ruling class), low-politics or sectoral (micro) policies are influenced by many different groups. The opportunities for participation in public policy therefore do exist, through overlapping policy communities that exchange ideas and, through a process of 'enlightenment', highlight issues for the policy agenda or options for implementation. Even 'outsider' groups can affect the trajectory of policy through their direct action, especially if they receive media attention. Since health policies seldom reach the high-politics stakes (even health sector reform has not been perceived as endangering regimes – except perhaps in the USA where observers suggested in 1993 that the Clinton proposals for domestic health reform might lead to the President's downfall), many health policies are formulated and implemented in a policy space which allows significant interaction. This does not imply that pluralism as it exists is sufficient. In most countries there is room for more pluralistic negotiation on policy, with much wider consultation between groups. Even where the mechanisms for public consultation exist they are often not used. Robinson (1993) argues that although drawing on the views of local people through bottom-up public consultation is a required part of the process of setting priorities by health authorities in the UK, few health authorities have been explicit about how they obtain and use such information.

However, even 'bounded pluralism' may be a deceptive perception of what actually happens in many countries, and particularly at a time in history when bipolar politics have been subsumed in the market-dominated ideology of global capitalism. By the 1990s the world seems to have shrunk and the G7 nations are described as the 'executive committee of the modern bourgeoisie' (MacShane 1993), setting the agenda of the global political economy. The 'new imperialists', as the World Bank and IMF have been described, have laid down policy conditions for rescheduling debts and negotiating loans in eastern Europe as well as the Third World, intervening in domestic areas previously considered out of bounds. The political and economic growth of the European Union has been perceived as a threat to British sovereignty, as was demonstrated by calls for a referendum and strong dissension within the ruling Conservative Party over the signing of the Maastricht Treaty in 1993. Hanlon (1991) has referred to the new missionaries recolonizing Mozambique, purporting to help through aid, but in fact undermining state structure and policy. Powerful international groupings work with each other to enforce policies. The mass media on the whole support ruling interests, and, in certain situations, are a reflection of the state. For example, during the 1991 Gulf War many inaccuracies (about the precision of weaponry, numbers killed, videos relayed) were claimed by governments and uncritically reported in the media (Pilger 1993). Ninety per cent of news comes from four Western news agencies. A few transnational companies dominate large areas of trade. In many Third World countries bilateral aid agencies have withheld aid until countries implemented the reform packages demanded by the financial institutions. Many NGOs are financed by aid agencies which lay down the rules of engagement in Third World countries. In corrupt states the national 'tropical gangsters' with 'their hands in the till' form power coalitions with the international 'tropical gangsters' from the World Bank and IMF (Klitgaard 1991).

These contentions are not formed from conspiracy theory: they are empirical representations of everyday life. And while they are described at the macro level of 'high politics', they influence what happens to politics-as-usual policies on the ground. In those countries where the health budget is largely being provided from external sources (in the early 1990s health expenditure of many countries in Africa was largely dependent on external funds) health policy is being radically redefined to encourage private-sector provision, to relieve ministries of health of service delivery, and to change financing mechanisms.

The context of public participation in policy making then is fore-shortened: the agenda is set elsewhere and the policies are formulated by narrow policy circles at international and national levels. In some countries, the policy space is extremely limited, with market ideology and economic recession setting the boundaries for both participation and policy options. At the same time, however, the paradigmatic leap in the content of health policy all over the world also offers opportunities for change which may be stimulating and which may, in the longer run, open the process of policy making to different, and more, participants.

Thus, even in a climate of relatively limited participation in public policy, there are challenges to existing power relations and ideologies. Scholars from the Third World (alone, or together with academics from industrialized countries) are increasingly expressing alternative views to current conventional wisdom on ways to deal with economic crisis (Stewart, Lall and Wangwe 1993) or on reforms within the international system (Saksena 1993). The public is in general more sophisticated and educated than three decades ago, and able to challenge and express sceptism over policy reforms. Zimbabweans have dubbed their government's economic structural adjustment programme (ESAP) the 'Extreme Suffering of the African People', and public debate on the effects of the programme and what needs to be done about it has been widespread and sustained throughout the country. The growth of NGOs, many of which are independent of government and particular interests, is also a sign of increased civic challenge, which may be translated into new social movements and public protest (Wignaraja 1993) but may also create debate within existing formal institutions. As the opportunities for more open media increase, so debate and alternatives to current thinking may be voiced. For example, democracy is under immense pressure in many countries, as it becomes clear that pluralist democracy cannot simply be introduced into any country at any stage of its history.

The search for alternative political forms which are more appropriate to the twentieth century has begun – not only for those countries transforming from authoritarian to more democratic systems, but also for the liberal democracies disillusioned with current corruption and feelings of powerlessness. Debate is being initiated, even in the mass media, questioning the appropriateness and sustainability of liberal democratic models for Third World or eastern European countries (Leftwich 1993), and raising the possibility of political systems based on 'communitarian' relationships in place of individualism or collectivism (Boswell 1993; Etzioni 1993).

Shaping change: process

All countries, developed and developing, are facing change in the health sector, brought about by the economic recession and a shifting political ideology which favours an increased role for the private sector in health care. Periods of political or economic change or crisis are known to be fertile for reviewing and evaluating past policies. Debate may have been stimulated externally or internally, but the call for change in the health sector has been a major preoccupation for all health policy makers.

Those countries which have traditionally relied on a market in health care are exploring policy instruments which will make greater use of regulation and planning. And those countries which have traditionally relied on planning and regulation, are moving towards a more competitive approach. In Britain the health sector is being restructured into a 'managed market' combining some of the principles of the private sector with those of public provision. Managed markets are based on the premise that the private sector which focuses primarily on profits will never meet basic health needs efficiently and equitably, but that the traditional bureaucratic national health system was insufficiently cost-effective or responsive to consumer needs. The move in Britain is towards introducing managed competition between providers and purchasers (Ham et al. 1990). As we saw in previous chapters, this paradigmatic change in British health policy was announced by the prime minister of the time, without consultation, without basic research or necessary information, fuelled by the conviction politics of private market ideology. It has been hotly debated, and many disagree with its basic premises, but the managed market is being introduced nevertheless, and will change the face of health care in Britain in the 1990s.

In the poorest Third World countries, the change in health policy has been no less paradigmatic, although from different starting points. In many countries the structure of health care provision has been unchanged for decades. In Asia and Latin America plurality and private-sector care have dominated many weak ministries of health. In Africa ministries of health were responsible for most health care provision, but were modelled on pre-independence organizations and remained basically unaltered. Economic constraints, political change and donor conditionality have forced changes to thinking about the financing of health services, and countries are currently exploring different funding options such as health insurance (Abel-Smith 1992) as well as structural changes in health systems themselves, with redefinitions of the role of the ministry of health (Cassells 1992).

However, here another layer of complexity must be added. Although this book has used a framework of analysis which can be used for developed and developing countries, this does not deny that there are huge differences between such countries. In another context Manor (1991) calls for 'thick description' and an end to 'parsimonious models'. As examples quoted throughout the chapters demonstrate, the policy environment in many Third World countries is constrained, in comparison with developed countries, by an absolute scarcity of funds, by a paucity of information, by values which favour personal over organizational loyalty, by a lack of managerial and administrative skills, and by poor communications networks and limited structures of accountability. All of these factors affect responses to policy, whether at the phase of problem identification, formulation or implementation and the extent of participation in the policy process.

Nevertheless, while change is often painful, it also provides opportunities. Political change, especially where wrought through democratic means, can open up the policy environment. New faces are brought in, new ideas are given credence, new coalitions of interests are formed. Incremental change is characteristic of the policy process during long periods – and decision-making studies in the UK suggest that most health policies over past decades have been more concerned with policy maintenance than with policy change (Pettigrew et al 1992). Even primary health care policy was not implemented in as radical a form as was originally envisaged, and the rhetoric of change was never matched by a major reallocation of funds between primary and secondary care. In the few exceptions, such as Tanzania, the shift in resources was limited in size and duration.

From the 1980s, however, the continuity and stability of a relatively incremental policy process has been replaced by the upheaval of paradigmatic change, and the old incrementalist or rational models of policy making are less useful. We need new dimensions for thinking about transformational change rather than incremental change; we have to differentiate between modes of change – imposed from outside or initiated from inside – whether we are looking at countries or organizations. Clearly one mode will affect action and reaction differently from the other mode. An institution (or government) with new leadership may well expect change, and welcome it, especially where it is presented as an antidote to previous corruption, maldistribution of resources or institutional paralysis. This does not mean it will not be threatening to some while welcomed by others. Where change is imposed from outside, different dimensions need consideration: is the need for change generally recognized, or do significant groups oppose it? Are the changes proposed compatible with existing values? Does change threaten regime security, and if so, who are the main risk takers?

While the mode of change is important – imposed from outside or initiated internally – so is the context. Policy making in health, and consequent planning strategies, have largely assumed an expansionary context. Yet from the early 1980s health policy making has in fact been taking place in resource-thin, contracting environments. As Cumper (1993) argues from experience in Jamaica, policy makers have reacted to economic constraints by making administrative adjustments (closing hospitals, laying off health personnel) instead of trying to develop methods for rationing health care in order to plan for contraction. New realities demand new strategies and new techniques but also new processes. Technical analysis cannot ignore political analysis. Policy prescriptions have to take into account local political conditions and interests, otherwise they are likely to fail.

In conclusion, this book is a tool. It offers a framework for understanding how health policies are made, who influences policy, and how. It provides a macro view of power and the policy process, interwoven with micro view examples at various international, national and subnational levels. It uses theories and models eclectically to help us understand a complex world, but as I conclude, I must warn against taking a simplistic, static or superficial position. The prevailing message I hope to leave is that – as health workers, students, researchers, teachers, trade unionists, activists or even policy makers – we can all influence the policy environment. Understanding the policy environment will allow us to operate more effectively in the promotion of policy change.

Bibliography

Abel-Smith, B. (1992) 'Health insurance in developing countries: lessons from experience', *Health Policy and Planning* 7: 215–26.

Abel-Smith, B. and Rawal, P. (1992) 'Can the poor afford "free" health services? A case study of Tanzania', *Health Policy and Planning* 7: 329–41.

Achebe, C. (1988) *Anthills of the Savannah*, Picador: London.

Aitken, J. (1992) *Conflict or complicity? Different 'cultures' within a bureaucracy in Nepal*, Unpublished paper, Liverpool School of Tropical Medicine: UK.

Allen, C. (1950) 'World health and world politics', *International Organization* 4: 27–43.

Allen, M. (1993) 'Worldly wisdom', *New Statesman & Society* 21 May: xii–xiii.

Anderson, J. (1975) *Public policy making*, Nelson: London.

Andrain, C. (1988) *Political change in the Third World*, Unwin Hyman: Boston.

Archer, C. (1983) *International organizations*, Unwin Hyman: London.

Barros, F., Vaughan, J.P. and Victora, C. (1986) 'Why so many caesarean sections? The need for a further policy change in Brazil', *Health Policy and Planning* 1: 19–29.

Bateman, D. (1993) 'The selected list', *British Medical Journal* 306: 1141.

Beaton, G.H., Martorell, R., L'Abbe, L., Edmonston, B., McCabe, G., Ross, A.C. and Harvey, B. (1992) *Effectiveness of vitamin A supplementation in the control of young child morbidity and mortality in developing countries*, University of Toronto: Toronto.

Benatar, S. (1991) 'Medicine and health care in South Africa – five years later', *The New England Journal of Medicine* 325: 30–36.

Bennett, S. and Tangcharoensathien, V. (1994) 'A shrinking state? Politics, economics and private health care in Thailand', *Journal of Public Administration and Development*, forthcoming.

Berger, P. (1974) *Pyramids of sacrifice*, Penguin: Harmondsworth.

Birch, A. (1993) *The concepts and theories of modern democracy*, Routledge: London.

Black, N. (1992) 'The relationship between evaluative research and audit', *Journal of Public Health Medicine* 14: 361–6.

Blondel, J. (1990) *Comparative government*, Philip Allan: New York.

Boswell, J. (1993) 'Building better relationships is the basis for a new world order', *Guardian*, 11 October.

Brandeau, M., Lee, H., Owens, D., Sox, C., and Wachter, R. (1993) 'Policy analysis of human immunodeficiency virus screening and intervention: an overview of modeling approaches', *AIDS & Public Policy Journal* 5: 119–31.

British Journal of Addiction (1991) 'Conversations with Sir Richard Doll', 86: 365–77.

Brockington, F. (1975) *World health*, Churchill Livingstone: London.

208

Brown, C. (1982) *A study of local institutions in Kgatleng district, Bostswana*, Applied Research Unit, Ministry of Local Government and Lands, Gaborone.

Bulmer, M. (ed.) (1986) *Social science and social policy*, Allen and Unwin: London.

Buse, K. (1993) *The World Bank and international health policy: genesis, evolution and implications*, unpublished M.Sc. dissertation, London School of Hygiene and Tropical Medicine and London School of Economics.

Buse, K. (1994) 'Spotlight on international agencies: the World Bank', *Health Policy and Planning* 9: 95–9.

Camp, S. (1993) 'Population: the critical decade', *Foreign policy* 90: 126–45.

Camp, S. and Lasher, C. (1989) *International family planning policy – a chronicle of the Reagan years*, unpublished paper, Population Crisis Committee: Washington.

Cassells, A. (1992) *Implementing health sector reform*, unpublished paper prepared for the Health and Population Division, Overseas Development Administration, London.

Cassels, A. and Janovsky, K. (1992) 'A time of change: health policy, planning and organization in Ghana', *Health Policy and Planning* 7: 144–54.

Castle-Kanerova, M. (1992) 'Social policy in Czechoslovakia', in: Deacon, B., Castle-Kanerova, M., Manning, N., Millar, F., Orosz, Szalai, J. and Vidinova, A. *The New Eastern Europe*, Sage Publications: London.

Cernea, M. (1991) *Using knowledge from social science in development projects*, World Bank discussion paper: Washington.

Chapman, S. and Wai Leng, W. (1990) *Tobacco control in the third world: a resource atlas*, International Organization of Consumers Unions: Penang, Malaysia.

Chatterjee, P. (1992) 'How to waste $5 billion a year' *Guardian*, 7 November 1992.

Chetley, A. (1986) *The politics of babyfoods*, Frances Pinter: London.

Chetley, A. (1992) *From policy to practice: the future of the Bangladesh national drugs policy*, International Organization of Consumers Unions: Penang, Malaysia.

Clark, J. (1991) *Democratizing development*, Earthscan: London.

Cleaves, P. (1980) 'Implementation amidst scarcity and apathy: political power and policy design', in: Grindle, M. (ed.) *Politics and Policy Implementation in the Third World*, Princeton University Press: New Jersey.

Cliff, J. (1993) 'Donor-dependence or donor control? The case of Mozambique', *Community Development Journal* 28: 237–44.

Cliff, J. and Noormohammed, A.R. (1988) 'South Africa's destabilization of Mozambique', *Social Science and Medicine* 27: 717–22.

Clift, C. (1988) 'Aid co-ordination: are there any lessons to be learnt from Kenya?', *Development Policy Review* 6: 115–37.

Cobb, R.W. and Elder, C.D. (1983) *Participation in American politics: the dynamics of agenda-building*, Johns Hopkins University Press: Baltimore.

Cohen, J. (1992) 'Foreign advisers and capacity building: the case of Kenya', *Public Administration and Development* 12: 493–510.

Collier, J. (1989) *The health conspiracy*, Century: London.

Collins, C. (1989) 'Decentralization and the need for political and critical analysis', *Health policy and planning* 4: 168–71.

Commission on Health Research for Development (1990) *Health research*, Oxford University Press: Oxford.

Constantino-David, K. (1992) 'The Philippine experience in scaling-up', in: Edwards, M. and Hulme, D. (eds), *Making a difference*, Earthscan: London.

Cox, R.W. and Jacobson, H.K. (1973) *The anatomy of influence: decision making in international organizations*, Yale University Press: New Haven.

Crane, B.B. and Finkel, J.L. (1989) 'The United States, China and the United Nations Population Fund: dynamics of US policy making', *Population and Development Review* 15: 23–59.

Crenson, M. (1971) *The unpolitics of air pollution*, Johns Hopkins University Press: Baltimore.

Cumper, G. (1986) 'Neglecting legal status in health planning: nurse practitioners in Jamaica', *Health Policy and Planning* 1: 30–36.

Cumper, G. (1993) 'Should we plan for contraction in health services? The Jamaican experience', *Health Policy and Planning* 8: 113–21.

Curtis, M. (ed.) (1990) *Introduction to Comparative Government*, Harper Collins: London.

Dahlgren, G. (1990) 'Strategies for health financing in Kenya – the difficult birth of a new policy', *Scandinavian Journal of Social Medicine, Supplement 46*: 67–81.

Daily Gazette (1993) 'City Council accused of defying government policies', 9 August.

Danziger, J. (1991) *Understanding the political world*, Longman: New York and London.

Daulaire, N.M.P., Starbuck E.S., Houston R.M. et al. (1992) 'Childhood mortality after a high dose of vitamin A in a high risk population', *British Medical Journal* 304: 207–10.

Dean, M. (1992) 'Margaret Thatcher's tobacco temptation, *The Lancet* 340: 294–5.

Dean, M. (1992) 'AIDS and the Murdoch press', *The Lancet* 339: 1286.

Delamothe, T. (1992) 'Health care in Russia', *British Medical Journal* 340: 1432–4.

Department of Health (1992) *The effects of tobacco advertising on tobacco consumption*, Economic and Operational Research Division, Dept of Health: UK.

De Roo, A. and Marse, H. (1990) 'Understanding the central–local relationship in health care: a new approach', *International Journal of Health Planning and Management* 5: 15–25.

Desowitz, R. (1991) *The malaria capers*, W.W. Norton & Co.: New York.

Dick, M. (1984) 'If you don't know Niassa you don't know Mozambique', in Walt, G. and Melamed, A., *Mozambique: towards a people's health service*, Zed Books: London.

Djukanovic, V. and Mach, E. (1975) *Alternative approaches to meeting basic health needs*, Unicef-WHO: Geneva.

Downs, A. (1972) 'Up and down with ecology – "the issue attention cycle"', *Public Interest* 32: 38–50.

Dror, Y. (1989) *Public policy making re-examined*, Transaction Publishers: New Brunswick and Oxford.

Dunwoody, S. and Peters, H. (1992) 'Mass media coverage of technological and environmental risks: a survey of research in the United States and Germany', *Public Understanding Science* 1: 199–230.

Easton, D. (1965) *A framework for political analysis*, Prentice-Hall: New Jersey.

The Economist (1992) 'Paying for peacekeeping', 16 May: 16.

Edge, S. (1993) 'State that starts from the bottom', *Guardian* 27 May: 14.

Elgstrom, O. (1992) *Foreign aid negotiations*, Avebury: Aldershot.

Enthoven, A.C. (1985) *Reflections on the management of the National Health Service*, Nuffield Provincial Hospitals Trust: London.

Escudero, J. (1981) 'Democracy, authoritarianism, and health in Argentina', *International Journal of Health Services* 11: 559–72.

Etzioni, A. (1967) 'Mixed-scanning: a third approach to decisionmaking', *Public Administration Review* 27: 385–92.

Etzioni, A. (1993) *Public policy in a new key*, Transaction Publishers: New Brunswick and London.

Evans, G. and Newnham, J. (1992) *The dictionary of world politics: a reference guide to concepts, ideas and institutions*, Harvester Wheatsheaf: London.

Fiedler, J. (1988) 'El Salvador's Ministry of Health, 1975–1986: a provisional performance assessment', *Health Policy* 10: 177–206.

Fiedler, J. (1991) 'Child survival and the role of the ministry of health in Ecuador: progress, constraints and reorganization', *Health Policy and Planning* 6: 32–45.

Finkle, F. and Crane, B. (1976) 'The World Health Organization and the population issue: organizational values in the United Nations', *Population and Development Review* 2: 367–93.

Foltz, A. (1992) *Assuring health sector policy reforms in Africa: the role of non-project assistance*, paper presented at the American Public Health Association Annual Meeting, 11 November.

Foltz, A. and Foltz, W. (1991) 'The politics of health reform in Chad', in Perkins, D. and Roemer, M. *Reforming economic systems in developing countries*, Harvard University Press: Cambridge.

Foster, S. (1993) 'Thirteen lessons learned 1981–1993', unpublished *R & D Feedback*, 15 April: 24–5, Centers for Disease Control: Atlanta.

Fox, D. (1990) 'Health policy and the politics of research in the United States', *Journal of Health Politics, Policy and Law* 15: 481–99.

Fox, P. (1989) 'From senility to Alzheimer's Disease: the rise of the Alzheimer's disease movement', *Milbank Quarterly* 67: 58–102.

Frieden, T. and Garfield, R. (1987) 'Popular participation in health in Nicaragua', *Health Policy and Planning* 2: 162–70.

Gadomski, A., Black, R., Mosley, H. (1991) 'Constraints to the potential impact of child survival in developing countries', *Health Policy and Planning* 5: 235–45.

Gerein, N. (1986) 'Inside health aid: personal reflections of a former bureaucrat', *Health Policy and Planning* 1: 260–6.

Ghai, D. (1992) *the IMF and the South: the social impact of crisis and adjustment*, Zed Books: London and New Jersey.

Ghana VAST Study Team (1993) 'Vitamin A supplementation in northern Ghana: effects on clinic attendances, hospital admissions, and child mortality', *The Lancet* 374: 7–12.

Gilson, L. (1992) *Value for money? The efficiency of primary health facilities in Tanzania*, Ph.D. thesis, University of London.

Godfrey, N. (1990) 'International aid and national health policies for refugees: lessons from Somalia', *Journal of Refugee Studies* 3: 110–34.

Godwin, P. (1992) 'Yes men', *New Statesman & Society*, 5 June: 18–19.

Goffman, I. (1961) *Asylums: essays on the social situation of mental patients and other inmates*, Anchor Books, New York.

Gonzalez-Block, M., Leyva, R., Zapata, O., Loewe, R. and Alagon, J. (1989) 'Health services decentralization in Mexico: formulation, implementation and results of policy', *Health Policy and Planning* 4: 301–15.

Grant, J. (1993) 'World Bank's world development report. Letter to the editor', *The Lancet* 342: 440.

Grant, W. (1984) 'The role of pressure groups', in Borthwick, R. and Spence, J. (eds), *British Politics in Perspective*, Leicester University Press: Leicester.

Green, A. (1993) *An introduction to health planning in developing countries*, Oxford University Press: Oxford.

Greenberg, M. (1992) 'Impediments to basing government health policies on science in the United States', *Social Science and Medicine* 35: 531–40.

Grindle, M. and Thomas, J. (1991) *Public choices and policy change*, Johns Hopkins Press: Baltimore.

Guardian (1993) 'NHS shortages cause deaths of 1000 newborn babies a year', 10 June: 8.

Gulhati, R. (1990) 'Who makes economic policy in Africa and how?', *World Development* 18: 1147–61.

Gunatilleke, G. (1984) *Intersectoral linkages and health development*, WHO Offset Publication 83, WHO: Geneva.

Hague, R. and Harrop, M. (1982) *Comparative government: an introduction*, Macmillan: London.

Hague, R., Harrop, M. and Breslin, S. (1992) *Comparative government and politics*, Macmillan: London.

Hall, A. (1992) 'From victims to victors: NGOs and empowerment at Itaparica', in Edwards, M. and Hulme, D., *Making a difference*, Earthscan: London.

Hall, P., Land, H., Parker, R. and Webb, A. (1975) *Change choice and conflict in social policy*, Heinemann: London.

Ham, C. and Hill, M. (1986) *The policy process in the modern capitalist state*, Wheatsheaf: Sussex.

Ham, C., Robinson, R. and Benzeval, M. (1990) *Health check: health care reforms in an international context*, Kings Fund Institute: London.

Hancock, G. (1989) *Lords of Poverty*, Macmillan: London.

Hanlon, J. (1991) *Mozambique: who calls the shots?*, James Currey: London.

Hardon, A. (1992) 'Consumers versus producers: power play behind the scenes', in Kanji, N. et al., *Drugs policy in developing countries*, Zed Books: London.

Harrod, J. (1988) 'UN specialized agencies: from functionalist intervention to international cooperation', in Harrod, J. and Schrijver, N. (eds) *The UN under attack*, Gower: Aldershot.

Harrop, M. (ed.) (1992) *Power and policy in liberal democracies*, Cambridge University Press: Cambridge.

Hazzard, S. (1973) *Defeat of an ideal*, Macmillan: London.

Hazzard, S. (1989) 'Reflections: The United Nations and Waldheim', *The New Yorker* 25 September: 63–99.

Headey, B. (1974) *British Cabinet Ministers*, George Allen and Unwin: London.

Healey, J. and Robinson, M. (1992) *Democracy, governance and economic policy*, Overseas Development Institute: London.

Herman, E. and Chomsky, N. (1988) *Manufacturing Consent*, Pantheon Books: New York.

Higgins, J. (1980) 'The unfulfilled promise of policy research', *Social Policy and Administration* 14: 195–208.

Hoggart, R. (1978) *An idea and its servants: UNESCO from within*, Chatto and Windus: London.

Hogwood, B. and Gunn, L. (1984) *Policy analysis for the real world*, Oxford University Press: Oxford.

Holm, J. (1988) 'Botswana: a paternalistic democracy', in Diamond, L., Linz, J. and Lipset, S. (eds) *Democracy in developing countries Vol. II*, Lynne Rienner: Boulder, Colo.

Howes, M. (1992) 'Linking paradigms and practice', *Journal of International Development* 4: 375–96.

Howes, M. and Sattar, M.G. (1992) 'Bigger and better? Scaling up strategies pursued by BRAC 1972–1991', in Edwards, M. and Hulme, D. *Making a difference*, Earthscan: London.

Hunter, D. and Pollitt, C. (1992) 'Developments in health services research: perspectives from Britain and the United States', *Journal of Public Health Medicine* 14: 164–8.

Hushang, A. (1982) *Politics and process in the specialized agencies of the United Nations*, Gower: Aldershot.

Ignatieff, M. (1992) 'The grey emptiness inside John Major', *The Observer* 15 November: 25

Illich, I. (1971) *Celebration of awareness*, Calder & Boyars: London.

Illich, I. (1973) *Deschooling Society*, Calder & Boyars: London.

Illich, I. (1975) *Medical nemesis: the expropriation of health*, Calder & Boyars: London.

Imo State Evaluation Team, (1989) 'Evaluating water and sanitation projects: lessons from Imo State, Nigeria', *Health Policy and Planning* 4: 40–49.

Jacques, M. (1991) 'Africa: Has Bob lost his voice?' Interview with Bob Geldof, *Marxism Today*, August, pp. 24–7.

Jasanoff, S. (1993) 'Skinning scientific cats', *New Statesman & Society* 26 February: 29–30.

Jeffery, R. (1986) 'Health planning in India 1951–84: the role of the Planning Commission', *Health Policy and Planning* 1: 127–37.

Joffe, M. (1993) 'Health protection and the European Community', *British Medical Journal* 306: 1629–30.

Jordan, A. and Richardson, J. (1987) *British politics and the policy process*, Unwin Hyman: London.

Judge, A. (1978) 'International institutions: diversity, borderline cases, functional substitutes and possible alternatives', in Taylor, P. and Groom, A. (eds) *International Organization: A Conceptual Approach*, Pinter: London.

Justice, J. (1986) *Plans, policies and people*, University of California Press: Berkeley.

Kanji, N., Munishi, G., and Sterkey, G. (1989) *Case study on Tanzania*, prepared for External Evaluation on WHO's Action Programme on Essential Drugs KIT–LSHTM: Amsterdam-London.

Kanji, N., Hardon, A., Harnmeijer, J.W., Mamdani, M. and Walt, G. (1992) *Drugs policies in developing countries*, Zed Books: London.

Karns, M. and Mingst, K. (eds) (1990) *The United States and multilateral institutions*, Unwin Hyman: Boston.

Karpf, A. (1988) *Doctoring the media*, Routledge: London.

Keane, J. (1988) 'Reform of the rump', *New Statesman & Society*, 8 December: 29–32.

Kingdon, J. (1984) *Agendas, alternatives and public policies*, Little Brown & Co.: Boston.

Klein, R. (1990) 'Research, policy and the national health service', *Journal of Health Politics, Policy and Law* 15: 501–23.

Klinmahorm, S. and Ireland, K. (1992) 'NGO–government collaboration in Bangkok', in Edwards, M. and Hulme, D. *Making a difference*, Earthscan: London.

Klitgaard, R. (1991) *Tropical Gangsters*, I.B. Tauris & Co.: London.

Koehn, P. (1983) 'The role of public administrators in public policy making: practice and prospects in Nigeria', *Public Administration and Development* 3: 1–26.

Korman, N. and Glennester, H. (1985) *Closing a hospital: the Darenth Park Project*, Occasional Papers in Social Administration, 78, Bedford Square Press: London.

Korten, D. (1989) 'The community: master or client. A reply', *Public Adminstration & Development* 9: 569–75.

The Lancet (1992) 'Contraception is not the best development', 340: 1155.

The Lancet (1993) 'Editorial: World Bank's cure for donor fatigue', 342: 63–4.

Lee, K. and Mills, A. (1982) *Policy-making and planning in the health sector*, Croom Helm: London.

Leftwich, A. (1993) 'Voting can damage your wealth', *The Times Higher* 13 August: 11–13.

Leichter, H.M. (1979) *A comparative approach to policy analysis: health care policy in four nations*, Cambridge University Press: Cambridge.

Leichter, H. (1989) 'Lives, liberty and seat belts in Britain: lessons for the United States', *International Journal of Health Services* 16: 213–26.

Le Vine, V. (1979) 'Parliaments in Francophone Africa' in Smith, J. and Musolf, L. (eds), *Legislatures and development*, Duke University Press, Durham, N. Carolina.

Lindblom, C. (1959) 'The science of muddling through', *Public Administration Review* 19: 79–88.

Lindblom, C. (1979) 'Still muddling, not yet through', *Public Administration Review* 39: 517–26.

Livingstone, K. (1987) *If voting changed anything, they'd abolish it*, Collins: London.

Lowi, T. (1964) quoted in Palmer G. and Short, S. (1989) *Health care and public policy*, Macmillan: Australia.

Macalister, M. (1992) 'The $225,000,000,000 habit', *The Observer Magazine*, 8 November.

McClintock, C. (1980) 'Reform government and policy implementation: lessons for Peru', in Grindle, M., *Politics and policy implementation in the Third World*, Princeton University Press: New Jersey.

McGrew, A. and Wilson, M. (1982) *Decision making*, Manchester University Press: Manchester.

Mackay, J. (1990) in Chapman, S. and Wai Leng, W. *Tobacco control in the third world: a resource atlas*, International Organization of Consumers Unions: Penang, Malaysia.

McLaren, R.I. (1980) *Civil servants and public policy*, Wilfred Laurier Press: Canada.

McNamara, R. (1981) *The McNamara Years at the World Bank: Major Policy Addresses of R.S. McNamara 1968–1981*, World Bank: Washington.

McPherson, M. and Radelet, S. (1991) 'Economic reform in The Gambia: policies, politics, foreign aid and luck', in Perkins, D. and Roemer, M. *The reform of economic systems in developing countries*, Harvard University Press: Cambridge, Mass.

Macrae, J., Zwi, A., and Birungi, H. (1993) *A healthy peace? Restructuring and reform of the health sector in a post-conflict situation – the case of Uganda*, unpublished report, London School of Hygiene and Tropical Medicine, UK, and Makerere University, Uganda.

MacShane, D. (1993) 'The new age of the internationals', *New Statesman & Society*, 30 April: 23–6.

Mamdani, M. and Ross, D. (1989) 'Vitamin A supplementation and child survival: magic bullet or false hope?', *Health Policy and Planning* 4: 273–94.

Manderson, L. and Aaby, P. (1992) 'Can rapid anthropological procedures be applied to tropical diseases?', *Health Policy and Planning* 7: 46–55.

Manor, A. (1991) *Re-thinking third world politics*, Longman: London.

Marger, M. (1993) 'The mass media as a power institution', in Olsen, M. and Marger, M., *Power in modern societies*, Westview Press: Boulder.

Martin, E. (1992) 'Human service organizations: an Australian perspective', *Social policy and administration* 26: 320–35.

Mbiti, D., Mworia, F. and Hussein, I. (1993) 'Cost recovery in Kenya', letter to *The Lancet* 341, 376.

Meacher, M. (1980) 'How the mandarins rule', *New Statesman*, 5 December: 14–15.

Milio, N. (1987) 'Making healthy public policy: developing the science by learning the art', *Health Promotion* 2: 263–74.

Mills, A., Vaughan, J., Smith, D., Tabibzadeh, I. (1990) *Health system decentralization*, World Health Organization: Geneva.

Mingst, K .(1990) 'The United States and the World Health Organization', in Karns, M. and Mingst, K. (eds), *The United States and multilateral institutions*, Unwin Hyman: Boston.

Morgan, L. (1993) *Community participation in health*, Cambridge University Press: Cambridge.

Morley, D. and Lovel, H. (1986) *My name is today*, Macmillan: London.

Mosley, P. (1991) 'Britain, the World Bank and structural adjustment', in Bose, A. and Burnell (eds) *Britain's overseas aid since 1979* Manchester University Press: Manchester.

Mwabo, G. (1993) *Health care reform in Kenya 1963–1993: lessons for policy research*, paper presented at the Conference on Health Sector Reform in Developing Countries, 10–13 September, New Hampshire, USA.

Nandan, G. (1993) 'Out of date vaccines given to Indian Children', *British Medical Journal*, 306; 1499.

Negrine, R. (1989) *Politics and the mass media in Britain*, Routledge: London.

Nelkin, D. (1991) 'AIDS and the news media', *Milbank Quarterly* 69: 293–307.

Nelson, B. (1990) 'The agenda-setting function of the media: child abuse', in Graber, D.A. (ed.), *Media power in politics*, CQ Press: Washington.

Newell, K. (1988) 'Selective primary health care: the counter revolution', *Social Science and Medicine* 26: 903–6.

The Nordic UN Project (1991) *The United Nations: Issues and Options*, Almqvist and Wiksell International: Sweden.

O'Connor, R. (1980) *Managing health systems in developing areas*, D.C. Heath & Co: Lexington.

Olson, M. (1982) *The rise and decline of nations*, Yale University Press: New Haven.

Oxfam (1992) 'Oxfam fights aid cuts', *Oxfam Campaigner*, Winter 1992.

Pallister, D. and Norton-Taylor, R. (1992) 'Concern grows over "revolving door"', *Guardian* 9 September: 5.

Palmer, G., and Short, S. (1989) *Health care and public policy*, Macmillan: Australia.

Panday, D. (1989) 'Administrative development in a semi-dependency: the experience of Nepal', *Public Administration and Development* 9: 315–29.

Parry-Williams, J. (1992) 'Scaling up via legal reform in Uganda', in Edwards, M. and Hulme, D., *Making a difference*, Earthscan: London.

Patton, M. et al. (1977) 'In search of impact: an analysis of the utilization of federal health evaluation research', in Weiss, C., *Using Social Research in Public Policy Making*, Lexington Books: Lexington.

Pedalini, L., Dallari, S. and Barber-Madden, R. (1993) 'Public health advocacy on behalf of women in Sao Paulo: learning to participate in the planning process', *Journal of Public Health Policy* 14: 183–96.

Perkins, D. and Roemer, M. (1991) *The reform of economic systems in developing countries*, Harvard University Press: Cambridge, Mass.

Pettigrew, A., Ferlie, E. and McKee, L. (1992) *Shaping strategic change*, Sage: London.

Pilger, J. (1993) 'The brave new media world', *New Statesman & Society* 11 June: 14–15.

Read, M. (1992) 'Policy networks and issue networks: the politics of smoking', in Marsh, D. and Rhodes, R., *Policy networks in British Government*, Clarendon Press: Oxford.

Rebelo, J. (1990) quoted in *Nation-wide Debate on the Draft Constitution*, Dossier 5, Mozambique Information Office: London.

Reich, M. (1993) *The politics of health sector reform in developing countries: three cases of phar-*

maceutical policy, paper presented at Conference on Health Sector Reform in Developing Countries: Issues for the 1990s, New Hampshire, 10–13 September.

Reich, M. (1994) 'Bangladesh pharmaceutical policy and politics', *Health Policy and Planning*, 9: 2.

Richardson, J., Gustafsson, G., and Jordan, G. (1982) 'The concept of policy style', in Richardson, J. (ed.) *Policy styles in Western Europe*, George Allen and Unwin: London.

Roberts, A. and Kingsbury, B. (1988) *United nations, divided world*, Clarendon Press: Oxford.

Robinson, R. (1993) 'Economic evaluation and health care: the policy context', *British Medical Journal* 307: 994–6.

Rondinelli, D. (1983) *Decentralization in developing countries*, Staff Working Paper 581, World Bank: Washington DC.

Rosenhead, J. (1992) 'Politics of the gut reaction', *Guardian* 5 May: 17.

Rossi, P. and Wright, S. (1979) 'Evaluation research: an assessment of theory, practice and politics', in Pollitt, C. et al. (eds) *Public policy in theory and practice*, Hodder & Stoughton: London.

Sabatier, P. (1991) 'Toward better theories of the policy process', *Political science and politics* 24: 144–56.

Saksena, K.P. (1993) *Reforming the United Nations*, Sage Publications: New Delhi.

Sandbrook, R. (1993) 'Live and learn', *New Statesman & Society* 22 January: 29–30.

Sanders , D. (1992) 'The state and democratization in PHC: community participation and the village health worker programme in Zimbabwe', in Frankel, S., *The community health worker*, Oxford University Press: Oxford.

Save the Children Fund (UK) (1993) *Sustainability in the health sector: Uganda case study*, unpublished document: London.

Scotch, R. (1989) 'Politics and policy in the history of the disability rights movement', *Milbank Quarterly* 67: 380–400.

Seers, D. (1977) 'The meaning of development', *International development review* XI, 2: 2–7.

Sen, A. (1983) 'The battle to get food', *New Society*, 13 October: 54–7.

Sharma, K. (1993) 'Controlling the hand that cures', *The Hindu*, 30 June.

Sharpe, L.J. (1977) 'The social scientist and policymaking: some cautionary thoughts and transatlantic reflections', in Weiss, C. (ed.) *Using social resarch in public policy making*, Lexington Books: Lexington.

Sikkink, K. (1986) 'Codes of conduct for transnational corporations: the case of the WHO\UNICEF code', *International Organization* 40: 817–40.

Simms, M. (1987) 'Run a pressure group and change the law', *British Medical Journal* 295: 772–3.

Simon, H. (1957) *Administrative behaviour* (2nd edn), Macmillan: London.

Smith, B. (1977) *Policy making in British government*, Martin Robertson: London.

Smith, C. (1991) 'Networks of influence: the social sciences in the UK since the war', Chapter 5 in Wagner P., Weiss, C., Wittrock B. and Wollman H., *Social sciences and modern states*, Cambridge University Press: Cambridge.

Smith, G. and May, D. (1993) 'The artificial debate between rationalist and incrementalist models of decision-making', in Hill, M. (ed.) *The policy process: a reader*, Harvester Wheatsheaf: London.

Smith, R. (1992) 'Hype from journalists and scientists', *British Medical Journal* 304: 730.

Sommer, A., Tarwotjo, I., Hussaini, G. and Susanto, D. (1983) 'Increased mortality in children with mild vitamin A deficiency', *The Lancet* Ii: 585–8.

Stebbins, K.R. (1991) 'Tobacco, politics and economics: implications for global health', *Social Science and Medicine* 33: 1317–26.

Stedward, G. (1987) 'Entry to the system: a case study of Women's Aid in Scotland' in: Jordan, A. and Richardson, J., *Government and pressure groups in Britain*, Clarendon Press: Oxford.

Stewart, F., Lall, S. and Wangwe, S. (eds) (1993) *Alternative devevlopment strategies in Subsaharan Africa*, Macmillan: London.

Strong, P. and Berridge, V. (1990) 'No-one knew anything: some issues in British AIDS policy', in Aggleton, P., Davies, P., and Hart, G. (eds) *AIDS: individual, cultural and policy dimensions*, Falmer: Brighton.

Taylor, P. (1984) *The smoke ring: the politics of tobacco*, Bodley Head: London.

Taylor, P. (1991) 'The United Nations system under stress: financial pressures and their consequences', *Review of International Studies* 17: 365–87.

Thomas quoted in Bulmer (1986), *op cit.*

Thomason, J., Newbrander, W. and Kolehmainen-Aitken (eds) (1991) *Decentralization in a developing country: the experience of Papua New Guinea and its health service*, The Australian National University: Canberra.

Ugalde, A. (1978) 'Health decision making in developing nations: a comparative analysis of Colombia and Iran', *Social Science and Medicine* 12: 1–7.

UNDP (1992) *Human development report*, Oxford University Press: Oxford.

UNICEF (1984) *Overview of evaluative activities in UNICEF*, unpublished document E/ICEF/1984/L.3, UNICEF: New York.

Urquhart, B. (1990) 'The United Nations and its discontents', *The New York Review of Books*, 15 March: 11–16.

Valdes Brito, J. and Henriquez, J. (1983) 'Health status of the Cuban population', *International Journal of Health Services* 13: 479–86.

Waddington, C. (1992) *Health economics in an irrational world – the view from a regional health administration in Ghana*, Ph.D. thesis, University of Liverpool.

Wagner, P. and Wollmann, H. (1986) 'Fluctuations in the development of evaluation research: do "regime shifts" matter?', *International Social Science Journal* 38: 205–18.

Walker, J.L. (1981) 'The diffusion of knowledge, policy communities and agenda setting: the relationship of knowledge and power', Chapter 4 in Tropman J., Dluhy, M.J. and Lind, R., *New strategic perspectives on social policy*, Pergamon Press: New York.

Walt, G. (1976) *Policymaking in Britain: A comparative study of fluoridation and family planning 1960–1974*, Ph.D. Thesis, University of London.

Walt, G. (ed) (1990) *Community health workers in national programmes: just another pair of hands?*, Open University Press: Milton Keynes.

Walt, G. (1993a) 'WHO under stress: implications for health policy', *Health Policy* 24: 125–44.

Walt, G. (1993b) 'Health policy in the Third World', in Webster C. (ed.) *Caring for health: History and diversity*, Open University Press: Milton Keynes.

Walt, G. and Cliff, J. (1986) 'The dynamics of health policy in Mozambique 1975–1985', *Health Policy and Planning* 1: 148–57.

Walt, G. and Harnmeijer, J. (1992) 'Formulating an essential drugs policy: WHO's role', in Kanji, N., Hardon, A., Harnmeijer, J., Mamdani, M. and Walt, G. *Drugs policy in developing countries*, Zed Books: London.

Weiss, C. (1977) in Bulmer, M (1986) *op cit.*

Weiss, C. (1991) 'Policy research: data, ideas or arguments?', Chapter 14 in Wagner et al. (1991), *Social Sciences and Modern States*, Cambridge University Press: Cambridge.

Wells, C. (1987) *The UN, UNESCO and the politics of knowledge*, Macmillan Press: London.

West, K.P., Katz, J., Shrestha, S.R., Le Clerq, S.C., Khatry, S.K., Pradhan, E.K., Pokrhel, R.P. and Sommer, A. (1993) 'Abstract: Impact of periodic vitamin A supplementation on early infant mortality in Nepal', in *Toward comprehensive programs to reduce vitamin A deficiency*, a report of the XV International Vitamin A Consultative Group Meeting, Arusha, Tanzania 8–12 March, IVACG: Washington.

Wignaraja, P. (ed) (1993) *New social movements in the South* Zed Books: London.

Willetts, P. (1993) *Transnational actors and changing world order* International Peace Research Institute, Meiji Gakuin University: Japan.

Williams, D. (1987) *The specialized agencies and the United Nations* C. Hurst & Co: London.

Wolffers, I. (1992) *Health in Bangladesh* VU University Press: Amsterdam.

Wood, H. (1980) *Third class ticket* London: Penguin Books.

Woodroffe, C. (1992) Medical abortion and the availability of RU486 – are women's rights being ignored in developing countries? *Health Policy and Planning* 7: 77–81.

World Bank (1980) *Health Sector Policy Paper*, World Bank: Washington.

World Bank (1987) *Financing Health Services in Developing Countries: An Agenda For Reform*, World Bank: Washington.

World Bank (1990) *World Development Report*, Oxford University Press: Oxford.

World Bank (1991) *Annual Report 1991*, World Bank: Washington.

World Bank (1993a) *World Development Report: Investing in health*, Oxford University Press: Oxford.

World Bank (1993b) *Annual report*, World Bank: Washington.

World Health Organization (1991) *Tabular information on legal instruments dealing with HIV infection and AIDS*, Document WHO/GPA/HLE/91.1 WHO: Geneva.

Wright, P. (1990) 'Gesture politics', *New Statesman & Society* 1 June: 16–20.

Wright Mills, C. (1956) *The power elite*, Oxford University Press: Oxford.

Yishai, Y. (1993) 'The hidden agenda: abortion politics in Israel', *Journal of Social Policy* 22: 193–212.

Index

abortion, 105, 196; anti- lobby, 63, 175; illegal, 183; policy, 18, 169
Abortion Law Reform Association (UK), 106, 110
acyclovir drug, 187
advisers: foreign, 89; position of, 88–9
advocacy groups, 111, 116
Afghanistan, 91
ageing population, growth of, 64
agenda: definition of, 53; process of setting, 8
agrarian reform, 166
aid: bilateral, 151; foreign, 58; implementation of, 158
aid donors, 85, 136, 157; assertiveness of, 159; demands by, 83; effect on health policies, 5, 33, 84
AIDS, 65, 86, 91, 103, 106, 129, 136, 137, 143, 154, 186; networks, 115; support organization (Uganda), 116; testing for, 154; transmission of, 196; treatment of, 187
alcohol: advertising of, 14; policy on, 22; production of, 61; trade in, 146; use of, 191
Alma Ata Declaration, 128
Alzheimer's Disease movement, 115
Angola, 21
apartheid, 11
Arab League, 123
Argentina, 25, 30
asbestos, dangers of, 192
Association of the British Pharmaceutical Industry (ABPI), 90, 104
associations, rights of, 36
asthma, cure for, 187
audit, use of, 180

Australia, 19, 74, 93
authoritarian-inegalitarian systems, 24–6
AZT drug, 186

baby foods, regulation of, 138, 139
Bandung Conference, 9
Bangladesh, 66, 107, 130, 169; drugs policy in, 170–3; health policy in, 55
Bangladesh Medical Association (BMA), 55, 170, 172
Bangladesh Rural Advancement Committee (BRAC), 106
battered children, 70
Belgium, 19
Bhopal chemical disaster, 192
Bill of Patients' Rights, 99
Blondel, J., 7, 19, 20
Bolivia, 25
Bosnia, sick children from, 69
Botswana, 27, 74, 155
bottom-up approaches to implementation, 155–7
Brazil, 25, 31, 99, 120, 193
breast cancer, screening for, 183
breastfeeding, 39, 179; substitutes, 140 (code on, 141, 148)
British American Tobacco (BAT), 114, 146
British Medical Association (BMA), 102, 113
budgetary control, 159
bureaucracy, 38, 76, 77, 82, 154, 166; impartial, 82; power of, 95

caesarian sections, 31–2
Cambridge school, 181